Baby Names 2019

Eleanor Turner

white
LADDER

Acknowledgments

I would like to extend my utmost gratitude to Beth Bishop at Crimson Publishing for her patience and guidance throughout this project. To the many individuals and families I've had the fortune to doula for over the years, and who have graciously allowed me to share their baby names with the world, thank you. Love and appreciation also goes to Michael Turner, who has stuck around and offered endless helpful suggestions while I've worked on these wonderful books for the last nine years. And finally, the greatest thanks go to my own children, Owen Henri, Jasper Hugh, and Josie May. I fall more in love with them, and their names, every day.

This eighth edition published by White Ladder, an imprint of Crimson Publishing Ltd, in 2018.

© 2011, 2012, 2013, 2014, 2015, 2016, 2017, 2018 Crimson Publishing Ltd

ISBN 978 1 910336 54 0

Front cover: AMR Image/iStock.com

Printed and bound in Denmark by Nørhaven, Viborg

Contents

Author's note

Baby names vary widely in spelling and pronunciation. To simplify things, this book usually lists each name only once: under the most common initial and spelling. If a name has a common alternate spelling with a different initial, it may also be listed under that letter.

Information relating to statistics and trends in baby names is based on the most recent data at the time of going to press.

Introduction

I have a confession to make. As I sat down to write the latest edition of this wonderful book I discovered our family would have another little addition to name. And I smugly thought that, because I've been writing about baby names for the better part of a decade now, finding a name for this little one would be easy. And yet, there I was, as daunted by the task as everyone else, feeling the clock tick by every week and still no name to claim. I finally had to take my own carefully crafted advice and really pay attention to how to track down that elusive, yet perfect, baby name.

Look, I really get it! Names are simultaneously fascinating, daunting, and hilarious. As soon as you know a baby is on its way, everyone around you is demanding to know exactly what names are on your "hit" list and offering up their own "miss" lists (even if you didn't ask ...) Everyone— from your dear Aunt Ethel to the man checking out your groceries —has an opinion on what this new baby should be called, and all you want to do is figure out a name that you can spell, pronounce, and doesn't clash with your last name.

Well, the good news is that it really doesn't have to be complicated at all. As daunting as it might sound at first, choosing a name for your baby is one of the most enjoyable and best decisions you get to make as a new parent. You are being given free rein to be as creative as possible, to honor a family member or celebrity you admire, or to find meaning in the dozens of names you've loved over the years. Who doesn't like the sound of that?

Did you know that the names Noah and Liam are popular in every single state in the US?

Or that the name Aurora is one of the Top 5 baby girl names in Alaska, but not anywhere else?

Ever considered calling your baby Choice, Poet, or Music?

Or are you just curious what oddball baby names celebrities have chosen this year?

Baby Names 2019 is here to take you through your options and solve your baby-naming dilemmas. It's updated annually, so it always includes the nation's most popular names, celebrity choices, and names making a comeback. We've included dozens of lists to provide you with inspiration and, of course, some downright bizarre names children have been given over the years (usually by celebrities). Learn what teachers *really* think about the names in their classrooms, and discover which names are still America's favorites.

Also, be sure to keep an eye out for all the facts and figures we've got for you—including what names are most popular in each state—so you can impress your friends and family with all this new-found naming knowledge you've picked up. It's okay: we'll even let you take the credit.

Remember, picking a baby name should be fun! Grab a pencil and get started. I guarantee you your hit list will be full of ideas by the time we're through.

Happy naming!

Eleanor Turner

Part One

1 Current baby-naming trends

Liam leaps while Emma endures

There was big news in the world of baby names this year! For the first time ever, the name Liam became the nation's most popular name for baby boys, rudely shoving previous number one Noah off his podium. Even more remarkably, Oliver and Ethan pushed perennial favorite Michael—listed in the Top 10 for literally decades—down to 12th place. Michael has sat in the Top 10 since World War II, which is why 2018's data is so astonishing. Poor Michael—what did he ever do to us?

Emma has now maintained her place at the top of the girls' charts for the fourth year in a row, which is kind of remarkable, but in a similar story to the boys' list, Emily has been bumped out of the Top 10 for the first time in nearly 30 years. However, despite the current political upheaval, baby names are at least one thing the entire country can agree on! More than 19,700 baby girls were given the name Emma in the latest baby names data (released by the Social Security Administration, SSA), and nearly 19,000 were given the name Liam.

This is rather incredible when you consider that, until a few years ago, either Jacob or Michael had remained the top choice for parents of newborn baby boys in the US for over 50 years. Jacob has been given to more babies (4.89 million and counting), but Michael has claimed the top spot more often (44 times), so the fact that Liam has arrived to rock his spot at the top is pretty unusual. In fact, Jacob is teetering dangerously on the edge of the Top 10 in 2019, just like his old pal Michael, which might say more about broader baby naming and political trends than just about anything else.

The four new entries to enter either the boys' list or the girls' list were Logan, Oliver, Amelia, and Evelyn, all of which were waiting in the wings in last year's Top 20. Interestingly, these new admissions demonstrate a departure for American families, moving away from the traditional Biblical leanings that have typically dominated the charts. I don't know about the rest, but I'm blaming Wolverine for the dramatic rise in popularity for Logan. Seems like the X-Men have a lot to answer for …

The Nation's Top 10

Boys	Girls
1. Noah	1. Emma
2. Liam	2. Olivia
3. William	3. Ava
4. Mason	4. Sophia
5. James	5. Isabella
6. Benjamin	6. Mia
7. Jacob	7. Charlotte
8. Michael	8. Abigail
9. Elijah	9. Emily
10. Ethan	10. Harper

Charlotte landed a spot in seventh place. Once a consistently popular name in the US, appearing exclusively in the Top 100 from 1908 to 1953, it had dropped dramatically by 1982. However, in the last decade it's seen a sharp uptick in use, and last year clawed its way to number seven. Of course, it was helped along by a certain Royal toddler, who also just became a new big sister to little brother Louis. Pronounced "Lou-ee", this Princely name was last seen in the Top 20 way back in 1914, which means it's ready for a comeback.

Charlotte has now become so fashionable that even shortened versions of it are gaining momentum: Charlie entered the Top 1,000 for baby girls in 2005 and in subsequent years has leaped nearly 800 places to 154th place. Charlie has also remained a steady favorite for parents of little boys, as it has climbed nearly 250 spots since the year 2000 in the boys' charts, landing last year in position 214.

Royal leading ladies

Now that Prince Harry's married to Meghan Markle, watch for the names Meghan and Megan to hit the charts next year. Currently in 883rd and 499th place respectively, they're almost guaranteed to be affected by the "Royal Effect" and bounce back to their pre-millennium Top 50 positions next year. Megan adn Meghan are both Welsh names meaning "pearl," which is rather delightful considering how many jewels the newest duchess will be wearing over the coming years.

Creatures of habit

Let's look a little further into what's trending right now: namely, the traditional and simple. Humans are creatures of habit, and traditional names feel as familiar to us as a pair of cozy jammies. What's interesting about recent trends is that no matter how many new and unusual names enter the most popular baby name lists each year, you will always see the majority of babies given the same familiar and traditional names of the past. The Top 10 names for both boys and girls seem to stay pretty fixed each year, and the recent lists are no different.

Jacob, Michael, Noah, and William have all appeared in the Top 20 boys' names every year since 2008, and the girls' names Ava, Emma, Sophia, and Isabella have also stayed put. The world has changed a lot since 2008, but apparently our taste in names has not.

There are a couple of theories as to why we're all giving our kids the same names, year after year. Personally, I think there's something to be said for the "minimalism" movement. Lately, we've taken to simplifying our lives and streamlining our possessions and choices like never before. The same could be said of names: why pick an unusual or complicated one when a classic one will do? Why search among thousands when you have a perfectly wonderful one right in front of you? Your baby will have enough mess and "stuff" already, so let's at least make their name nice and simple.

The other theory is that parents are choosing names they've heard for so long that they feel safe and familiar. Just take a look at the Top 10 (the first six spots for baby girls end in -a), or the highest climbers (seven of the ten biggest climbers for baby girls end in either -a, -ie, -y, or a similar sound). This means that most names ending in -a or -ie/-y are immensely popular for little girls right now ... even the sneaky ones like the spelling of Saoirse (which is actually pronounced Ser-sha, thanks to its Irish Gaelic roots).

There's a comfortable pattern to the way we name our children that has prevailed for almost 20 years now, and other old-fashioned names, such as Eleanor, Henry, James, and Josephine, have climbed the popularity ranks in the Top 100 lists, along with their alternate spellings of Ellie, Harry, Jack, and Josie.

Thinking outside the box

Have you ever raised your eyebrows when you heard a friend's baby name choice? (I know I have.) Well, there might be a reason for that.

A little inertia

Ryan Gosling helped actor Saoirse Ronan with her major PR problem when promoting a movie—namely, that nobody knows how to pronounce her name! Gosling helpfully provided an explanation that it was "Ser-sha ... like inertia," and the memo seems to have worked. A cinema in Minnesota reportedly wanted to help its patrons remember this tip, and even listed the explanation next to the Irish actor's name on their billboard.

Despite our oh-so-traditional leanings when it comes to the names coasting at the top of the charts, research shows we are actually seeing more variation than ever before in the rest of the list. In the 1950s, the Top 25 boys' names and the Top 50 girls' names were given to half of all babies born in that decade. Think about that for a moment: half of *all* babies born in the 1950s were given one of either 25 boys' names or 50 girls' names. That's astonishing.

To reach the same figure now, you would have to include the Top 143 boys' names and the Top 253 girls'. That's everything from Liam (1st) to Eric (143rd), and Emma (1st) to Hope (253rd). In fact, if you look over the last decade, the percentage of babies given names in the Top 1,000 gets smaller every year: ten years ago 73.51% of registered births appeared in the Top 1,000 names, but last year it was only 72.91%. This means there is a far greater variety of names, spellings, and pronunciations than ever before, even though the names at the very top of the charts remain traditional and stable.

Statistical stuff

	Boys	Girls
Individual names registered	14,160	18,309
Total registrations	1,834,490	1,711,811
Top names	Liam (18,728 babies)	Emma (19,738 babies)
Babies with names in Top 10	146,914	143,559
Top 10 names as percentage	8% of all names	8.4% of all names
Highest climbers	Wells (up 504 places)	Ensley (up 1,461 places)
Biggest fallers	Riaan (down 421 places)	Julianne (down 263 places)

One explanation for this is that parents have begun to give their children names more unusual than their own. A parent who was one of a dozen Jennifers in their class in the 1980s or '90s might not want the same experience for their children. Alternatively, a parent who has a slightly unusual name and enjoyed that experience growing up might feel confident about giving their offspring an even more unique name. If the trend for seeking out unique names continues into 2019 and beyond, you might start to see even stranger and stranger spellings …

> Some of the US's quirkiest baby names over the last year have included Choice, Klever, Poet, and Superior for boys; and Godiva, Music, Psalms, and Stetson for girls.

Every year, the SSA releases a report on the biggest climbers and fallers, and most years these names tend to be the quirkiest. The names at the top of these lists have the greatest jumps in popularity, although it doesn't necessarily mean they are widely used across the USA. In fact, it's the opposite. The biggest climbers are always those further down the charts—if ten families chose a name last year, but then 20 families choose it this year, that's an increase of 100%. The same percentage increase for Liam would need an additional 19,000 families to choose the name. So a rarely used name can jump several hundred spots in a single year, despite only having a handful of families choosing it for their little ones. Here's a short breakdown of the Top 10 game-changers:

Biggest winners		Biggest losers	
Boys	**Girls**	**Boys**	**Girls**
Wells	Ensley	Riaan	Julianne
Kairo	Oaklynn	Kylo	Wendy
Caspian	Dream	Kolby	Milania
Nova	Oaklyn	Uriiah	Montserrat
Colson	Melania	Kamdyn	Nathaly
Kace	Emberly	Jamar	Jayden
Kashton	Octavia	Giovani	Jessa
Koa	Paisleigh	Nickolas	Tenley
Gatlin	Yara	Chad	Aryana
Bjorn	Kehlani	Jair	Ciara

So why do names increase or decrease so dramatically in a single year? I mean, look at what happened to Kylo, which was top of the winners charts last year and now finds itself in second place on the losers list. My personal theory is that Lucasfilms made the same error as the rest of us: they thought Kylo Ren was going to be the big hit among Star Wars fans (as demonstrated by the hoards of toys left on shelves) and it turns out we all much preferred Rey and Finn anyway. Both of those names jumped up last year too, by the way, although they didn't make these particular lists: Finn is now in 167th place and Rey jumped up 100 places to spot 769. The Force will keep those trends going in 2019, I'm sure.

Well, just like everything else, names fall in and out of fashion. The popularity of names tends to ebb and flow, and in the case of Melania and Milania, it could be attributed to the simultaneous popularity and unpopularity of the nation's First Lady. However, this could also just as easily be a flash in the pan, and appear nowhere on any list next year! It all depends on what happens in 2019.

Prince Louis

The most influential Royal baby name of recent years was that chosen by Prince William and the Duchess of Cambridge for their third child. Four days after his birth, it was announced that Will and Kate's second son would be called Louis Arthur Charles. It's a great choice, with a nod to several important people in the couple's life. First off, Louis is the name of Prince William's great-great uncle, Louis Mountbatten, who was a strong influence on Prince Charles as he grew up, and who acted as a surrogate grandfather to him. Second, Arthur is a fitting tribute to the current Queen of England as it's the middle name of her own father King George VI, and Charles ... well, you just can't go wrong with naming your son after Will's own father,

Trendy or tragic?

One new trend over the last few years has been the increase in mystical-themed names, such as Caspian, Nova, and Dream. In fact, of the hundreds of names to show large jumps in popularity, this category made up a significant proportion. Nova was a huge climber for baby boys last year, along with Dream for girls, demonstrating how much parents are enjoying giving their children big, powerful names. It was probably helped along by Rob Kardashian and Blac Chyna's decision to name their daughter that recently, too. Other choices included God, Messiah, Thor, and Zeus for baby boys last year, and little girls were given the names Goddess, Jewels, Luna, Lyra, and Star.

Also, there's clearly a desire for getting back to nature, with Briar, Ridge, Shepard, and Wilder all big climbers in 2018 for little boys, along with Emerald and Sunny for baby girls. Meanwhile, parents seeking to follow the trends of the Kardashians went with a whole host of K names last year, including Kairo, Kace, Kashton, Koa, Kehlani, and Khari. I'll leave it up to you to decide if this particular trend is also your style.

Entertain us, baby

Everything, from films and TV to books and blogs, shapes the world of baby names.

The biggest influences to hit screens in recent years were the Star Wars franchise, Game of Thrones, and anything produced by Disney, but also some unexpected ones. Read on to discover if your love of binge watching Netflix during bouts of pregnancy-induced insomnia can technically be classified as research.

Even though Solo: A Star Wars Story wasn't actually a Luke Skywalker story, because the franchise has been so huge any time a new movie in canon is released, it never fails to ensure the names of the original characters pop up in the charts again... as well as some new ones. Luke hasn't dropped out of the Top 30 since 2014, and Leia, which hadn't appered in the Top 1,000 since 1980 until a few years ago, is suddenly in 279th place and still climbing. The same story is happening for Finn, which didn't exist in the SSA's rankings until the year 2000, and is now in 167th place! Han could do with a boost though: only 29 babies were called that last year, and not a single one was called Chewie. Now a tragedy, that is.

Other influential movies included Incredibles 2, which helped push the name Violet into a stronger place on the charts at position 48. When the original movie was released in 2004, Violet sprang up a whopping 200 places in a single year, and it doesn't show signs of slowing down yet. It may have been aided by the fact Violet has appeared in other shows, like Downton Abbey, and fits into the mold of being so-old-it's-cool-again. Elsewhere, in the realm of comic book movies, Avengers: Infinity War might have helped the name Scarlett move a little ahead in the charts to 18th place, and why not? Being named after the actor playing Black Widow might be a fun story to tell as you grow up!

Small-screen style

Tell me you didn't fall in love with the gorgeous costuming and acting in *The Crown*? And now tell me you're not seriously considering the names George, Elizabeth, Philip, Margaret, or Winston for your new baby. No one could blame you for being sucked into such a feast for the eyes. Anyway, continuing the theme of period dramas, *Call the Midwife* has allowed fun go-getter Trixie to swish up the charts and go from literally zero babies with that name to appearing in the Top 1,400. If you fancy a vintage name from everyone's favourite set of mid-century midwives, options include Cynthia, Jenny, Julienne, and Monica.

Other big TV shows included *Orange is the New Black*, *The Handmaid's Tale*, *This Is Us*, and *Sneaky Pete*. Heart-wrenching NBC drama *This is Us* may be partially responsible for the recent popularity of the names Milo and Sterling, after actors Milo Ventimiglia and Sterling K. Brown, and it's been well established for several years now that the reason Piper has swept up the charts since 2013 is directly related to everyone's favorite prison comedy-drama *Orange Is the New Black*. Even Amazon Prime's surprise hit *Sneaky Pete* could be held accountable for the recent burst of interest in the name Otto, with the name entering the top 500 for the first time in 60 years, and while there aren't many parents selecting Offred as an appropriate choice of name for their infant daughters, *The Handmaid's Tale* has helped actor Elisabeth Moss's name sneak ahead in the charts. Her particular spelling jumped 100 places since Season One was released, while the more traditional Elizabeth remained solidly in the Top 20.

> When *Unbreakable Kimmy Schmidt* star Ellie Kemper had her baby in 2016 she reportedly forgot to publicly announce her son's name. When quizzed about it several months later, she said, "Oh no, he has a name! That's so funny; it's James! What if we were so mortified by his name we were like, 'Don't tell anyone!'?"

The sporting year

Names of sporting heroes are often an inspiration for new parents, particularly those with moving stories. When figure skater Adam Rippon took home his Winter Olympics bronze medal (and then won a far more important victory on *Dancing With the Stars* ...) he saw his name pop up again in the charts. His backstory is incredibly inspiring, and it seems there are a lot of parents who agree.

Stars of the NFL always make an impression on new parents, and the New England Patriots' Tom Brady, MVP winner of Super Bowl 51 and voted the number one NFL Player of the 2017–18 season, proved that once again. The name Brady showed a slight uptick in babies with that name in 2017 into 2018, and Thomas ended up in the Top 50! Football legend Peyton Manning has seen literally thousands of babies be given his name; there were 1,000 baby boys and a whopping 3,200 baby girls called Peyton in the most recent SSA list.

There is a history of successful athletes creating baby name trends: Jackie Robinson, the first African-American baseball player to play professionally, and one of the great legends of the sport, increased the popularity of both the name Jack (for boys) and Jackie (for girls) during the peak of his fame in the US. He can be credited, in large part, for the continuous popularity of these names even in the 21st century—particularly after the film based on his life, *42: The True Story of an American Legend*, came out a few years ago and brought new attention to his story.

> An Israeli couple called their baby girl Like after the Facebook button. Their other children are called Pie and Vash, which means honey.

Celebrity power

The previous edition of this book took a sorrowful tone when we analyzed the sad return of celebrities choosing totally normal and benign names for their children. However, it looks like we spoke too soon …

Celebrities are, apparently, fickle creatures, and in general, last year they enjoyed more outlandish baby name trends—which is what we've all come to love and expect from them. The Kardashians had a beautiful run on unique names in 2018, starting with Kim's Chicago, Kylie's Stormi, and Khloe's True. No other babies in the USA were named Chicago last year, according to the SSA's data, and only a small handful were called True and Stormi. As always though, the Kardashians are true trendsetters, and it will be interesting to see how those names change in the rankings over the next few years.

Elsewhere, Aaron Paul went with the delightfully cute Story Annabelle for his newborn daughter, and rapper Macklemore chose the deliciously bonkers Colette Koala for his. Macklemore follows in the footsteps of actor Zooey Deschanel, who has chosen wildlife-themed middle names for her own children in recent years: Elsie Otter and Charlie Wolf.

Recent celebrity babies

Alexis Olympia (Serena Williams and Alexis Ohanian)

Axel Strahl (Seth Meyers and Alexi Ashe)

Beckett Richard (Michael Phelps and Nicole Phelps)

Chicago (Kim Kardashian and Kanye West)

Colette Koala (Macklemore and Tricia Davis)

Ennis Howard (Kirsten Dunst and Jesse Plemons)

Francisco (Lin-Manuel Miranda and Vanessa Nadal)

Frida (Brigitte Nielsen and Mattia Dessi)

Gio Grace (Adam Levine and Behati Prinsloo)

Hart (Miranda Kerr and Evan Spiegel)

Hayes (Jessica Alba and Cash Warren)

Jack (Rosie Huntington-Whiteley and Jason Statham)

Louis Arthur Charles (Prince William and the Duchess of Cambridge)

Luke Richard (Eddie Redmayne and Hannah Bagshawe)

Miles Theodore (Chrissy Teigen and John Legend)

Minnie Theodora (Jack Osbourne and Lisa Osbourne)

Remy Anne (Billy Joel and Alexis Roderick)

Romeo Alejandro David (Alec Baldwin and Hilaria Baldwin)

Santiago Enrique (Eva Longoria and José Antonio Bastón)

Stormi (Kylie Jenner and Travis Scott)

Story Annabelle (Aaron Paul and Lauren Paul)

Tiana Gia (Dwayne "The Rock" Johnson and Lauren Hashian)

True (Khloe Kardashian and Tristan Thompson)

Other celebrities are a little more tame in their choices, such as Chrissy Teigen and John Legend's son Miles – joining big sister Luna – and Luke, the baby boy of *Fantastic Beasts* star Eddie Redmaye. And then there are the Latin and Hispanic choices of several celebrities too, most of whom can credit their own ancestry for the selections: Gio Grace, from Adam Levine; Francisco from *Hamilton* composer and star Lin-Manuel Miranda; Romeo Alejandro David, the fifth child of Alec Baldwin; and Tiana Gia, Dwayne Johnson's second baby girl.

In 2017, Beyoncé and Jay Z applied to trademark the names Rumi Carter and Sir Carter for their twin girl and boy, echoing their actions when their daughter Blue Ivy Carter was born in 2012.

State differences

What's interesting about US baby name statistics is that there is such variety in the popularity of names across different states and territories. Olivia was a favorite name for baby girls in almost every state, and only the good people of Wyoming chose not to favour it.

However, only 16 states chose Liam for their top spot and a mere five picked Noah. This is in contrast to the national lists, in which Liam appears in first place and Noah in second.

It seems as though geography can have a major impact on baby-naming decisions, and population density can certainly change the rankings. States with smaller populations, like Wyoming or Vermont, usually have slightly different names making up their Top 5 each year. Alaska, for example, has Aurora for baby girls, which isn't found in any of the other states listed. The reasoning for this is simple: fewer babies born means each baby name chosen carries greater weight. For Logan to make the number one spot in Delaware it needed only 56 parents to choose it; to have the same impact and overtake Noah in Texas, it would need over 1,900. Likewise, only 45 babies were called Nora in South Dakota, but it still claimed fifth place.

The most popular baby girl name given in any mainland US state was Emma in California, with over 2,700 registrations. Likewise for boys it was Noah in California, with some 2,500 registrations. The names with the fewest picks but still able to claim a top spot were Evelyn in Vermont with 34 registrations, and Liam in Wyoming with 30. So find your state in the lists following lists—and make sure your baby won't have another ten Emmas or Noahs in their class!

Top 5 baby girl names by state

State	Rank 1	Rank 2	Rank 3	Rank 4	Rank 5
Alabama	Ava	Olivia	Emma	Harper	Amelia
Alaska	Emma	Olivia	Aurora	Isabella	Sophia
Arizona	Emma	Isabella	Olivia	Mia	Sophia
Arkansas	Emma	Olivia	Ava	Harper	Isabella
California	Emma	Mia	Olivia	Sophia	Isabella
Colorado	Emma	Olivia	Charlotte	Evelyn	Isabella
Connecticut	Olivia	Emma	Ava	Mia	Sophia
Delaware	Olivia	Ava	Charlotte	Isabella	Emma
Dist. of Columbia	Ava	Olivia	Eleanor	Genesis	Elizabeth
Florida	Isabella	Emma	Olivia	Sophia	Ava
Georgia	Ava	Olivia	Emma	Isabella	Charlotte
Hawaii	Emma	Olivia	Aria	Ava	Chloe
Idaho	Emma	Olivia	Charlotte	Evelyn	Harper
Illinois	Olivia	Emma	Ava	Sophia	Isabella
Indiana	Emma	Olivia	Amelia	Charlotte	Harper
Iowa	Harper	Emma	Olivia	Charlotte	Evelyn
Kansas	Emma	Olivia	Ava	Harper	Evelyn
Kentucky	Emma	Ava	Olivia	Harper	Isabella
Louisiana	Olivia	Ava	Emma	Amelia	Harper
Maine	Charlotte	Olivia	Emma	Harper	Amelia
Maryland	Ava	Olivia	Emma	Sophia	Charlotte
Massachusetts	Emma	Olivia	Charlotte	Sophia	Isabella

Baby Names 2019

State	Rank 1	Rank 2	Rank 3	Rank 4	Rank 5
Michigan	Emma	Ava	Olivia	Charlotte	Amelia
Minnesota	Olivia	Evelyn	Emma	Charlotte	Nora
Mississippi	Ava	Emma	Olivia	Paisley	Amelia
Missouri	Olivia	Ava	Emma	Amelia	Harper
Montana	Olivia	Emma	Harper	Ava	Charlotte
Nebraska	Emma	Olivia	Amelia	Charlotte	Evelyn
Nevada	Emma	Mia	Isabella	Sophia	Olivia
New Hampshire	Charlotte	Evelyn	Emma	Olivia	Amelia
New Jersey	Emma	Olivia	Isabella	Mia	Sophia
New Mexico	Mia	Sophia	Idsabella	Olivia	Ava
New York	Olivia	Emma	Sophia	Mia	Ava
North Carolina	Ava	Emma	Olivia	Isabella	Charlotte
North Dakota	Emma	Harper	Olivia	Amelia	Ava
Ohio	Emma	Ava	Olivia	Harper	Charlotte
Oklahoma	Emma	Olivia	Harper	Ava	Isabella
Oregon	Emma	Olivia	Sophia	Charlotte	Evelyn
Pennsylvania	Emma	Olivia	Ava	Charlotte	Sophia
Rhode Island	Charlotte	Emma	Olivia	Sophia	Isabella
South Carolina	Ava	Emma	Olivia	Charlotte	Harper
South Dakota	Emma	Olivia	Harper	Evelyn	Nora
Tennessee	Ava	Olivia	Emma	Amelia	Harper
Texas	Emma	Mia	Isabella	Sophia	Olivia
Utah	Olivia	Emma	Charlotte	Evelyn	Hazel
Vermont	Evelyn	Olivia	Charlotte	Emma	Harper
Virginia	Olivia	Ava	Emma	Charlotte	Isabella
Washington	Olivia	Emma	Evelyn	Ava	Isabella
West Virginia	Emma	Olivia	Harper	Paisley	Amelia
Wisconsin	Emma	Olivia	Evelyn	Charlotte	Ava
Wyoming	Emma	Harper	Ava	Avery	Charlotte

Top 5 baby boy names by state

State	Rank 1	Rank 2	Rank 3	Rank 4	Rank 5
Alabama	William	James	Elijah	John	Noah
Alaska	James	Liam	Wyatt	William	Noah
Arizona	Liam	Noah	Sebastian	Alexander	Julian
Arkansas	Elijah	William	Noah	Liam	Mason
California	Noah	Sebastian	Liam	Ethan	Matthew
Colorado	Liam	Oliver	William	Noah	Benjamin
Connecticut	Noah	Liam	Logan	Jacob	Michael
Delaware	Logan	Noah	Liam	Mason	Michael
Dist. of Columbia	James	Alexander	Henry	Noah	Benjamin
Florida	Liam	Noah	Lucas	Elijah	Matthew
Georgia	William	Noah	Mason	Elijah	James
Hawaii	Liam	Noah	Mason	Elijah	Logan
Idaho	Oliver	Liam	William	James	Mason
Illinois	Noah	Liam	Benjamin	Logan	Alexander
Indiana	Oliver	Liam	Elijah	Noah	William
Iowa	Oliver	Liam	Henry	Lincoln	Wyatt
Kansas	Oliver	William	Liam	Jackson	Henry
Kentucky	William	Elijah	Noah	Liam	James
Louisiana	Liam	Noah	Mason	Elijah	William
Maine	Oliver	Lincoln	Liam	Owen	Wyatt
Maryland	Liam	Noah	James	Logan	Jacob
Massachusetts	Benjamin	William	Liam	Lucas	Noah
Michigan	Liam	Noah	Oliver	Lucas	Mason
Minnesota	Oliver	William	Henry	Liam	Theodore
Mississippi	William	John	James	Mason	Elijah
Missouri	William	Liam	Oliver	Noah	Elijah
Montana	James	Liam	Liam	Oliver	Henry

Baby Names 2019

State	Rank 1	Rank 2	Rank 3	Rank 4	Rank 5
Nebraska	Oliver	Liam	William	Henry	Noah
Nevada	Liam	Noah	Elijah	Michael	Sebastian
New Hampshire	Logan	Henry	Mason	Owen	Oliver
New Jersey	Liam	Noah	Matthew	Michael	Jacob
New Mexico	Noah	Santiago	Elijah	Liam	Daniel
New York	Liam	Noah	Jacob	Lucas	Jospeh
North Carolina	William	Noah	Liam	James	Mason
North Dakota	Oliver	Henry	Liam	Noah	William
Ohio	Liam	Carter	Noah	William	Lucas
Oklahoma	William	Liam	Noah	Elijah	James
Oregon	Oliver	Liam	Henry	Benjamin	William
Pennsylvania	Liam	Noah	Logan	Benjamin	Mason
Rhode Island	Lucas	Liam	Noah	Julian	Mason
South Carolina	William	Noah	Mason	James	Liam
South Dakota	Oliver	Owen	Lincoln	Liam	William
Tennessee	William	Elijah	James	Noah	Mason
Texas	Noah	Liam	Sebastian	Mateo	Elijah
Utah	Oliver	Liam	William	James	Benjamin
Vermont	Wyatt	William	Oliver	Liam	Noah
Virginia	Liam	William	Noah	James	Benjamin
Washington	Liam	Oliver	Noah	William	Benjamin
West Virginia	Liam	Mason	Elijah	Grayson	Carter
Wisconsin	Henry	Oliver	Liam	William	Logan
Wyoming	Liam	Wyatt	Carter	James	Logan

2 Predictions for the coming year

Future trends

Looking forward, we predict the Top 10 names will probably go largely unchanged for both boys and girls, but based on some trends from previous years, we can make some predictions. As parents grow more globally aware and the demographics of North America change, we may see more culturally and ethnically diverse names appearing in these lists, such as Mahnoor and Dandre.

Along the same theme, we will continue to see a pattern of the US adopting trends from other countries—particularly the UK, Australia, and New Zealand. Trends in these countries have been moving steadily towards shorter, cuter names and even using nicknames as first names, such as Ellie, Bobby, Jamie, and Max, and the US has been slowly following suit for a couple of years now. These countries are also fans of using very traditional names, and look back to their country's heritage for inspiration (such as royal or literary names). The same thing is starting to happen in the USA, and it's possible we'll see some very old names coming back into style—perhaps even inspired by the Puritans or the

Founding Fathers. Look out for some virtuous Puritan names such as Mercy, Temperance, and Gideon, or even Alexander (Hamilton), Benjamin (Franklin), and of course George (Washington).

Top 10 names from 1919		Top 10 names from 1969	
Boys	**Girls**	**Boys**	**Girls**
1. John	1. Mary	1. Michael	1. Lisa
2. William	2. Helen	2. David	2. Michelle
3. James	3. Dorothy	3. James	3. Jennifer
4. Robert	4. Margaret	4. John	4. Kimberly
5. Charles	5. Ruth	5. Robert	5. Melissa
6. George	6. Mildred	6. William	6. Amy
7. Joseph	7. Virginia	7. Christopher	7. Angela
8. Edward	8. Elizabeth	8. Mark	8. Mary
9. Frank	9. Frances	9. Brian	9. Tammy
10. Thomas	10. Anna	10. Richard	10. Laura

Speaking of history, the 100-year rule helps us understand how baby names regain popularity, with names that were popular at the end of World War I and at the start of the Roaring Twenties once again on every parent's list. And it doesn't seem to be failing, with names that were in the 1919 Top 100 likely appearing in 2019 as well. Look at William and James, and Anna and Charlotte. The reverse is true, too; names that were popular only 50 years ago are now as unfashionable as the clothing we once wore. Think about Lisa, Brian, or Tammy, or any of the names we learned from *Mad Men*. However, some names we used to use are still our top picks, simply because they're considered so timeless they've never really gone out of style (William and James definitely fit this mold).

Predicted 2019 baby names

Boys		Girls	
1. Liam	6. Benjamin	1. Emma	6. Mia
2. Noah	7. Oliver	2. Olivia	7. Charlotte
3. Logan	8. Elijah	3. Ava	8. Abigail
4. William	9. Jacob	4. Sophia	9. Amelia
5. James	10. Mason	5. Isabella	10. Evelyn

For girls' names, it's certain that those ending in -a/-er will continue to dominate the Top 20 for at least a while longer. There are currently 12 names in that group that end in -a/-er, and of those 12, six moved up places from the year before (Amelia, Aria, Ella, Harper, Isabella, and Victoria); four stayed put (Ava, Emma, Mia, and Olivia), and only two moved down (Sofia and Sophia). Other similar-sounding names in the Top 20 include Avery, Emily, and Evelyn, which presumably means that names ending in -y or -ie sounds will also stick around for a few more years, as well as Charlotte and Scarlett. To top it all off, two of the Top 20 names are so similar they're essentially the same name with a different spelling: Sophia and Sofia. In fact, there are only three names that don't fit into one of the -a or -y/-ie molds—Abigail, Elizabeth, and Madison—and all of those are such "classics" that they, too, have grown considerably in popularity over the last ten years.

With boys' names, trends are a little harder to predict. There are definitely names that sound very similar in the Top 20 though, such as Liam and William, and Aiden, Benjamin, Ethan, Jackson, Logan, and Mason. Also, names beginning with J or M are pretty big right now (Jackson, Jacob, James, and Joseph; and Mason, Matthew, and Michael), and if you really want to dig deep, a great many of the names in the boys' list are straight from the Bible: Alexander, Benjamin, Daniel, David, Elijah, Ethan, Jacob,

James, Joseph, Lucas, Matthew, Michael, and, of course, Noah. There is a great deal more shuffling in the ranks going on in the boys' names list, with huge differences over the last ten years—especially in names listed outside the Top 10. Therefore, it's probable that parents expecting baby boys in 2019 will be following trends such as traditional or religious names instead.

Most popular biblical names

According to data from the SSA, these are the most popular names taken from the Bible for the last 100 years:

1. James	6. Joseph
2. John	7. Thomas
3. Michael	8. Christopher
4. David	9. Daniel
5. Mary	10. Matthew

In general, US parents prefer to give their children full-length names rather than shortened versions or nicknames, although, as mentioned previously, this trend may start to decline in the coming years. Elizabeth (13th) appears higher up the charts than Ellie (44th) and Libby (1068th). We see this over and over again: Jacob (ranked 10th) is more popular than Jake (248th); Abigail (10th) is higher than Abby (4509th); and Eve (436th) is much further down the charts than Evelyn (12th).

However, in some cases, a short version or a nickname actually now ranks higher than the traditional name it's taken from. The name Ella (16th last year), for example, is a shortened version of Eleanor (35th), while Leo (61st) is a shortened version of either Leon (245th) or Leonardo (97th); both of these shorter names are certainly more widespread than the longer ones. In parts of Europe this is particularly fashionable right now, so perhaps in 2019 we will see more of a European flair to our baby-naming game.

Liberal Lena or conservative Kim?

What about the theory that you can tell the political leanings of a family by the name a parent gives their child? Well, in a study conducted at the University of Chicago, researchers noticed that parents with more liberal leanings tended to give names that contained softer sounds, like -a and -l. Examples included Ella, Sophia, Liam, and Lena. Parents with more conservative views chose names with harder or stronger sounds, like -d, -b, -t, and -k. Examples of those names were Kurt, Kim, Donald, and Bryce. However, the researchers also noted that the level of education each parent obtained had as much of an impact as their political viewpoint: well-educated parents chose unusual names, but with traditional spellings (such as Atticus or Finnegan), and less educated parents chose traditional names with more unusual spellings (such as Andruw instead of Andrew). So, while it's true that politicians and political stances definitely affect baby name trends, it might have quite a lot to do with levels of education as well.

Goings-on in 2019

Other influences on the names parents choose in 2019 may come from the worlds of sport, politics, and royalty. In 2019 there are a couple of major sporting events, and athletes who perform well at them will no doubt become inspirational for new parents. Other than the usual run of baseball's World Series, college basketball's March Madness, and of course, football's Super Bowl 53, we will also be observing some international events such as the athletics World Championships and the FIFA Women's World Cup.

There is a chance that not only sport stars themselves, but also the names they choose for their own children might prove influential. It wouldn't be the first time: Dallas Cowboys defensive end Datone Jones chose the name Laila for his baby girl, citing a great admiration for boxer Muhammad Ali and Ali's daughter Laila Ali; and Arizona Cardinals cornerback Patrick Peterson chose the name Paityn for his little girl, after NFL quarterback legend Peyton Manning. Watch out for athletes that perform well at the World Championships and Superbowl, and possibly even what they name their children!

So what of politics? If nothing else, you can't say that 2018 wasn't an eventful year for our country, and if the trend continues, 2019 will follow suit. But the question is, how will political events and headlines affect the names we give our babies? Well, one thing is for certain: while very few parents are turned on to the name Donald (it's been in steady decline since 1934 and hasn't been in the Top 200 since 1999), more and more of us are choosing the name Melania for our daughters. The name jumped a massive 720 spots last year, making it the fifth-highest climber of all names on the list, and it will be interesting to see what happens as our extraordinary political climate continues in 2019.

The idea that we don't name our children after our politicians isn't new, mind you. Neither Barack nor Obama appeared in the Top 1,000 at any point during the former president's two terms, and despite the name Hillary scoring high in the years preceding the election, it hasn't appeared there again since. However, Barack Obama's daughters are named Malia and Sasha, and the name Malia jumped a whopping 350 places the year Obama was first elected and has continued to grow in popularity ever since. Sasha, which was already fairly common, also jumped a further 100, although it has struggled to broach the Top 500 since the Obamas left the White House.

> When Pope Francis I was elected a few years ago, there was a flurry of parents choosing to honor him. The name Francis jumped nearly 20 places last year alone and Frances (for baby girls) also moved up to almost hit the Top 40. In fact, Francis is now the most popular name for baby boys in Italy.

Banned names around the world

@—China
Akuma (meaning "devil")—Japan
Anus—Denmark
Chow Tow (meaning "smelly head")—Malaysia
Dalmata (meaning "Dalmatian")—Italy
Gesher (meaning "bridge")—Norway
Monkey—Denmark
Ovnis (meaning "UFO")—Portugal
Q—Sweden
Sor Chai (meaning "insane")—Malaysia
Stompy—German

There's always the chance of a regal influence, particularly with celebrities such as the Kardashians and Lil' Kim choosing names like Reign and Duke. Queen Elizabeth is now Britain's longest-reigning monarch, since she has been on the throne longer than the 63 years and seven months Queen Victoria reigned. It's possible, although extremely unlikely, that she will choose to step down for her eldest son Prince Charles, sparking renewed interest in both her name and his. The name Elizabeth is in 13th place in the US right now, and has held firm in the Top 20 for over 50 years. Victoria is in 19th place, and it too has been in about the same place for over decades. Both are considered such classic names that it's hard to imagine them disappearing entirely.

A law in Sonora, Mexico, states parents cannot give their babies names that are defined by authorities as "derogatory, pejorative, discriminatory or lacking in meaning." Names on the published list include Twitter, Burger King, Hitler, Facebook, Harry Potter, Escroto (Spanish for scrotum), and Batman.

America's strange choices

According to the website BabyCenter.com, parents are choosing some pretty imaginative names. Users recently registered the following names for their children:

Boys	Girls
Axel	Journey
Avaan	Niamey
Bello	Princess
Major	Wynter
New	Zaylee

Significant upcoming dates

So what else might influence baby names? How about anniversaries? No, we don't mean your wedding anniversary, or the first time your significant other brought you coffee at work, but rather significant worldly events that are acknowledged during the year. When these dates pop up in the media it can remind expecting parents of names that had been forgotten to the past, and they can therefore become useful inspiration. Coming up in 2019 …

- 10th anniversary of the Miracle on the Hudson, when Captain Chelsey "Sully" Sullenberger successfully performed an emergency landing on the River Hudson in New York after his plane struck a flock of geese.

- 25th anniversary of the attack on figure skater Nancy Kerrigan by rival Tonya Harding and her ex-husband Jeff Gillooly.

- 25th anniversary of the release of the original *Lion King* movie, so look out for Simba and Nala to become more popular again.

- 40th anniversary of the publication of Douglas Adams' *Hitchhiker's Guide to the Galaxy*, and the 50th anniversary of the first time an episode of *Monty Python's Flying Circus* was broadcast on TV. Did you know Douglas Adams was also briefly part of the writing team for the infamous comedy series? Well, now you do.

- 80th anniversary of the start of World War II. Watch out for Franklin and Truman to make an appearance again … although probably not Adolf.

- 100th anniversary of the passing of the Nineteenth Amendment in the USA, granting women the right to vote. You can thank Susan B. Anthony and Elizabeth Cady Stanton for helping our ancestral sisters catch up with other countries across the pond.

- 200th anniverary of the birth of author and poet Walt Whitman, and 100 years for J.D. Salinger, the latter being the author of every angst-ridden teenage boy's favourite book *Catcher in the Rye*. It's also Sir Arthur Conan Doyle's 160th birthday.

Most popular names of all time

Boys	Girls
1. James	1. Mary
2. John	2. Patricia
3. Robert	3. Jennifer
4. Michael	4. Linda
5. William	5. Elizabeth
6. David	6. Barbara
7. Richard	7. Susan
8. Joseph	8. Jessica
9. Thomas	9. Sarah
10. Charles	10. Margaret

Showbiz babies

As always, pop culture will probably be the most prominent influence on baby names in the coming year. Celebrities with new arrivals from the stork include Eva Longoria, Rachel McAdams, and Kirsten Dunst. The choices of names these and other pregnant celebrities make are particularly noteworthy, and they may well influence the choices made by the general population.

Celebrity bumps ahead

Rebecca Hall and Morgan Spector

Claire Danes and Hiugh Dancy

Cat Deeley and Patrick Kielty

Hilary Duff and Matthew Koma

Kat Von D and Leafar Sayers

Rachel Weisz and Daniel Craig

Kate Hudson and Danny Fujikawa

Michael Bublé and Luisana Lopilato

Tom Daley and Dustin Lance Black

The year 2019 looks like being a pretty stonking one for new films. Disney is doubling-down on the success of the live-action remakes of *Cinderella*, *Beauty and the Beast*, and *The Jungle Book*, by releasing not one ... not two... but three new versions of some classic animations. Get set to relive your childhood (and probably cry your eyes out) through *Aladdin*, *Dumbo*, and *The Lion King*. The latter's release is being carefully timed to coincide with the 25th anniversary of the original cartoon—which makes me personally feel very old indeed. Disney is also crowning itself "King of the Sequel" again, by releasing *Toy Story 4*, *Frozen 2*, and what seem to be several thousand superhero films under their Marvel banner.

Names that are featured in these films stand a good chance of influencing baby names if past trends are repeated. *Frozen 2*, for example, will almost definitely spike interest in the names Elsa and Anna again. After its release in late 2013, Elsa jumped 250 places into the Top 250, and Kristoff appeared in the charts for the first time ever! It's entirely possible the sequel will introduce us to a new cast of lovable characters whose names we just have to have for our children. And as for *Aladdin*, well. Jasmine was stuck in the middle of the charts for years and years before the early 1990s, but since then it's remained steadfastly in the Top 100. Last year it slipped to position 130, but 2019 could be the year it breaks the Top 50.

Big and Small Screen baby names

Boys	Girls
Finn	Aria
George	Elizabeth
Graham	Elsa
Han	Jasmine
Jonathon	Jhaleesi
Kylo	Nala
Lincoln	Piper
Philip	Rey
Ryan	Trixie
Winston	Yasmin

Harry's back! (Sort of ...)

Did you miss the Wizarding World of Harry Potter? You weren't alone. We turned out in droves to see the newest big screen addition to the Harry Potter/Fantastic Beasts universe in 2018, *Fantastic Beasts: The Crimes of Grindelwald*. While Newt Scamander might not be popping up on birth certificates any time soon, it did bring the delightful Albus Dumbledore back into our lives and the entire Harry Potter-naming phenomenon back into the charts.

Fictional characters with hidden meanings in their names

Bran Stark (*Game of Thrones*)—bran is an old Welsh name from the word for "raven".

Darth Vader (*Star Wars*)—darth is related to "dark" or "death"; vader is Dutch for "father".

Frodo Baggins (*The Lord of the Rings*)—from fród, meaning "wise by experience" in Old English.

Katniss Everdeen (*The Hunger Games*)—from the katniss plant, meaning "archer" in Latin.

Nyota Uhura (*Star Trek*)—from the Swahili term for "star freedom".

Remus Lupin (*Harry Potter*)—Remus was an ancient Roman orphan raised by wolves; lupinus is the Latin word for "wolfish".

As for the influence the small screen could wield on our collective baby-naming psyche, *Dr Who* is a good place to start. After the success of the first female Time Lord's series in 2018, another series is predicted to be equally as good in 2019. Maybe it's time for the names Graham, Ryan, and Yasmin to break away from the rest of the pack?

And everyone likes zombies … right? Well, according to newest data about popular zombie series *The Walking Dead*, we at least love naming our babies after them. Walker, Abraham, Sasha and Maggie have all been big climbers since the show was first broadcast, and a new series in 2019 will have a similar impact. In fact, British actor Andrew Lincoln has seen his own name move up the charts recently – Lincoln is now in 41st place and has jumped over roughly 150 spots in ten years.

Other popular TV programs set to air in 2019 include *Game of Thrones*, *Empire*, *The Blacklist*, and another season of *Orange is the New Black*.

As some of you may be heavily pregnant, so you're putting your feet up and watching some TV, you may be influenced by some of these shows. What about Tyrion (Lannister, *Game of Thrones*), Raymond "Red" (Reddington, *The Blacklist*), Piper (Chapman, *Orange is the New Black*) … or even Cookie (Lyon, *Empire*)? We're not even joking: for a detailed look at how *Game of Thrones* has impacted baby names, see page 13.

Reality series will continue to influence our decisions—especially after Kylie Jenner named her daughter Stormi last year and 35 parents promptly followed suit. Kim Kardashian and singer/rapper Kanye West named their daughters North (also known as Nori, which is a lot cuter) and Chicago, and their son Saint. The names North and Saint both picked up steam last year, with 17 babies called North and 138 called Saint (that's a 50% increase for each name), although Chicago wasn't given to a single baby last year! Sister Khloe chose a family name for her newborn last year too: apparently the name True was also the name of her great-grandfather and grandfather. Celebrities: they choose family names just like the rest of us!.

Prince's goodbye Kiss

Following the death of pop legend Prince in 2016, there was a sudden uptick in parents choosing to add the name Prince to their baby's birth certificate. The trend continued into 2017 too, and included Princedavid, Princeamir, Princemichael, and, of course, just plain Prince—which jumped up 50 places to 345th place. A fitting tribute, this also fits neatly into the current trend for Royal baby names.

3 How to choose a name

Your baby-naming checklist

- Fall in love with the name(s) you've chosen. Pick a name that makes you smile because, if you love it, hopefully your child will too.

- Don't listen to other people. Sometimes grandparents and friends will offer you baby-naming "advice," which may not always be welcome. If you've got your heart set on a name, keep it a secret until after the birth. Trust your own instincts: they will come in handy later.

    > Norwegian baby-naming law is so strict that Norwegians are only allowed to use names that appear on an approved list. Parents who break this law have been fined and even jailed! Banned names include Gesher (meaning bridge), and anything that could be mistaken for a surname.

- Find a name with meaning. Having a name that has a back story helps your child understand their significance in the world, so whether you name them after a religious saint or prophet, an important political figure, or a hero in a Greek tragedy, ensure they know where their name came from. They may just be inspired to be as great as their namesake.

- Have fun. Picking out names should be fun. Laughing at the ones you'd never dream of choosing can really help you narrow it down to the ones you would. You can also experiment with different spellings, pronunciations, or variations of names you like, or go to places where you might feel inspired.

- Expand your mind. Don't rule out the weird ones just yet! As a teenager I went to school with a girl named Siam. Her parents had conceived her on a honeymoon trip to Thailand and gave her the country's former name. She loved growing up and having an unusual name, as I'm sure Penelope Scotland (Kourtney Kardashian and Scott Disick's daughter) and Winnie Fallon do too. (Jimmy Fallon's daughter is named after the New Hampshire lake where he proposed to his wife.)

  > The shortest baby names are only two letters long (Al, Ed, Jo, and Ty), but the longest could be any length imaginable.
  > Popular 11-letter-long names include Bartholomew, Christopher, Constantine, and Maximillian.

- Try it out. While you're pregnant, talk to your baby and address it using a variety of your favorite names to see if it responds. There are numerous stories of names being chosen because the baby kicked when it was called Charlie or Aisha, but was suspiciously silent when it was called Dexter or Mildred, so see if it has a preference! Try writing names down and sticking them to your fridge, practicing a few signatures, or saying one out loud enough times to see if you ever get sick of it.

- Do *not* pick the name of an ex. No matter how lovely you think your ex's name is, it would take a very understanding partner to allow you to pick it for your baby. Just steer clear of any names you know will cause problems to other people, paying particular attention to your partner and loved ones.

> How's this for a tip? Awesomebabyname.com will let you pick a name based on what domain names are available, in case you want to get ahead of your child's celebrity status and start their online visibility early.

- What if you can't agree? This is probably the trickiest problem to solve in the baby-naming process. It's wise to research a number of names you and your partner are both interested in and make a point of discussing your reasons for liking or disliking them long before the baby is due to be born. The labor and delivery room is probably not the best place to argue as you'll both be tired, emotional, and at least one of you will be in pain. Avoid sticking to your guns on a name one of you really isn't happy with because it might lead to your baby being caught in the middle.

- Compromise is the name of the game. You could try compromising and picking two middle names so you both have a name in there that you love; or you could each have five names you're allowed to "veto," but no more. Whichever way you go about it, it is important that you both eventually agree on the name you are giving your baby, even if it means losing out on the one you've had your heart set on.

- Use your app. With all the new technology literally at our fingertips, how about putting some of it to good use? There are hundreds of new apps for smartphones and tablets that promise to help you narrow down the endless lists of potential names to the one you'll love.

Think to the future

One important aspect of naming your child is thinking ahead to their future. Will the name you've chosen stand the test of time? Will names popular in 2019 remain popular in 2059? Will they be able to confidently enter a room and give a crucial business presentation with an awkward or unpronounceable name? Will they be able to hand their business card over to a potential client without that client looking bemused? Even sooner, can they survive the potential minefields of elementary school and junior high with a name that could easily be shortened to something embarrassing? Would you want to try catching criminals as Sheriff Apple Blossom or have other politicians take you seriously with a name like Senator Fortune Scarlett? You don't want to give your child a name they just cannot live with for the rest of their life, so make your choice based on what's appropriate for an adult as well as a child. To make this easier you might want to choose a longer name that can be shortened or extended as your child desires.

Popular names from the past

Boys	Girls
Abraham	Agatha
Arthur	Bertha
Edmund	Clara
Emmett	Edith
Franklin	Gladys
Gilbert	Mabel
Jasper	Pearl
Neville	Theodora
Percival	Wilhelmina
Vincent	Winifred

If your child doesn't like the name you've given them because their first and surnames make a funny combination, they may choose to use just their first name professionally as an adult. An old colleague of mine goes by "Shiney" only—omitting her surname on business cards and emails because it's a euphemism for male genitalia.

The topical website Buzzfeed.com once ran an article on people with funny names who were caught on camera. Living among us are Dr Whet Fartz, horse riding judge Willie Stroker, and store district manager Rick Roll ... which is probably only funny if you've ever been "rickrolled" online. At the same time another article appeared, listing all the reasons why having an unusual name is a hassle—examples given were not ever being able to find your name on novelty souvenirs, coffee shop baristas not knowing how to spell or pronounce your name for your order, and other people giving you "fun, new" nicknames because they can't be bothered with your given name. I say we just ask those same baristas to call us Duchess or Duke and have done with it.

> Another Buzzfeed article in 2018 asked users to submit the strangest names they'd ever come across. The accuracy of the submissions cannot be verified for accuracy, but did include the glorious Guitar, Gamble, Peachy, Random, and twins Nikola and Tesla. There's an idea: give your baby a name so obscure they appear in future pop news articles twenty years from now!

Stereotypes—true or false?

Will the name you choose actually affect your child's life? Will names that seem clever make your child brainier? Will names with positive meanings make your child a happier person? The answer is … possibly.

One thing you should consider is how your child's name will be perceived by the outside world. Typically, judgments are passed on a person before they are met, and made purely based on their name, such as at job interviews or in school. A survey of 3,000 teachers found that 49% of them make assumptions about their pupils based on their names alone. Topping the "naughty" charts were Callum, Connor, and Jack for boys; and Chelsea, Courtney, and Chardonnay for girls. On the other hand, the names in the "clever" category were Alexander, Adam, and Christopher for boys; and Elizabeth, Charlotte, and Emma for girls.

Research has also indicated that certain names are more likely to provoke strong responses in people. A study analyzed the number of stickers given to children as rewards for good behavior. Children named Abigail and

Jacob are more likely to be praised for being well-behaved than children named Beth and Josh; and children who do not shorten their name or go by nicknames are more likely to be better behaved, too.

Inspirational names		Aspirational names	
Destiny	Joy	Armani	Ferrari
Happy	Peace	Aston	Jaguar
Heaven	Serenity	Bugatti	Mercedes
Hope	Unique	Chanel	Porsche
Innocence	Unity	Dolce	Prada

Along the same lines, a study conducted by the Hebrew University of Jerusalem in 2017 found that we subconsciously act like stereotypes of our names, and that other people can pick up on it. They asked students to guess the names of faces they were shown, and the students were able to correctly match them twice as often as expected. So think carefully about the names on your favorites list, and consider what types of personalities tend to have these names. If you don't like the answers, it might be time to reconsider. (But you can probably relax: Herbert was the name suggested to be most associated with an idiot and only 80 baby boys were given that last year, so you're probably safe.)

And finally, a recent university study suggests that names are particularly important for language development in early childhood. Apparently, a child's name is one of the first words they can identify (probably from all that cooing into the cot that goes on when they're born), and they use it to learn how to construct and deconstruct sentences. Their name anchors the sentence spoken to them, enabling them to pick out other familiar words and sounds, and put them all together to identify the meaning of the entire thing. Brainy stuff!

Eccentric names

There are lots of advantages to having an eccentric name. For one thing, people will never forget your child's name, and if they do something influential with their life their name could become an inspiration for other parents. On the other hand, a quirky name often requires a quirky personality. If you don't think your genes could stand up to a name like Satchel or Zizi, perhaps it's time to think of one a little more run-of-the-mill.

An eccentric name often says more about the parents than the child, and their own personalities may affect the personality of their child in a significant way. A conventional family that names its baby John will probably find he becomes a conventional child, whereas a quirky family that names its baby Zanzibar will find he develops a quirky personality. The name itself is not the leading factor; it's the eccentric or conventional behavior encouraged by the parents who chose the name that's important.

Children who are told they have inherited an ancestor's name or are named after an influential character from history might be more driven and focused than children who are told disappointingly, "We just liked the sound of it." As a parent, therefore, it seems it's okay to pick an unusual name if you have a story or reason behind it. So naming your child Atticus (after Atticus Finch from Harper Lee's To Kill a Mockingbird, once known for being a strong and moral character), or even Harper (like the Beckhams and every other celebrity a few years ago did), may not be a bad idea ...

Ivy League names

Alcott	Graydon
Arthur	Katherine
Beatrice	Martha
Caroline	Robert
Charles	Victoria

However, be warned: there is also new research from baby website Bounty.com which says that as many as one in five parents regret their choice of baby name. Of the 3,000 parents interviewed, 20% said they no longer thought the unusual choice of spelling or pronunciation was appropriate. Around 8% said they were tired of

> ## Names that sound "clever"
>
> | | |
> |---|---|
> | Abner | Shanahan |
> | Cassidy | Todd |
> | Haley | Ulysses |
> | Penelope | Washington |
> | Portia | Wylie |

people mispronouncing their child's name, and 10% thought the novelty of the original pick had worn off. They also said they would now pick a new name which had not occurred to them or been an option before.

One possible way to avoid potential regret or humiliation is to download the SSA's hard data on the most recent baby-name choices, and scour the names down at the bottom of the lists for inspiration. You are likely to find a wealth of unusual and currently unpopular names there, but it's comforting to know that your child won't be the only one in the world with that name. Suggestions from last year's data include Aneka, Dollie, Lynea, Retta, and Zeya for girls; and Blair, Hernando, Olly, Rolf, and Yogi for boys.

While avoiding any kind of possible connection to a fictional character is nigh on impossible, you can help make things easier for your child by educating them about their namesake and encouraging them to read more about them. Stay up to date with new cartoons and children's characters to prepare both yourself and your child for preschool and childhood. That way they can be proud of their name and have ammunition if things get rough in the schoolyard.

Controversial names adopted by real people

Adolf Hitler	Jezebel
Beelzebub	Lucifer
Desdemona	Mussolini
Hannibal Lecter	Stalin
Himmler	Voldemort

Masculine or feminine?

How do we define what makes a name masculine or feminine? Well, it may be to do with the sounds the letters create, either when written down or spoken aloud. Harder-sounding combinations (-ter, -it, -ld) tend to be found in masculine names, and softer-sounding combinations (-ie, -ay, -la) are more associated with feminine names. You therefore end up with Sophia, Joanie, and Bella; or Harold, Walter, David, and Oscar. If you're planning on choosing a feminine-sounding name, approach with caution: recent research suggests that girls who are given particularly "girly" names—think Tiana, Kayla, or Isabella—are much more likely to misbehave when they reach school age. These "feminine" girls were also far less likely to choose subjects at school like math and science, while their sisters with more masculine names—such as Morgan, Alexis, and Ashley—were encouraged to excel in these courses.

Nowadays, names are becoming more androgynous and loads of names appear in both boys' and girls' lists: Madison, Riley, Hayden, and, of course, Alex—some form of which appears in the Top 100 for both boys and girls every year. Therefore, if you want a more gender-neutral name for your new arrival, you won't be alone.

Gold-digger names

According to a survey by background-check website DirtSearch.org, the following names are supposedly more likely to belong to "gold diggers":

1. Jennifer
2. Jessica
3. Michelle
4. Lisa
5. Ashley

6. Amanda
7. Melissa
8. Stephanie
9. Nicole
10. Angela

But what about your own gender? Does the fact you're a man or woman mean you're more likely to pick certain names for your child? Well, it looks like this isn't the case, but there might be an element of truth to it. Apparently, mothers are prone to picking names that are similar to, or exactly the same as, their maiden name, if they got rid of it when they got married. This system allows a mother to pass on a part of her own lineage, as well as the father's. A lot of celebrities do this, too, allowing a child to either use their middle name as an additional surname, or ignore it altogether. Either way, it ensures the famous mom's name gets to stick around a bit longer!

Another recent study found that mothers tend to win the argument over who gets to pick the final name of a newborn, with four in ten moms ignoring the choices selected by dads, and one in ten dads just simply backing down. However, four in ten couples don't make the final decision until after the baby is born, and a third will argue about it before settling—but hey, at least they're talking about it!

Cartoon characters named after real people

Yogi Bear (named after baseball player Yogi Berra)

Buzz Lightyear (named after astronaut Buzz Aldrin)

Alvin, Simon, and Theodore Chipmunk (named after record executives)

Calvin and Hobbes (named after the theologian John Calvin and philosopher Thomas Hobbes)

Homer, Marge, Lisa, and Maggie Simpson (named after creator Matt Groening's family members)

Teenage Mutant Ninja Turtles (all named after Renaissance painters: Raphael, Michelangelo, Donatello, and Leonardo da Vinci)

Nicknames

Nicknames are unavoidable. They can range from the common—Mike from Michael, Sam from Samantha—to the trendy, funny, or downright insulting. Don't be put off if the name you love has an unfortunate nickname associated with it, though—if you don't encourage the use of nicknames, chances are they won't stick. Another way to avoid embarrassing nicknames is to select one for your child that you actually like so that others don't even get a mention. Call your daughter Elizabeth by the name Liz, Lizzie, or Libby if you don't like Betty or Beth, and no one will even consider the alternatives. You can pre-empt possible nicknames to some extent by saying the name you've chosen out loud and trying to find rhymes for it. This is a clever way to avoid children's chants and nursery rhyme-type insults, such as Dora the Explorer or Georgie Porgie. But don't be too concerned about schoolyard chants—most children are subjected to them at some point and emerge unscathed.

> Pronunciation matters: A Swedish couple was once banned from naming their child "Brfxxccxxmnpccccllllmmnprxvclmnck-ssqlbb11116," which they claimed was pronounced "Albin."

Your surname

Try to avoid first names that might lead to unfortunate phrases when combined with your surname, to prevent a lifetime of embarrassment for your child. The best way to work out if this might happen is to write down all the names you like alongside your child's surname and have someone else read them out loud. This second pair of eyes and ears might just spot something you didn't. The age of the internet has given parents a wonderful new weapon in their baby-naming arsenal: the search engine. Before you settle on anything final, try searching for any examples of the complete first, middle, and surname of your new baby. You may find out that your baby has an ax-murderer namesake—or, like one of my colleagues, the same name as a well-known porn star.

Initials

What surname will your baby have? Will it lend itself easily to amusing acronyms when coupled with certain first and middle names? My brother-in-law was going to be called Andrew Steven Schmitt before he was born, until his parents realized at the last minute what his initials would spell ...

Bizarre baby names from around the country

Boys	Girls
Aero	Ace
Burger	Kaixin
Donathan	Leeloo
Espn	Monalisa
Haven'T	Rogue
Kix	Sesame
Pawk	Thinn
Rysk	Yoga
Zaniel	Zealand

It's also worth taking the time to think about how credit cards display names or how your child's name would look written out on a form. Nobody should have to go through life known as S. Lugg because their parents didn't think that far ahead.

Using family names

Some families have a strong tradition of using names for babies that come from the family tree. There are families where naming your son Augustine VIII is simply not an option—it's a rule. Another way families do this is to give children the name of their parent of the same sex and add "Junior" (Jr.) to the end. This could only create a problem if that child then decides to carry on the tradition and name their child after themselves—after all, who wants to be known as Frederick Jr. Jr.?

There are pros and cons to using family names.

- **Pros:** Your child will feel part of a strong tradition, which will create a sense of security for them and help make them feel a complete member of the family. If you're having a problem selecting a name you and your partner both agree on, this is a very simple solution and will make your new child's family very happy.

- **Cons:** You might not actually like the name that's being passed down. Naming your child the 12th Thumbelina in a row might not actually hold the same attraction for you as for the generation before. Another drawback could be if the cultural associations with a name have changed in your lifetime and it is no longer appropriate.

One way to include a family name is to compromise. You could use the name as a middle name, or refer to your baby by a nickname instead. Another possible solution is to use monikers—if your family is insisting your daughter be called Jade, maybe you could choose Giada instead. Or if your partner is determined the next child be called Michael after himself, and it turns out to be a girl, choose Michaela in its place. In many Jewish families the tradition is to take the name of a deceased relative and give it to a new baby. If this thought fills you with dread, you could opt for a possible solution a lot of families adopt, which is to use the first initial instead. If you're not keen on Solomon, pick Samuel; if you don't like Ruth, choose Rebecca.

Spellings and pronunciation

Once you've finally agreed on a name, it's time to consider how you wish it to be spelled and pronounced. Some parents love experimenting with unusual variations of traditional names, while others prefer names to be instantly recognizable. Try to avoid making a common name too long or too unusual in its spelling as this will be the first thing your child learns how to write. They will also have to spell it out constantly during their lifetime, as other people misspell or mispronounce their name. Substituting the odd "i" for a "y" isn't too bad, but turning the name Jonathan into Jonnaythanne doesn't do anyone any favors.

> **"Text speak" spellings**
>
> Camron
> Conna
> Ema
> Esta
> Flicity
> Jayk
> Lora
> Patryk
> Samiul
> Summa
> Wilym

A palindrome name is a name that is spelt the same backwards and forwards, as with Bob, Elle, Eve, and Hannah.

According to the journal *Scientific American*, participants in one particular study were more likely to believe statements made by people with names they could pronounce, and distrust statements from those they could not. The study only used names from countries outside of the USA, to adjust for pre-existing prejudices, and found that the harder to pronounce the name, the less trustworthy the statement coming from the person seemed to be. Interesting stuff, and worth thinking about if you're debating whether to add that extra "xyz" to your baby's name.

Middle names

Giving your child a middle name is generally acknowledged to be standard practice these days. In fact, it has become fairly uncommon to name a child without a middle name, although the use of second and third names only became popular around the turn of the 20th century. Before then, giving a child a middle name was seen as a status symbol; it was only really used when a man married a higher-class woman and they wanted to keep the woman's maiden name as a reminder of the child's heritage. Once the fashion caught on, it became popular to give more than one middle name to children of status, but it's only been since the 1900s that it has become standard for everyone.

Regardless of your status, a middle name can have just as much of an impact as a first name, so your choice for your own baby should be made as carefully as the decision about their first name.

> New Zealand has a law that states baby names cannot exceed 99 characters, including first, middle, and surnames.

Here are some common trends to help you choose.

- Opposite-length names. It has become popular to give a child either a long first name and short middle name (e.g. Jennifer Ruth, Nicholas John), or vice versa.

- Name from the family tree. Honoring your ancestors is another current trend. Parents are looking back to their own lineage for interesting, unusual, or influential names.

- Unusual names. Parents who aren't brave enough to give their child an out-there name as a first name are using it as a middle name.

- Maiden name or other parent name. It is becoming increasingly common to use a parent's first name, or mother's maiden name, as a middle name for a baby.

You may have already decided what middle name to give your child due to tradition or culture, in which case the following advice may be moot. In some Hispanic cultures, for example, middle names are often the mother's surname or another name to promote the matriarchal lineage. Similarly, parents who have not taken each other's surnames or are not married may choose to give their child one surname as a middle name and one as a surname so both parents are represented. Other traditions use an old family name, passed down to each first-born son or daughter, to encourage a sense of family pride and history. A decision about what middle name to pass on may have therefore already been made for you, even before your own birth.

Sweden has a pretty strict naming law, enacted in 1982, which says: "First names shall not be approved if they can cause offense or can be supposed to cause discomfort for the one using it, or names which for some obvious reason are not suitable as a first name." However, the Swedish government did recently approve the use of "Google" as a middle name, so there's that.

Many people actually choose to go by their middle name instead of their first name, so it could be seen as a safety net if you're worried your child won't like their name.

Celebrities who go by their middle name

Antonio Banderas (José Antonio Domínguez Banderas)

Ashton Kutcher (Christopher Ashton Kutcher)

Bob Marley (Nesta Robert Marley)

Brad Pitt (William Bradley Pitt)

Kelsey Grammer (Allen Kelsey Grammer)

Reese Witherspoon (Laura Jeanne Reese Witherspoon)

Rihanna (Robyn Rihanna Fenty)

Will Ferrell (John William Ferrell)

Even the British Royal family likes to give many middle names. Prince Charles's full name is Charles Philip Arthur George Mountbatten-Windsor, and Prince William is William Arthur Philip Louis Mountbatten-Windsor. The newest heir to the throne is, of course, Prince Louis Arthur Charles, named after Lord Louis Mountbatten, the father of Queen Elizabeth, and of course his grandfather Prince Charles. Big sister Princess Charlotte Elizabeth Diana was named after the current queen and her late grandmother, Diana Spencer; and then there's her elder brother, Prince George Alexander Louis, named after King George VI and Lord Louis Mountbatten.

Naming twins, triplets, and more

If you have discovered you are expecting multiples, congratulations! Naming multiples needn't be any different to naming a single child … unless you want it to be. You could stick to the same process everyone else does, by picking an individual name for each individual child. Even "Octomom" Nadya Suleman chose eight different names for her octuplets, although they do all sound reasonably similar and biblical:

Isaiah, Jeremiah, Jonah, Josiah, Maliyah, Makai, Nariyah, and Noah. All eight children also share the middle name Angel.

Of course, when all's said and done you can just stick to giving each child a name unique to them. For triplets, quads, and more, this is probably an easier choice than twisting your head around three names with the same meaning, or trying to create four anagrams you like for all of your babies. Some parents do like to use a theme, though, such as going down the alphabet (think Alastair, Benjamin, Christopher, and David), or doing what the famous acting Phoenix clan did and giving each child a name to do with nature: River, Rain, Leaf (now Joaquin), Liberty, and Summer.

Twin names with the same meaning

Bernard and Brian (strong)

Daphne and Laura (laurel)

Deborah and Melissa (bee)

Dorcas and Tabitha (gazelle)

Elijah and Joel (God)

Eve and Zoe (life)

Irene and Salome (peace)

Lucius and Uri (light)

Lucy and Helen (light)

Sarah and Almira (princess)

The Clooney and Carter twins

Amal and George Clooney welcomed their twins into the world in June 2017. They chose the traditional names Alexander and Ella. Many were surprised the couple did not choose to reference Amal's Lebanese heritage.

At the time of going to press, Beyoncé and Jay Z have applied to trademark the names Rumi Carter and Sir Carter, leaving us to assume these are their choices for their baby girl and boy. It's thought Rumi could be in reference to the 13th-century poet and Muslim scholar Jalaluddin al-Rumi.

There are a few things to keep in mind when naming twins or multiples, but they are at least pretty simple ones.

- Don't use very long names. You will often find yourself needing to write both names down, or calling both children down for dinner, so use shorter versions of the names you like, such as Max for Maximilian, or Eve for Evangeline.

- Don't get too complicated. Stick with traditional spellings if possible, like Cameron instead of Kammeryn and Elizabeth instead of Alyzybeth.

- Don't forget that your babies are still individuals. If you use names that sound so similar you often mix them up, your children may get frustrated as they get older and other people confuse them. Instead, keep those nearly identical names you love as middle names and use this opportunity to explore more individual first names to match your babies' unique personalities.

> The official Guinness World Record for the most siblings baptized with the same initial is held by a Canadian family, who had ten sons and six daughters named with the letter E. However the unofficial challenger to this would be the notorious Duggar family, whose 19 children all have names starting with J.

Celebrity twin names of the past few years

Alexander and Ella (George and Amal Clooney)

John and Gus (Julie Bowen and Scott Phillips)

Myla Rose and Charlene Riva, *and* Leo and Lenny (two sets for Roger and Mirka Federer!)

Poppy and Charlie (Anna Paquin and Stephen Moyer)

Rumi and Sir (Beyoncé and Jay Z)

Tristan and Sasha (Chris Hemsworth and Elsa Pataky)

Victoria and Ysabel (Michael Jordan and Yvette Jordan)

Around the world in popular baby names

Country	Girls	Boys
England	Olivia, Amelia, Emily	Oliver, George, Harry
Wales	Olivia, Amelia, Ella	Oliver, Jacob, Noah
Scotland	Olivia, Emily, Isla	Jack, Oliver, James
Northern Ireland	Emily, Grace, Olivia	James, Jack, Oliver
Republic of Ireland	Emily, Emma, Amelia	Jack, James, Daniel
Netherlands	Emma, Tess, Sophie	Noah, Sem, Lucas
Germany	Emma, Hannah, Mia	Ben, Jonas, Leon
Sweden	Alice, Alicia, Olivia	William, Oscar, Liam
Norway	Sofie, Nora, Emma	Jakob, Lucas, Emil
Iceland	Emilã, Emma, Elisabet	Alexander, Aron, Mikael
Portugal	Maria, Matilda, Leonor	João, Rodrigo, Francisco
Spain	Maria, Lucia, Paula	Alejandro, Daniel, David
New Zealand	Charlotte, Harper, Isla	Oliver, Jack, Noah
Australia	Charlotte, Olivia, Mia	Oliver, William, Jack
South Africa	Precious, Princess, Amahle	Junior, Blessing, Gift

Part Two

Boys' names
A–Z

Baby names vary widely in spelling and pronunciation. To simplify things, this book usually lists each name only once: under the most common initial and spelling. If a name has a common alternate spelling with a different initial, it may also be listed under that letter.

A Boys' names

Aaron

Hebrew, meaning "mountain of strength." In the Bible, Aaron was the older brother of Moses and the first high priest of Israel.

Abasi

Egyptian Arabic, meaning "male"; Swahili, meaning "stern."

Abdiel

Hebrew, meaning "servant of God." Also the name of an important seraph in Milton's *Paradise Lost*.

Abdul
(alt. Abdullah)

Arabic, meaning "servant of God." Often followed with a suffix indicating who Abdul is the servant of (e.g. Abdul-Basit, servant of the creator).

Abel

Hebrew, meaning "breath" or "breathing spirit." The biblical son of Adam and Eve who was killed by his brother Cain.

Abelard

German, meaning "resolute."

Aberforth

Gaelic, meaning "mouth of the river Forth." Name of Dumbledore's brother in the *Harry Potter* series.

Abner

Hebrew, meaning "father of light." Abner was the commander of Saul's army in the Bible.

Abraham
(alt. Abram; abbrev. Abe)

Hebrew, meaning "exalted father." Famous Abrahams include President Abraham Lincoln and Abraham Van Helsing—the vampire hunter and doctor in Bram Stoker's *Dracula*.

Absalom
(alt. Absalon)

Hebrew, meaning "father/leader of peace." The name of King David's favorite son in the Bible, and one of Chaucer's curly-haired characters in *The Canterbury Tales*.

Acacio

Greek origin, meaning "thorny tree." Now widely used in Spain.

Ace

Latin, meaning "unit." Also used to mean "number one" or "the best."

Achebe

Yoruba, meaning "may the earth protect us."

Achilles

Greek, mythological hero of the Trojan War, whose heel was his only weak spot.

Achim

Hebrew, meaning "God will establish"; Polish, meaning "The Lord exalts." Also a shortened form of Joachim.

Ackerley

Old English, meaning "oak meadow."

Adam
(alt. Adome, Admon)

Hebrew, meaning "man" or "earth." The biblical creation story names Adam as the first man on Earth.

Adão

Portuguese variant of Adam, meaning "earth."

Addison

Old English, meaning "son of Adam." Also used as a female name.

Ade

Yoruba, meaning "peak" or "royal." A common name in Nigeria.

Adelard

French or German, meaning "brave" or "noble." Became popular in Canada during the 19th century.

Adin

Hebrew, meaning "slender" or "voluptuous"; Swahili, meaning "ornamental."

Aditya

Sanskrit, meaning "belonging to the sun." Refers to the offspring of Aditi—the mother of the gods.

Adlai

Hebrew, meaning "God is just," or sometimes "ornamental."

Adler

Old German, meaning "eagle."

Adley

English, meaning "son of Adam." Also used as a girls' name.

Adolf

(alt. Adolfo, Adolph)

Old German, meaning "noble majestic wolf." Popularity of the name plummeted after World War II, for obvious reasons.

Adonis

Phoenician, meaning "Lord." Adonis was the god of beauty and desire in ancient Greek mythology.

Adrian

(abbrev. Ade)

Latin origin, meaning "from Hadria," a town in northern Italy.

Adriel

Hebrew, meaning "of God's flock." Adriel was one of Saul's sons-in-law in the Bible.

Aeneas

Greek/Latin origin, meaning "to praise." Name of the hero who founded Rome in Virgil's *Aeneid*.

Aero

Greek, meaning "air."

Aeson

Greek, after the father of Jason in ancient Greek mythology.

Afonso

Portuguese, meaning "eager noble warrior." King Afonso of Portugal was nicknamed "The Conqueror" during the Middle Ages.

Agamemnon

Greek, meaning "leader of the assembly." Figure in mythology who commanded the Greeks at the siege of Troy.

Agathon

Greek, meaning "good" or "superior." The name of a tragic poet in ancient Greece.

Agustin

Latin/Spanish, meaning "venerated."

Ahab

Hebrew, meaning "father's brother." Name of the obsessed captain in Herman Melville's *Moby-Dick*.

Ahijah

Hebrew, meaning "brother of God" or "friend of God." Common name in the Bible.

Ahmed

Arabic/Turkish, meaning "worthy of praise." Also one of the prophet Muhammad's many given names.

Aidan

(alt. Aden, Aiden)

Gaelic, meaning "little fire." Derives from Aodh, the name of a Celtic sun god.

Aidric

Old English, meaning "oaken."

Airyck

Old Norse, from Eric, meaning "eternal ruler."

Ajani

Yoruba, meaning "he fights for what he is"; Sanskrit, meaning "of noble birth."

Ajax

Greek, meaning "mourner of the Earth." A Greek hero from the siege of Troy.

Ajay

Hindi, meaning "unconquerable." One of the most popular names in India.

Ajit

Sanskrit, meaning "invincible." Another name for Shiva or Vishnu in Hindu mythology.

Akeem

Arabic, meaning "wise or insightful." Popular name in Nigeria.

Akio

Japanese, meaning "bright man." Akio Morita was one of the founders of Sony.

Akira

Japanese, meaning "intelligent." Also the name of one of the most successful Japanese anime films of all time.

Akiva

Hebrew, meaning "to protect" or "to shelter." Rabbi Akiva is an important figure in the Jewish faith.

Akon

American English, meaning "flower." Made popular after rapper Akon.

Aksel

Hebrew/Danish, meaning "father of peace."

Aladdin

Arabic, meaning "servant of Allah." Character in *The Arabian Nights*, made popular by Disney.

Alan

(alt. Allan, Allen, Allyn, Alun)

Gaelic or Old French, meaning "rock." One of the oldest names still widely used in Western countries, dating back to the 11th century.

Alaric

Old German, meaning "noble regal ruler." Also the name of a king who helped bring about the fall of the Roman Empire.

Alastair

(alt. Alasdair, Alastor, Allister; abbrev. Al, Ali)

Greek/Gaelic, meaning "defending men." Also the name of a demon in *Supernatural*.

Alban

Latin, meaning "from Alba"; Welsh and Scottish Gaelic word for "Scotland."

Alberic

Germanic, meaning "Elfin king."

Albert

(alt. Adalberto, Adelbert, Alberto, Elbert)

Old German, meaning "noble, bright, famous." Prince Albert was the husband of Queen Victoria.

Albus

(alt. Albin)

Latin, meaning "white." Albus Dumbledore is headmaster of Hogwarts School in the *Harry Potter* series.

Alcaeus

Greek, meaning "strength." The name of an ancient Greek poet.

Alden

Old English, meaning "old friend."

Aldis

Latvian, meaning "from the old house."

Aldo

Latin, meaning "the tall one." Also the name of the main gorilla character in *Planet of the Apes*.

Aldric

English, meaning "old king."

Aled

Welsh, meaning "child" or "offspring."

Aleph

Hebrew, meaning "first letter of the alphabet," or "leader." The aleph is the first character of many Middle Eastern alphabets.

Alessio

Italian, meaning "defender."

Alexander

(alt. Alexandro, Alessandro, Alejandro; abbrev. Al, Alec, Alek, Alex, Alexei, Sandro, Sandy, Xander, Zander)

Greek, meaning "defending men." Alexander the Great was an undefeated fourth-century king whose empire stretched from Greece to modern Pakistan. The abbreviation Alexei is enduringly popular in Russia.

Alfonso

Germanic/Spanish, meaning "noble and prompt, ready to struggle." Alfonso Cuarón is the director of *Gravity*. Alfonso Ribeiro is known for *Fresh Prince of Bel Air* and *America's Funniest Home Videos*.

Alford

Old English, meaning "old river/ford."

Alfred

(alt. Alfredo; abbrev. Alf, Alfi, Alfie)

English, meaning "elf" or "magical counsel." Name of legendary English king Alfred the Great.

Algernon

(abbrev. Algie)

French, meaning "with a moustache." A popular name for the nobility in 18th- and 19th-century England. *Flowers for Algernon* is a novel by Daniel Keyes.

Ali

(alt. Allie)

Arabic, meaning "noble, sublime."

Alijah

Hebrew, meaning "the Lord is my God."

Alois

German, meaning "famous warrior." Also the name of Adolf Hitler's father.

Alok

Sanskrit, meaning "cry of triumph."

Alon

Hebrew, meaning "oak tree." A popular name in Jewish communities.

Alonso

(alt. Alonzo)

Germanic, meaning "noble and ready."

Aloysius

Italian saint's name, meaning "fame and war."

Alpha

First letter of the Greek alphabet and synonymous with "beginning."

Alphaeus

Hebrew, meaning "changing." Father of two of the Apostles in the Bible.

Alpin

Gaelic, meaning "related to the Alps." The House of Alpin was a dynasty of Scottish kings.

Altair

Arabic, meaning "flying" or "bird." Altair is one of the brightest stars seen in the night sky.

Alter

Yiddish, meaning "old man."

Alton

Old English, meaning "old town."

Alvin

(alt. Alvie)

English, meaning "friend of elves." Often associated with *Alvin and the Chipmunks*.

Alwyn
(alt. Alwen)
Welsh, meaning "wise friend."

Amachi
African, meaning "who knows what God has brought us through this child."

Amadeus
Latin, meaning "God's love." One of composer Wolfgang Amadeus Mozart's many given names.

Amadi
Igbo, meaning "appeared destined to die at birth." Often given to babies who survive against the odds.

Amado
Spanish, meaning "God's love."

Amador
Spanish, meaning "one who loves." Two towns in California were named after rancher José María Amador.

Amari
Hebrew, meaning "given by God." Used for both boys and girls.

Amarion
Arabic, meaning "populous, flushing." Made popular after R&B singer Omarion.

Amasa
Hebrew, meaning "burden." Found in the Bible.

Ambrose
Greek, meaning "undying, immortal." St. Ambrose of Milan was one of the four original doctors of the Church.

Americo
Germanic, meaning "ever powerful in battle."

Amias
Latin, meaning "loved."

Amir
Arabic, meaning "chieftain" or "commander." Amir or Emir is a title for a high-ranking sheikh in many Muslim communities.

Amit
Hindi, meaning "infinite." One of the many name of the Hindu god Shri Ganesha.

Ammon
Hebrew, meaning "the hidden one." The Ammonites were an ancient group of people named in the Bible.

Amory
German/English, meaning "work" and "power."

Amos

Hebrew, meaning "encumbered" or "burdened."

Anacletus

Latin, meaning "called back" or "invoked." Also the name of the third Pope.

Anakin

American English, meaning "warrior." Made famous by Anakin Skywalker in the *Star Wars* films.

Ananias

Greek/Italian, meaning "answered by the Lord." Ananias Dare was the first baby born to English parents in the New World, making him the first ever "modern" American.

Anastasius
(alt. Anastasios)

Greek, meaning "resurrection." A very popular name for popes, emperors, and saints.

Anatole

French, meaning "sunrise."

Anders

Greek, meaning "lion man." A very popular name in Sweden.

Anderson

English, meaning "male." Anderson Cooper is a TV host.

Andrew
(alt. Andreas, Andre, Andy)

Greek, meaning "man" or "warrior." Andrew Lincoln is known for his role in *The Walking Dead*.

Androcles

Greek, meaning "glory of a warrior." *Androcles and the Lion* was a well-known folktale in the second century, and influenced Aesop's *Fables*.

Angel

Greek, meaning "messenger." A very popular name in Hispanic communities. Used for both boys and girls.

Angelo

Italian, meaning "angel."

Angus
(abbrev. Gus)

Scottish, meaning "one choice." Name of Merida's horse in *Brave*.

Anil

Sanskrit, meaning "air" or "wind."

Anselm

German, meaning "helmet of God." St. Anselm was an influential figure in the formation of Christianity.

Anson

English, meaning "son of Agnes." Anson Jones was the last independent President of Texas, before it became incorporated into the USA.

Anthony
(alt. Antony; abbrev. Ant, Tony)
English, from the old Roman family name. *Antony and Cleopatra* is a Shakespearean play about the romance between Roman general Mark Antony and Cleopatra of Egypt.

Antipas
Hebrew, meaning "for all or against all." Herod Antipas is acknowledged as being responsible for the executions of John the Baptist and Jesus Christ in the Bible.

Antwan
(alt. Antoine)
Old English, meaning "flower."

Apollo
Greek, meaning "to destroy." Greek god of poetry, music, and the sun.

Apostolos
Greek, meaning "apostle." The Apostolos is a text believed to have been written by one of the Apostles.

Ara
Armenian, from the legendary king of the same name.

Aragorn
Literary, used by Tolkien in *The Lord of the Rings* trilogy.

Aram
Hebrew, meaning "Royal Highness." Also the name of an ancient region in modern-day Syria.

Aramis
Latin, meaning "swordsman." One of the three musketeers in Alexandre Dumas's novel.

Arcadio
Greek/Spanish, meaning "paradise."

Archibald
(alt. Archie)
Old German, meaning "genuine/bold/brave."

Ardell
Latin, meaning "eager, burning with enthusiasm."

Arden
Celtic, meaning "high."

Ares
Greek, meaning "ruin." Son of Zeus and Hera, and the Greek god of war.

Ari
Hebrew, meaning "lion" or "eagle." Also used to refer to an important man in Hebrew.

Arias
Germanic, meaning "lion." Sometimes used as a spelling variation of Eric.

Ariel

Hebrew, meaning "lion of God."
One of the archangels, the angel of
healing and new beginnings.

Arild

Old Norse, meaning "battle
commander."

Aris

Greek, meaning "best figure."
Popular name in Greece.

Ariston

Greek, meaning "the best." Also the
name of Plato's father.

Aristotle

Greek, meaning "best." Also an
ancient Greek philosopher.

Arjun

Sanskrit, meaning "bright and
shining." Taken from Arjuna, an
ancient and legendary archer.

Arkady

Greek, region of central Greece.
Popular throughout Eastern
Europe.

Arlan

Gaelic, meaning "pledge" or "oath."

Arlie

Old English place name, meaning
"eagle wood."

Arliss

(alt. Arlis)

Hebrew, meaning "pledge." A 1990s
sitcom.

Arlo

Spanish, meaning "barberry
tree."

Armani

(alt. Armand)

Old German, meaning "soldier." A
well-known Italian designer.

Arnaldo

Spanish, meaning "eagle power."

Arnav

Indian, meaning "the sea."

Arnold

(abbrev. Arnie)

Old German, meaning "eagle ruler."
Arnold Schwarzenegger is an actor,
former bodybuilder, and former
governor of California.

Arrow

English, from the common word
denoting weaponry.

Art

Irish, from the name of a warrior in
Irish mythology, Art Oenfer (Art the
Lonely). Also used as a shortened
form of Arthur.

Arthur
(alt. Artie, Artis)

Celtic, probably from "artos," meaning "bear." Made famous by the tales of King Arthur and the Knights of the Round Table.

Arturo

Celtic or Italian, meaning "strong as a bear."

Arvel

From the Welsh "Arwel," meaning "wept over." Arvel Crynyd appears in *Star Wars*, and Arvel the Swift in *The Elder Scrolls V: Skyrim*.

Arvid

English, meaning "eagle in the woods." Popular name in Scandinavia.

Arvind

Sanskrit, meaning "red lotus." Also derived from the word for "white lotus," upon which the Hindu goddess Lakshmi sits.

Arvo

Finnish, meaning "value" or "worth."

Asa

Hebrew, meaning "doctor" or "healer." Popular with Puritans in the 17th century.

Asante

African, meaning "thank you." Also the language of the Ashanti people.

Asher

Hebrew, meaning "fortunate" or "lucky." One of the 12 sons of Jacob in the Bible.

Ashley

Old English, meaning "ash meadow." Used for both boys and girls.

Ashok

Sanskrit, meaning "not causing sorrow." Popular in India and Sri Lanka.

Ashton

English, meaning "settlement in the ash-tree grove." The middle name of actor Ashton Kutcher (see page 52).

Aslan

Turkish, meaning "lion." The name of the lion from C. S. Lewis's *The Lion, The Witch and The Wardrobe*.

Asriel
(alt. Azriel)

Hebrew, meaning "God is my help." Lord Asriel is an important character in the "His Dark Materials" trilogy. Azriel is the name of the angel of death in Christianity and Judaism.

Astrophel

Latin, meaning "star lover."

Athanasios

Greek, meaning "eternal life." Extremely popular in ancient and modern Greece.

Atilio

Portuguese, meaning "father."

Atlas

Greek, meaning "to carry." In ancient Greek mythology Atlas was a Titan forced to carry the weight of the heavens.

Atlee

Hebrew, meaning "God is just."

Atticus

Latin, meaning "from Athens." Atticus Finch is a central character in Harper Lee's *To Kill A Mockingbird*.

Auberon

(alt. Oberon)

Old German, meaning "royal bear." Also the name of a Shakespearean fairy king.

Aubrey

Old German, meaning "power." Used for both boys and girls.

Auden

Old English, meaning "old friend." W. H. Auden is considered to be one of the most influential 20th-century poets.

Audie

Old English, meaning "noble strength." Audie L. Murphy was one of the most decorated US soldiers during World War II.

August

Latin, meaning "magnificent."

Augustus

(alt. Augustas; abbrev. Gus)

Latin, meaning "venerated." Also the name of a spoiled child in *Charlie and the Chocolate Factory*.

Aurelien

French, meaning "golden." An ancient Roman emperor.

Austin

Latin, meaning "venerated." Also the city in Texas.

Avi

Hebrew, meaning "father of a multitude of nations."

Awnan

Irish, meaning "little Adam."

Axel

Hebrew, meaning "father is peace." Made famous by Guns 'n' Roses frontman Axl Rose.

Azarel

(alt. Azaryah)

Hebrew, meaning "helped by God." Also the name of an evil spirit in the Bible.

Azuko

African, meaning "past glory." Popular in Japan.

Boys' names

Babe

American English, meaning "baby." George Herman "Babe" Ruth was a legendary baseball player.

Baden

German, meaning "battle." Also the name of a city in Switzerland known for its hot springs.

Bailey

English, meaning "bailiff." Baileys is a popular Irish crème liqueur.

Baird

Scottish, meaning "poet" or "one who sings ballads."

Bakari

Swahili, meaning "hope" or "promise."

Baker

English, from the word "baker."

Baldwin

Old French, meaning "bold, brave friend."

Balin

Old English, meaning "powerful and strong." Balin was one of the Knights of the Round Table.

Balthazar

Babylonian, meaning "protect the king." Also the name of one of the Three Wise Men in the Nativity.

Balwinder
(alt. Balvinder)

Hindi, meaning "merciful, compassionate."

Bannon

Irish, meaning "descendant of O'Banain."

Barack

African, meaning "blessed." Made popular by the 44th President of the United States Barack Obama.

Barclay

Old English, meaning "birch tree meadow," and Persian, meaning "messenger."

Barker

Old English, meaning "shepherd."

Barnaby
(abbrev. Barney)

Greek, meaning "son of consolation." *Barnaby Rudge* is one of Charles Dickens's less well-known novels.

Barnard

English, meaning "strong as a bear."

Baron

Old English, meaning "young warrior." A title given to certain men of nobility in Europe.

Barrett

English, meaning "strong as a bear."

Barron

Old German, meaning "old clearing."

Barry
(abbrev. Baz)

Irish Gaelic, meaning "fair haired." *Great Gatsby* film director Baz Luhrman's real name is Mark.

Bartholomew
(abbrev. Bart, Barty)

Hebrew, meaning "son of the farmer." Bartholomew "Bart" Simpson appears in *The Simpsons*.

Barton

Old English, meaning "barley settlement." The name of several towns in the UK.

Baruch

Hebrew, meaning "blessed." Also the name of a Jewish blessing ceremony.

Bascom

Old English, meaning "from Bascombe."

Bashir

Arabic, meaning "well educated" and "wise." Journalist Martin Bashir is known for his infamous interviews with Diana, Princess of Wales, and Michael Jackson.

Basil

Greek, meaning "royal, kingly." Also the name of the herb.

Basim

Arabic, meaning "smile." Popular in Arabic-speaking communities.

Bastien

Greek, meaning "revered."

Baxter

Old English, meaning "baker." One of the most popular names for towns across the USA.

Bayard

French, meaning "auburn haired." Bayard Rustin was one of Martin Luther King Jr.'s mentors and advisors during the Civil Rights Movement.

Bayo

Yoruba, meaning "to find joy."

Beau

French, meaning "handsome." Actor Beau Bridges' real name is Lloyd Vernet Bridges.

Beck

Old Norse, meaning "stream." Singer Beck Hansen is usually known as just "Beck."

Beckett

Old English, meaning "beehive" or "bee cottage."

Beckham

English, meaning "homestead by the stream." Finding popularity as a given name due to English soccer star David Beckham.

Belarius

Shakespearean, meaning "a banished lord." From Shakespeare's play *Cymbeline*.

Benedict

Latin, meaning "blessed." Made popular after actor Benedict Cumberbatch.

Benjamin

(abbrev. Ben, Benny)

Hebrew, meaning "son of the south." Benjamin Franklin was one of the Founding Fathers of the USA.

Bennett

French/Latin vernacular form of Benedict, meaning "blessed."

Benoit

French form of Benedict, meaning "blessed."

Benson

English, meaning "son of Ben." The title of the 1980s sitcom *Benson*.

Bentley

Old English, meaning "bent grass meadow." Popularity has increased since the shows *16 and Pregnant* and *Teen Mom* first aired.

Benton

Old English, meaning "town in the bent grass."

Beriah

Hebrew, meaning "in fellowship" or "in envy." The son of Asher in the Bible.

Bernard
(abbrev. Bernie)
Germanic, meaning "strong, brave bear."

Berry
Old English, meaning "berry." Also used as a shortened form of Bernard or Barry.

Berton
Old English, meaning "bright settlement." Berton Averre is the guitarist from The Knack.

Bertrand
(alt. Bertram; abbrev. Bert, Bertie)
Old English, meaning "illustrious." The name of a *Sesame Street* muppet. Bertram (Bertie) Wooster was one of P.G. Wodehouse's most beloved characters. Bert is also a shortened form of Albert.

Bevan
Welsh, meaning "son of Evan."

Bicknell
Old English, meaning "from Bicknell."

Bilal
Arabic, meaning "wetting, refreshing." Popular in many Muslim communities.

Birch
Old English, meaning "bright" or "shining." Also a type of tree.

Birger
Norwegian, meaning "rescue."

Bishop
Old English, meaning "bishop." Bishops are members of the Church who oversee several parishes and jurisdictions.

Bjorn
Old Norse, meaning "bear." Bjorn Ulvaeus was one of the founding members of ABBA.

Bladen
Hebrew, meaning "hero."

Blaine
Irish Gaelic, meaning "yellow." Has risen in profile due to David Blaine, known for his magic, illusions, and extreme stunts.

Blair
English, meaning "plain."

Blaise
French, meaning "lisp" or "stutter."

Blake
Old English, meaning "dark, black."

Blas
(alt. Blaze)
German, meaning "firebrand." Also the name of a mountain in the Alps.

Bo

Scandinavian, from Robert, meaning "bright fame." Also the name of the Obamas' pet dog.

Boaz

Hebrew, meaning "swiftness" or "strength." The name of an influential character in the Bible.

Boden
(alt. Bodie)

Scandinavian, meaning "shelter" or "messenger."

Bogumil

Slavic, meaning "God's favor."

Bond

Old English, meaning "peasant farmer." Often associated with the fictional character James Bond.

Boris

Slavic, meaning "battle glory." Boris Yeltsin was the president of Russia during the 1990s.

Boston
(alt. Bosten)

English, meaning "town by the woods."

Bowen

Welsh, meaning "son of Owen." The Bowen knot is a common sight in heraldic symbolism.

Boyd

Scottish Gaelic, meaning "yellow."

Bradley
(abbrev. Brad)

Old English, meaning "broad" or "wide." Actor Brad Pitt's full name is William Bradley Pitt.

Brady

Irish, meaning "large-chested." Name of the family in *The Brady Bunch*.

Bradyn
(alt. Braden, Bradan)

Gaelic, meaning "descendant of Bradan."

Bram

Gaelic, meaning "raven." Bram Stoker was the author of *Dracula*.

Brando

Old Norse, meaning "sword" or "flaming torch." Name of the movie star Marlon Brando.

Brandon
(abbrev. Bran)

Old English, meaning "gorse." Brandon "Bran" Stark is a main character in *Game of Thrones*.

Brandt

Old English, meaning "beacon."

Brannon

Gaelic, meaning "raven."

Branson

English, meaning "son of Brand."

Brant

Old English, meaning "hill."

Braulio

Greek, meaning "shining."

Braxton

English, meaning "Brock's town." Associated with Braxton Hicks contractions during pregnancy.

Brayden

Irish, meaning "broad meadow."

Brendan

Gaelic, meaning "prince." Actor Brendan Fraser is known for his role in the "Mummy" series.

Brennan

Gaelic, meaning "teardrop."

Brent

English, meaning "hill." Brent Seabrook currently plays for the Chicago Blackhawks.

Brenton

English, meaning "hill town."

Brett

(alt. Bret)

English, meaning "a Breton." Made popular by Poison lead vocalist Bret Michaels.

Brian

Gaelic, meaning "high" or "noble." Singer songwriter Brian Wilson was a founding member of The Beach Boys.

Brice

Latin, meaning "speckled."

Brier

French, meaning "heather." Also the name of a type of thorny plant.

Brock

Old English, meaning "badger." One of the more popular characters in the Pokémon franchise.

Broderick

English, meaning "ruler." Surname of the actor Matthew Broderick.

Brody

Gaelic, meaning both "ditch" and "brother." Brody Jenner is known for being part of the Jenner/Kardashian clan.

Brogan

Irish, meaning "sturdy shoe."

Bronwyn

(alt. Bronwen)

Welsh, meaning "fair breast." The spelling of Bronwyn is more common for baby boys, and Bronwen for baby girls.

Brooklyn

American English, from the New York City borough of the same name. Brooklyn Beckham is the eldest son of soccer star David and singer turned fashion designer Victoria Beckham.

Bruce

Scottish, meaning "high" or "noble." The former name of Olympian decathlete and Jenner/Kardashian clan member Caitlyn Jenner.

Bruno

Germanic, meaning "brown." Bruno Tonioli is a judge on *Dancing With The Stars*.

Bryant

English variant of Brian, meaning "high" or "noble." Associated with basketball legend Kobe Bryant.

Bryce

Scottish, meaning "of Britain."

Bryden

Irish, meaning "strong one."

Bryson
(alt. Brycen)

Welsh, meaning "descendant of Brice." Bryson was the name of an ancient Greek philosopher and also a mathematician from the same time.

Bubba

American English, meaning "boy." The restaurant chain Bubba Gump Shrimp Co. takes its name from the characters of Benjamin Buford "Bubba" Blue and Forrest Gump in the movie *Forrest Gump*.

Buck

American English, meaning "goat" or "deer," specifically a male deer.

Bud
(alt. Buddy)

American English, meaning "friend." Buddy has been used as a stage name by a number of musicians including Buddy Holly and Buddy Guy.

Burdett

Middle English, meaning "bird."

Burke

French, meaning "fortified settlement."

Burl

French, meaning "knotty wood."

Buzz

American English, from Busby, meaning "village in the thicket." Buzz Aldrin was the second man on the moon and Buzz Lightyear appears in Disney's "Toy Story" series.

Byron

Old English, meaning "barn." Famous Byrons include the poet Lord Byron.

C

Boys' names

Cabot

Old English, meaning "to sail."

Cade

(alt. Caden, Caiden, Kayden)

English, meaning "round, lumpy." A character in the novel *Gone With The Wind*.

Cadence

Latin, meaning "with rhythm." Poetry, music, and marching all have some type of cadence.

Cadogan

Welsh, meaning "battle glory and honor." Sir Cadogan is a knight in a painting in the *Harry Potter* series.

Caedmon

Celtic, meaning "wise warrior." An early English poet.

Caelan

Gaelic, meaning "slender."

Caerwyn

(alt. Carwyn, Gerwyn)

Welsh, meaning "white fort" or "settlement."

Caesar

(alt. Cesar)

Latin, meaning "head of hair." Made famous by the first Roman emperor, Julius Caesar.

Caetano

Portuguese, meaning "from Gaeta, Italy."

Caillou

French, meaning "pebble." Name of a children's cartoon character.

Cain

Hebrew, meaning "full of beauty." Brother of Abel in the Bible.

Cainan

Hebrew, meaning "possessor" or "purchaser."

Cairo

Egyptian city near Giza. Also home of the Great Pyramids.

Calder

Scottish, meaning "rough waters."

Caleb

(alt. Cal, Calen)

Hebrew, meaning "dog." A character in the Bible.

Calix

Greek, meaning "very handsome."

Callahan

Irish, meaning "contention" or "strife."

Callum

(alt. Calum)

Gaelic, meaning "dove." Very popular name in Ireland.

Calvin

(alt. Kalvin)

French, meaning "little bald one." Associated with the comic strip Calvin and Hobbes.

Camden

(alt. Kamden)

Gaelic, meaning "winding valley." A district in north London, UK, known for its market.

Cameron

Scottish Gaelic, meaning "crooked nose." Also the name of Ferris Bueller's best friend in Ferris Bueller's Day Off. Used for boys and girls.

Camillo

Latin, meaning "free born" or "noble."

Campbell

Scottish Gaelic, meaning "crooked mouth." The name of a famous brand of soup.

Canaan

Hebrew, meaning "to be humbled." A region heavily referenced in the Bible.

Candido

Latin, meaning "candid" or "honest." Candido Jacuzzi was the inventor of the Jacuzzi tub.

Canon

(alt. Cannon)

French, meaning "of the church." Originally given to members of a certain order in the Church.

Canton

French, meaning "dweller of corner." Also the name given to provinces of Switzerland.

Cappy

Italian, meaning "lucky." Can also be a nickname for Captain.

Carden

Old English, meaning "wool carder"—which refers to someone who would "card" wool to remove impurities from it.

Carey

Gaelic, meaning "love." Used for both boys and girls.

Carl
(alt. Carlo, Carlos, Karl)

Old Norse, meaning "free man." Carl Jung was a famous psychologist.

Carlton

Old English, meaning "free peasant settlement." Carlton is a character in the sitcom *The Fresh Prince of Bel Air*.

Carmelo

Latin, meaning "garden" or "orchard."

Carmen

Latin/Spanish, meaning "song." The title of an opera by French composer Georges Bizet. Used for boys and girls.

Carmine

Latin, meaning "song." Also the name of a bright-red pigment used in the production of red fruit juices.

Carnell

English, meaning "defender of the castle."

Carson
(alt. Carsten)

Scottish, meaning "marshdwellers." Carson Daly is a late night TV host.

Carter

Old English, meaning "transporter of goods." Jimmy Carter was the 39th President of the United States and Carter Camper is an American professional ice hockey player.

Cary

Celtic, meaning "love." Old Celtic river name. Cary Elwes is a current actor and Cary Grant was the stage name of the dashing English-American actor of the 1930s–1950s.

Case
(alt. Casey, Kace, Kacey, Kasey)

Irish Gaelic, meaning "alert" or "watchful."

Cash

Latin, shortened form of Cassius, meaning "empty, hollow." Associated with musician Johnny Cash.

Casimer

Slavic, meaning "famous destroyer of peace."

Cason

Latin, from Cassius, meaning "empty, hollow."

Casper
(alt. Kasper)

Persian, meaning "treasurer." The ghost character in *Casper the Friendly Ghost*.

Caspian

English, meaning "of the Caspy people." Taken from the children's novel *Prince Caspian*.

Cassidy

Gaelic, meaning "curly haired." Originated from the surname Caiside.

Cassius
(alt. Cassio)

Latin, meaning "empty, hollow." Legendary boxer Muhammad Ali's birth name was Cassius Clay.

Cathal

Celtic, meaning "battle rule." Variation of Charles.

Cato

Latin, meaning "all-knowing." Also the name of a character in *The Hunger Games*.

Cecil

Latin, meaning "blind." Cecil B. DeMille was a legendary film director.

Cedar

English, name of an evergreen tree.

Cedric

Welsh, meaning "spectacular bounty." Taken from Sir Walter Scott's novel *Ivanhoe*.

Celestino

Spanish/Italian meaning "heavenly."

Chad
(alt. Chadrick)

Old English, meaning "warlike, warrior." Also the name of an African country.

Chaim
(alt. Chayyim)

Hebrew, meaning "life."

Champion

English, from the word "warrior."

Chance

English, from the word "chance," meaning "good fortune."

Chandler

Old English, meaning "candle maker and seller." Made famous by Chandler Bing from 1990s sitcom *Friends*.

Charles
(alt. Charley, Charlie; abbrev. Chas)

Old German, meaning "free man." Charles, Prince of Wales, is heir to the British throne.

Chase
(alt. Chace)

Old French, meaning "huntermen." Actor Chace Crawford is known for his role on *Gossip Girl*.

Chaska

Native American name usually given to first son.

Che

Spanish, shortened form of José. Made famous by Che Guevara.

Chesley

Old English, meaning "camp on the meadow."

Chesney

English, meaning "place to camp." Also used as a girls' name.

Chester

Latin, meaning "camp of soldiers." Chester Arthur was the 21st President of the United States and Chester Bennington is the lead singer of rock band Linkin Park.

Chima

Old English, meaning "hilly land."

Christian
(abbrev. Chris)

English, from the word "Christian." Actor Christian Slater is known for his roles in *Heathers* and *Breaking In*.

Christopher
(alt. Christophe, Kristopher; abbrev. Chris, Kris)

Greek, meaning "bearing Christ inside." Christopher Columbus is credited with discovering America.

Cian

Irish, meaning "ancient." Father of Lug in Gaelic mythology.

Ciaran

Irish, meaning "black." Actor Ciaran Hinds is known for his voice work as Gree in *Rio 2*, and the Troll King in *Frozen*.

Cicero

Latin, meaning "chickpea." Also the Roman philosopher and orator.

Cimarron

City in western Kansas.

Ciprian

Latin, meaning "from Cyprus." Popular in ancient Rome.

Ciro

Spanish, meaning "sun." Also the title of a seventeenth-century opera.

Clancy

Old Irish, meaning "red warrior." Clancy has been a popular name for US actors, writers and sports stars. Also a character in *The Simpsons*.

Clarence

Latin, meaning "one who lives near the river Clare." Clarence Thomas is one of the current Associate Justices of the Supreme Court.

Clark

Latin, meaning "clerk." Superman's human name is Clark Kent.

Claude
(alt. Claudie, Claudio, Claudius)

Latin, meaning "lame."

Claus

Variant of Nicholas, meaning "people of victory." Associated with Santa Claus.

Clay

English, from the word "clay." Singer Clay Aiken is known for his appearances on American Idol.

Clement
(alt. Clem)

Latin, meaning "merciful." Also the taken name for 14 different popes.

Cletus

Greek, meaning "illustrious." Cletus Spuckler is a hillbilly character in The Simpsons.

Clifford
(alt. Clifton; abbrev. Cliff)

English, meaning "ford by a cliff." Associated with Bill Cosby's character Cliff Huxtable on The Cosby Show.

Clinton
(alt. Clint)

Old English, meaning "fenced settlement." Actor Clint Eastwood is known for dozens of movie roles, both as an actor and as a director.

Clive

Old English, meaning "cliff" or "slope." Clive Owen is an actor and Clive Davis is a record producer and record label executive.

Clyde

Scottish, from the river that passes through Glasgow. Also the name of one half of the bank robber duo Bonnie and Clyde.

Coby
(alt. Koby, Kobe)

Diminutive of Jacob, meaning "he who supplants." Also used as a girls' name.

Colden

Old English, meaning "dark valley."

Cole
(alt. Coley)

Old French, meaning "coal black." Composer Cole Porter is known for dozens of popular songs and musicals.

Colin

Gaelic, meaning "young creature." Actor Colin Firth is known for his roles in Pride and Prejudice and Love Actually. Colin Powell was a US secretary of state and is a retired army general.

Colson

Old English, meaning "coal black."

Colton

English, meaning "swarthy." Actor Colton Haynes is known for his role in *Arrow*.

Columbus

Latin, meaning "dove."

Colwyn

Welsh, from the river in Wales.

Conan

Gaelic, meaning "wolf." Comedian Conan O'Brien is known for his work as a late-night TV host.

Conley

Gaelic, meaning "sensible."

Connell

(alt. Connolly)

Irish, meaning "high" or "mighty."

Connor

(alt. Conrad, Conroy)

Irish, meaning "lover of hounds." Very popular name in Ireland.

Constant

(alt. Constantine)

English, from the word "constant." Popular with Puritans during the 17th century.

Cooper

Old English, meaning "barrel maker."

Corban

Hebrew, meaning "dedicated and belonging to God." Corban Knight currently plays for the Florida Panthers.

Corbett

(alt. Corbin, Corby)

Norman French, meaning "young crow."

Cordell

Old English, meaning "cord maker." An old term for people who made or sold cords.

Corey

Gaelic, meaning "hill hollow." Corey Hart currently plays for the Pittsburgh Pirates.

Corin

Latin, meaning "spear."

Cormac

Gaelic, meaning "impure son." American writer Cormac McCarthy is the author of modern classics *No Country for Old Men* and *The Road*.

Cornelius

(alt. Cornell)

Latin, meaning "horn." Cornelius Fudge is the Minister for Magic in the *Harry Potter* series.

Cortez

Spanish, meaning "courteous."

Corwin

Old English, meaning "heart's friend" or "companion."

Cosimo

(alt. *Cosme, Cosmo*)

Italian, meaning "order" or "beauty." Masculine form of Cosima.

Coty

French, meaning "riverbank." Refers to people who live on the French coast.

Coulter

English, meaning "young horse."

Courtney

Old English, meaning "domain of Curtis." Used for both boys and girls.

Covey

English, meaning "flock of birds."

Cowan

Gaelic, meaning "hollow in the hill."

Craig

Welsh, meaning "rock." Comedian Craig Ferguson is known for his work as a late night TV host.

Crispin

Latin, meaning "curly haired." A patron saint of shoemakers.

Croix

French, meaning "cross."

Cruz

Spanish, meaning "cross." Made famous after David and Victoria Beckham chose it for their third son.

Curran

Gaelic, meaning "dagger" or "hero."

Curtis

(alt. *Curt*)

Old French, meaning "courteous." Most popular in the US. Curtis Mayfield was a soul and R&B singer and Curtis LeMay was a general in the US Air Force during World War II.

Cutler

Old English, meaning "knife maker."

Cyprian

English, meaning "from Cyprus." Also the name of an early Christian bishop and writer.

Cyril

Greek, meaning "master" or "Lord." Associated with St. Cyril.

Cyrus

Persian, meaning "Lord." Cyrus the Great was a ruler of Persia in ancient times.

D

Boys' names

Dai
Welsh, meaning "darling."
Sometimes used as a girls' name.

Daichi
Japanese, meaning "great wisdom."

Daisuke
Japanese, meaning "lionhearted."

Dakari
African, meaning "happy."

Dakota
Native American, meaning "friend" or "ally." Both North and South Dakota take their names from the Native American tribe of the same name.

Dale
Old English, meaning "valley." Dale Earnhardt Jr. is one of the best-known NASCAR drivers.

Dallin
English, meaning "dweller in the valley."

Dalton
English, meaning "town in the valley."

Daly
Gaelic, meaning "assembly."

Damarion
Greek, meaning "gentle."

Damian
(alt. Damon)
Greek, meaning "to tame, subdue." Actor Damian Lewis is known for his role in *Homeland*.

Dane
Old English, meaning "from Denmark." Dane Cook is known for his stand-up comedy.

Daniel

(abbrev. Dan, Danny)

Hebrew, meaning "God is my judge." Daniel is mentioned several times in the Bible.

Dante

Latin, meaning "lasting." Name of the Italian 13th-century poet Dante Alighieri.

Darby

Irish, meaning "without envy." Name of the main character in Disney's *Darby O'Gill and the Little People*.

Darcy

Gaelic, meaning "dark." Mr. Darcy is a main character in Jane Austen's *Pride and Prejudice*.

Dario

(alt. Darius)

Greek, meaning "kingly." Dario Argento is an Italian film director known for his horror fims.

Darnell

Old English, meaning "the hidden spot."

Darragh

Irish, meaning "dark oak."

Darren

(alt. Darrian)

Gaelic, meaning "great." Darren Aronofsky is a Harvard-educated film director and producer.

Darrick

Old German, meaning "power of the tribe."

Darryl

(alt. Darrell, Daryl)

Old English, meaning "open." Comedian Darrell Hammond was known for his roles on *Saturday Night Live*. The spelling Daryl is more commonly used as a girls' name.

Darshan

Hindi, meaning "vision."

Darwin

Old English, meaning "dear friend." Often associated with naturalist and author Charles Darwin.

Dash

(alt. Dashawn)

American English, meaning "enlightened one." Dash is a character in Disney Pixar's *The Incredibles*.

Dashiell

French, meaning "page boy." Author Dashiell Hammett was known for his detective novels.

David

(alt. Daffyd, Davian; abbrev. Dave, Davey, Davie)

Hebrew, meaning "beloved." David was a king of Israel who killed the giant Goliath in the Bible.

Davis

Old English, meaning "son of David."

Dawson

Old English, meaning "son of David." Associated with 1990s drama *Dawson's Creek*.

Dax

(alt. Daxton)

French, from the town in southwestern France. Actor Dax Shepard is known for his role in *Parenthood*.

Dayal

Indian, meaning "kind."

Dayton

Old English, meaning "David's place." Also the name of a city in Ohio.

Dean

(alt. Dino)

Old English, meaning "valley." Actor Dean McDermott is known for his marriage to Tori Spelling.

Declan

Irish, meaning "full of goodness." Declan Porter is a character on *Revenge*.

Dedric

Old English, meaning "gifted ruler."

Deegan

(alt. Deagon, Daegan)

Irish, meaning "black-haired."

Deepak

(alt. Deepan)

Indian, meaning "illumination." Deepak Chopra is known for his work as a doctor and author.

Del

(alt. Delano, Delbert, Dell)

Old English, meaning "bright shining one."

Demetrius

Greek, meaning "harvest lover." One of the star-crossed lovers in Shakespeare's *A Midsummer Night's Dream*.

Dempsey

Irish, meaning "proud."

Denham

(alt. Denholm)

Old English, meaning "valley settlement."

Dennis

(alt. Denny, Denton)

English, meaning "follower of Dionysius." The main character in comic strip *Dennis the Menace*.

Denver

Old English, meaning "green valley."
City in Colorado.

Denzel
(alt. Denzil)

English, meaning "fort." Actor Denzel Washington is known for his roles in *Malcolm X* and *Philadelphia.*

Deon

Greek, meaning "of Zeus." The male version of Dionne.

Derek

English, meaning "power of the tribe." Dancer and choreographer Derek Hough is known for his work on *Dancing With The Stars.*

Dermot

Irish, meaning "free man." Actor Dermot Mulroney is known for his roles in *My Best Friend's Wedding* and *New Girl.*

Desmond
(abbrev. Des)

Irish, meaning "from south Munster." Former Archbishop Desmond Tutu is a high profile South African social activist.

Destin

French, meaning "destiny."

Devyn
(alt. Devin, Devon)

Irish, meaning "poet."

Long names

Alexander	Bartholomew
Christopher	Demetrius
Giovanni	Maximillian
Montgomery	Nathaniel
Sebastian	Zachariah

Dewey
(alt. Dewi)

Welsh, meaning "beloved." One of Donald Duck's three nephews.

Dexter
(alt. Dex)

Latin, meaning "right-handed." Became more popular since the massive success of TV drama *Dexter.*

Didier

French, meaning "much desired."

Diego

Spanish, meaning "supplanter." A character in children's cartoon *Dora the Explorer.*

Dietrich

Old German, meaning "power of the tribe."

Diggory

English, meaning "dyke." Cedric Diggory is a character in the *Harry Potter* series.

Dilbert

English, meaning "day-bright." Main character in the comic strip of the same name.

Dimitri

(alt. Dimitrios, Dimitris)

Greek, meaning "prince." Popular name for boys in Russia.

Dion

Greek, short form of Dionysius.

Dirk

Variant of Derek, meaning "power of the tribe." Famous Dirks include actors Dirk Bogarde and Dirk Benedict. Infamous Dirks include fictional porn star Dirk Diggler, from the film *Boogie Nights*.

Dominic

Latin, meaning "Lord." Actor Dominic Monaghan is known for his roles in *Lost* and *The Lord of the Rings*.

Donald

(alt. Donal, Donaldo; abbrev. Don, Donnie)

Gaelic, meaning "great chief." Famous Donalds include President Donald Trump, actor Donald Sutherland, and Donald Duck.

Donato

Italian, meaning "gift." Given name of the Italian sculptor Donatello.

Short names

Al	Ben
Dai	Ed
Jay	Jon
Max	Rio
Sam	Ty

Donnell

(alt. Donnie, Donny)

Gaelic, meaning "world fighter."

Donovan

Gaelic, meaning "dark-haired chief."

Doran

Gaelic, meaning "exile."

Dorian

Greek, meaning "descendant of Doris." The title character of Oscar Wilde's *The Picture of Dorian Gray*.

Douglas

(alt. Dougal, Dougie)

Scottish, meaning "black river." Author Douglas Adams is known for his novel *The Hitchhiker's Guide to the Galaxy*.

Draco

Latin, meaning "dragon." Draco Malfoy is a main character in the *Harry Potter* series.

Drake

Greek, meaning "dragon." Drake Bell is an American actor, TV personality, and musician.

Drew

Greek, from Andrew, meaning "man" or "warrior." Drew Carey is known for his work in comedy and as a TV host.

Dudley

Old English, meaning "people's field." The name of Harry's cousin in the *Harry Potter* series.

Duff

Gaelic, meaning "swarthy."

Duke

Latin, meaning "leader." Became popular as a first name after the birth of Giuliana and Bill Rancic's son Duke.

Duncan

Scottish, meaning "dark warrior." King Duncan is a character in Shakespeare's *Macbeth*.

Dustin

(alt. Dusty)

French, meaning "brave warrior." Actor Dustin Hoffman is known for his roles in *Rain Man* and *Tootsie*.

Dwayne

Irish Gaelic, meaning "swarthy." Actor Dwayne Johnson was known as "The Rock" during his professional wrestling career.

Dwight

Flemish, meaning "blond." Dwight D. Eisenhower was the 34th President of the United States.

Dwyer

Gaelic, meaning "dark wise one."

Dylan

(alt. Delyn, Dillon)

Welsh, meaning "son of the sea." Dylan Thomas was a famous Welsh poet.

E

E Boys' names

Eamon
(alt. Eames, Eamonn)

Irish, meaning "wealthy protector."
Eamonn Walker is known for his role
in *Oz*.

Earl
(alt. Earle, Errol)

English, meaning "nobleman,
warrior." Became popular after the
sitcom *My Name is Earl*.

Ebenezer
(abbrev. Ebb)

Hebrew, meaning "stone of help."
The main character in Charles
Dickens's *A Christmas Carol* is
Ebenezer Scrooge.

Edgar
(alt. Elgar)

Old English, meaning "wealthy
spear." Gothic author Edgar Allen
Poe wrote "The Raven," amongst
other poems.

Edison

English, meaning "son of Edward."
Thomas Edison was one of the most
influential American inventors.

Edmund

English, meaning "wealthy protector."
Sir Edmund Hillary became the first
Westerner to reach the summit of
Mount Everest, in 1953.

Edric

Old English, meaning "rich and
powerful."

Edsel

Old German, meaning "noble." Car
pioneer Henry Ford named his son
Edsel.

Edward
*(alt. Eduard; abbrev. Ed, Eddie, Eddy,
Ned, Ted)*

Old English, meaning "wealthy guard."
A character in the "Twilight" series.

Edwin

English, meaning "wealthy friend."

Efrain

Hebrew, meaning "fruitful."

Egan

Irish, meaning "fire."

Einar

Old Norse, meaning "battle leader." A popular name for boys in Iceland.

Eladio

Greek, meaning "Greek."

Elam

Hebrew, meaning "eternal." The son of Shem and of Noah in the Bible.

Eldon

Old English, meaning "Ella's hill."

Eldred

(alt. Eldridge)

Old English, meaning "old venerable counsel."

Elgin

Old English, meaning "high minded." Also the name of a town in Scotland.

Eli

(alt. Eliah)

Hebrew, meaning "high." Eli Whitney is credited with inventing the cotton gin.

Elijah

(alt. Elias, Elio, Ellis; abbrev. Eli)

Hebrew, meaning "the Lord is my God." Elias is the Greek form of the same name, Elio is the Spanish version and Ellis the Welsh version. Actor Elijah Wood played Frodo in The Lord of the Rings. Elias Disney was Walt Disney's father.

Ellery

Old English, meaning "elder tree."

Elliott

Variant of Elio, meaning "the Lord is my God." Elliot was the little boy in the classic film E.T.

Ellison

English, meaning "son of Ellis."

Elmer

(alt. Elmo)

Old English, meaning "noble"; Arabic, meaning "aristocratic." Associated with the children's characters Elmer the Elephant and Elmo from Sesame Street.

Elon

Hebrew, meaning "oak tree."

Elroy

French, meaning "king." A cartoon character in The Jetsons.

Elton

Old English, meaning "Ella's town." Sir Elton John is one of the most successful recording artists of all time.

Elvin

English, meaning "elf-like." Elvin Bale was a huge circus performer known for cannonball stunts.

Elvis

Figure in Norse mythology. Made famous by the singer Elvis Presley.

Emanuel
(alt. Immanuel, Imanol)

Hebrew, meaning "God is with us."

Emeric

German, meaning "work rule." St. Emeric was known for living a pure and pious life.

Emile
(alt. Emiliano, Emilio)

Latin, meaning "eager." Emile is Remy the rat's older brother in Disney's Ratatouille.

Emlyn

Welsh, from the UK town of Newcastle Emlyn.

Emmett

English, meaning "universal." Emmett Kelly was known for his role as Weary Willie, the Depression-era clown.

Emrys

Welsh, meaning "immortal." Said to be the birth name of the magician Merlin.

Enoch

Hebrew, meaning "dedicated." Enoch is an ancestor of Noah in the Bible.

Enrico
(alt. Enrique)

Italian form of Henry, meaning "home ruler."

Enzo

Italian, short for Lorenzo, meaning "laurel." Enzo Ferrari was the founder of the Ferrari car company.

Ephron
(alt. Effron, Efron)

Hebrew, meaning "dust."

Erasmo
(alt. Erasmus)

Greek, meaning "to love."

Eric

Old Norse, meaning "ruler." Famous Erics include legendary guitarist Eric Clapton.

Ernest
(alt. Ernesto, Ernie, Ernst)

Old German, meaning "serious." Author Ernest Hemingway wrote the novel The Old Man and the Sea, amongst others.

Erskine

Scottish, meaning "high cliff."

Erwin

Old English, meaning "boar friend."

Ethan

(alt. Etienne)

Hebrew, meaning "long lived." Ethan Hawke is an actor. Ethan Coen and his brother Joel are award-winning film producers and directors.

Eugene

Greek, meaning "well born." Eugene Allen was a butler at the White House for 34 years and the inspiration for the film *The Butler*.

Evan

Welsh, meaning "God is good." Evan Williams founded Twitter.

Everard

Old English, meaning "strong boar."

Everett

English, meaning "strong boar."

Ewan

(alt. Ewald, Ewell)

Old English, from Owen, meaning "well born" or "noble." Actor Ewan McGregor is known for his roles in *Moulin Rouge* and the *Star Wars* series.

Exton

English, meaning "on the river Exe."

Ezra

Hebrew, meaning "helper." Name of the poet Ezra Pound.

F

Boys' names

Fabian
(alt. Fabien, Fabio)
Latin, meaning "one who grows beans."

Fabrice
(alt. Fabrizio)
Latin, meaning "works with his hands."

Faisal
(alt. Faison)
Arabic, meaning "resolute."

Faron
Spanish, meaning "pharaoh," and Gaelic for "thunder."

Farrell
Gaelic, meaning "hero."

Faulkner
Latin, from "falcon."

Faustino
Latin, meaning "fortunate."

Felipe
(alt. Filippo)
Spanish, meaning "lover of horses."

Felix
(alt. Felice)
Italian/Latin, meaning "happy." Felix the Cat was first developed as a cartoon during the silent movie era.

Fennel
Latin, name of a herb.

Ferdinand
(alt. Fernando)
Old German, meaning "bold voyager." Ferdinand was a popular name for Roman emperors and kings of Spain, as well as Disney princes.

Fergus
(alt. Ferguson)
Gaelic, meaning "supreme man."
King Fergus is Merida's father in
Disney's *Brave*.

Ferris
Gaelic, meaning "rock." The lead
character from *Ferris Bueller's Day Off*.

Fidel
Latin, meaning "faithful." Fidel Castro
was president of Cuba from 1976 to
2008.

Finbarr
Gaelic, meaning "fair head."

Finian
Gaelic, meaning "fair." St. Finnian is
an important Irish saint.

Finlay
(alt. Finley)
Gaelic, meaning "fair-haired
courageous one." Actor Finlay
Robertson is known for his role in
Doctor Who.

Finn
Irish Gaelic, meaning "fair."
Associated with the novel
Huckleberry Finn and the latest *Star
Wars* episodes.

Finnegan
Gaelic, meaning "fair." *Finnegans
Wake* is a work by James Joyce.

Fintan
Gaelic, meaning "little fair one."
Fintan supposedly saved one of
Noah's granddaughters from the
flood.

Flavio
Latin, meaning "yellow hair." *Flavio* is
the name of an opera by Handel.

Florencio
(alt. Florentino)
Latin, meaning "from Florence."

Florian
(alt. Florin)
Slavic/Latin, meaning "flower,"
though it is a masculine name.
Popular in Germany and Switzerland
and the name of the patron saint of
Poland.

Floyd
Welsh, meaning "gray haired."
Floyd is the given name of two
title-winning American professional
boxers.

Flynn
Gaelic, meaning "with a ruddy
complexion." Flynn Rider is
Rapunzel's unlikely love interest in
Disney's *Tangled*.

Fortunato
Italian, meaning "lucky."

Forrest
(alt. Forest)

Old French, meaning "woodsman." Made popular by the movie *Forrest Gump*.

Foster

Old English, meaning "woodsman."

Fotini
(alt. Fotis)

Greek, meaning "light."

Famous male guitarists

Brian (May)

Carlos (Santana)

Chuck (Berry)

Eddie (Van Halen)

Eric (Clapton)

Frank (Zappa)

Jeff (Beck)

Jimi/Jimmy (Hendrix/Page)

Joe (Satriani)

Keith (Richards)

Prince (Rogers Nelson)

Francesco
(alt. Francis, Francisco, Franco, François)

Latin, meaning "from France." After the election of Pope Francis, Francesco has become the most popular name for baby boys in Italy.

Frank
(alt. Frankie, Franklin, Franz)

Middle English, meaning "free landholder." Famous Franks include singers Frank Sinatra and Frank Zappa, and 32nd US President Franklin D. Roosevelt.

Fraser
(alt. Frasier)

Scottish, meaning "of the forest men." *Frasier* was a 1990s sitcom revolving around main character, Dr. Frasier Crane.

Frederick
(alt. Fred, Freddie, Freddy)

Old German, meaning "peaceful ruler." There is a spelling or pronunciation variation of Frederick in virtually every Western language.

Furman

Old German, meaning "ferryman."

G Boys' names

Gabino
Latin, meaning "God is my strength."

Gabriel
(alt. Gale)
Hebrew, meaning "hero of God." An archangel of God.

Gael
(alt. Gale)
English, old reference to the Celts. Gale has increased in popularity since "The Hunger Games" series.

Gage
(alt. Gaige)
Old French, meaning "pledge."

Galen
Greek, meaning "healer." Name of an ancient Roman philosopher.

Galileo
Italian, meaning "from Galilee." Galileo Galilei was an important physicist during the Scientific Revolution.

Ganesh
Hindi, meaning "Lord of the throngs." One of the Hindu deities.

Gannon
Irish, meaning "fair skinned."

Gareth
(alt. Garth)
Welsh, meaning "gentle." Also the name of one of the Knights of the Round Table.

Garfield
Old English, meaning "spear field." Also the name of the cartoon cat.

Garland

English, as in "garland of flowers."

Garrett

(alt. Garet, Gared, Garratt, Garrod)

Derived in the Middle Ages from Gerald or Gerard. Garret the Great was a political powerhouse in fifteenth-century Ireland. Now most popular as a given name in the US and Ireland.

Gary

(alt. Garry, Geary)

Germanic, meaning "spear." The name peaked in popularity in the 1950s, when actor Gary Cooper won an Oscar. Modern Garys include actor Gary Oldman.

Gaspar

(alt. Gaspard)

Persian, meaning "treasurer." A children's cartoon character from *Gaspar and Lisa.*

Gaston

From the region in the south of France.

Gavin

(alt. Gawain)

Scottish/Welsh, meaning "little falcon." Gavin DeGraw and Gavin Christopher are both singers.

Gene

Greek, shortened form of Eugene, meaning "well born." Made popular by actor and dancer Gene Kelly.

Gennaro

Italian, meaning "of Janus."

Geoffrey

(abbrev. Geoff)

Old German, meaning "peace." Actor Geoffrey Rush appeared in *Shine* and the "Pirates of the Caribbean" series.

George

(alt. Giorgio)

Greek, meaning "farmer." Queen Elizabeth's great-grandson Prince George is now third in line for the British throne.

Gerald

(alt. Geraldo, Gerard, Gerardo, Gerhard)

Old German, meaning "spear ruler." Former President of the United States Gerald Ford is the only person to have served as both president and vice president without being elected to either position, thanks to two infamous resignations before him.

Geronimo

Italian, meaning "sacred name." Geronimo led the Apache Indians against the Spanish in the 19th century.

Gerry

English, meaning "independent." Famous Gerrys include singer Gerry Rafferty.

Gert

Old German, meaning "strong spear."

Gervase

Old German, meaning "with honor." Gervase Peterson is a long-time *Survivor* contestant.

Giacomo

Italian, meaning "God's son." Legendary womanizer Casanova's full name was actually Giacomo Girolame Casanova.

Gibson

English, meaning "son of Gilbert." The name of a legendary guitar company.

Gideon

Hebrew, meaning "tree cutter." A figure in the Bible.

Gilbert

(alt. *Gilberto*)

French, meaning "bright promise." One half of the famous comedy opera duo Gilbert and Sullivan.

Giles

Greek, meaning "small goat."

Gino

Italian, meaning "well born."

Giovanni

Italian form of John, meaning "God is gracious." Actor Giovanni Ribisi is known for his roles in *Friends* and *Avatar*.

Giulio

Italian, meaning "youthful."

Giuseppe

Italian form of Joseph, meaning "Jehovah increases."

Glen

(alt. *Glenn, Glyn*)

English, from the word "glen." Glenn Miller was a world-renowned big band director and composer.

Godfrey

German, meaning "peace of God." Associated with comedian Godfrey.

Gordon

Gaelic, meaning "large fortification." Gordon Ramsay is a chef and reality TV star.

Gottlieb

German, meaning "good love." One of composer Mozart's birth names was Gottlieb.

Graeme
(alt. Graham)
English, meaning "gravelled area."

Grant
English, from the word "grant."

Granville
English, meaning "gravelly town." Granville Woods was the first African-American electrical engineer after the Civil War.

Gray
(alt. Grey)
English, from the word "gray."

Grayson
English, meaning "son of gray."

Green
English, from the word "green." The Green Lantern is a superhero from DC Comics.

Gregory
(alt. Gregorio, Grieg; abbrev. Greg)
English, meaning "watcher." Actor Gregory Peck was known for his role in *To Kill A Mockingbird*.

Griffin
English, from the word "griffin." A mythological creature.

Guido
Italian, meaning "guide." Popularized after the show *Jersey Shore*.

Guillaume
French form of William, meaning "strong protector."

Gulliver
English, meaning "glutton." Made popular after the publication of *Gulliver's Travels* by Jonathan Swift.

Gunther
German, meaning "warrior." Gunther von Hagans is the *Body Works* artist.

Gurpreet
Indian, meaning "love of the teacher."

Gustave
(abbrev. Gus)
Scandinavian, meaning "royal staff."

Guy
English, from the word "guy." Chef Guy Fieri regularly appears on the Food Network.

H Boys' names

Habib

Arabic, meaning "beloved one."

Haden

(alt. Haiden, Hayden, Haydn)
English, meaning "hedged valley."

Hades

Greek, meaning "sightless." Name of the underworld in Greek mythology.

Hadrian

From Hadria, a north Italian city. The name of an influential Roman emperor.

Hadwin

Old English, meaning "friend in war."

Hakeem

Arabic, meaning "wise and insightful." Actor Hakeem Kae-Kazim is known for his role in *Hotel Rwanda*.

Hamid

Arabic, meaning "praiseworthy." Hamid Karzai was the president of Afghanistan 2004–14.

Hamilton

Old English, meaning "flat-topped hill." Alexander Hamilton was one of the nation's Founding Fathers.

Hamish

Scottish form of James, meaning "he who supplants."

Hampus

Swedish form of Homer, meaning "pledge." Hampus Lindholm currently plays for the Anaheim Ducks.

Hamza

Arabic, meaning "lamb." Also a letter in the Arabic alphabet.

Han

(alt. Hannes, Hans)

Scandinavian, meaning "the Lord is gracious." Han Solo is a central character in the *Star Wars* films.

Hank

German, form of Henry, meaning "home ruler." Singer Hank Williams was a country superstar.

Hansel

German, meaning "the Lord is gracious." *Hansel and Gretel* is a children's fairy tale by the Brothers Grimm.

Hardy

English, meaning "tough."

Harlan

English, meaning "dweller by the boundary wood."

Harland

Old English, meaning "army land." KFC was founded by Colonel Harland David Sanders.

Harley

Old English, meaning "hare meadow." Associated with the Harley Davidson motorcycle company.

Harmon

Old German, meaning "soldier."

Harold

Scandinavian, meaning "army ruler." Actor Harold Ramis was known for his roles in *Ghostbusters* and *Stripes*.

Harrison

Old English, meaning "son of Harry." Famous Harrisons include actor Harrison Ford.

Harry

Old German, form of Henry, meaning "home ruler." Famous Harrys include fictional character Harry Potter and singer Harry Styles.

Hart

Old English, meaning "stag."

Harvey

Old English, meaning "strong and worthy." The title character of the film *Harvey*, starring James Stewart.

Haskell

Hebrew, meaning "intellect."

Hassan

Arabic, meaning "handsome." Hassan Rouhani is the current president of Iran.

Heart

English, from the word "heart."

Heath

English, meaning "heath" or "moor." Actor Heath Ledger was known for his roles in *Brokeback Mountain* and *The Dark Knight*.

Heathcliff

English, meaning "cliff near a heath." Also the main male character in Emily Bronte's novel *Wuthering Heights*.

Heber

Hebrew, meaning "partner."

Hector

Greek, meaning "steadfast."

Henry

(alt. Hal, Hale, Henri, Hendrik, Hendrix)

Old German, meaning "home ruler." Eight kings of England were called Henry. Harry is often used as a name by boys given the name Henry, as with Prince Harry, who is officially Prince Henry of Wales.

Henson

English, meaning "son of Henry."

Herbert

(alt., Herb, Heriberto; abbrev. Bert, Herbie)

Old German, meaning "illustrious warrior." Herbert Hoover was the 31st President of the United States.

Herman

(alt. Herminio, Hermon)

Old German, meaning "soldier." Herman Melville was the author of *Moby-Dick*.

Hermes

Greek, meaning "messenger." Hermes was the messenger of the gods in Greek mythology.

Herschel

Yiddish, meaning "deer."

Hezekiah

Hebrew, meaning "God gives strength."

Hideki

Japanese, meaning "excellent trees." The prime minister of Japan during World War II was Hideki Tojo.

Hideo

Japanese, meaning "excellent name."

Hilario

Latin, meaning "cheerful, happy."

Hilary

(alt. Hillary)

English, meaning "cheerful." Sir Edmund Hillary became the first Westerner to reach the summit of Mount Everest, in 1953.

Hillel

Hebrew, meaning "greatly praised."

Hilliard

Old German, meaning "battle guard."

Hilton

Old English, meaning "hill settlement." The name of a large hotel chain.

Hiram

(alt. Hyrum)

Hebrew, meaning "exalted brother."

Hiro

Spanish, meaning "sacred name." Hiro is a character on *Heroes*.

Hiroshi

Japanese, meaning "generous."

Hirsch

Yiddish, meaning "deer."

Hobart

English, meaning "bright and shining intellect."

Hodge

English, meaning "son of Roger."

Hogan

Gaelic, meaning "youth." Became well known after the success of sitcom *Hogan's Heroes* in the 1960s. Also made famous by wrestler Hulk Hogan.

Holden

English, meaning "deep valley." Holden Caulfield is the teenage protagonist of *The Catcher in the Rye*.

Hollis

Old English, meaning "holly tree."

Homer

Greek, meaning "pledge." Famous Homers include the ancient Greek poet, and Homer Simpson from *The Simpsons*.

Honorius

Latin, meaning "honorable."

Horace

Latin, common name of the Roman poet Quintus Horatius Flaccus.

Houston

Old English, meaning "Hugh's town."

Howard

Old English, meaning "noble watchman." Famous Howards include Howard Carter, who discovered the tomb of King Tut, and Howard Hughes, the aviator and movie maker.

Howell

Welsh, meaning "eminent and remarkable."

Hoyt

Norse, meaning "spirit" or "soul," or Old English meaning "hill inhabitant." Hoyt Fortenberry is a character in *True Blood*.

Hristo

From Christo, meaning "follower of Christ."

Hubert

German, meaning "bright and shining intellect." Givenchy's founder was Count Hubert de Givenchy.

Hudson

Old English, meaning "son of Hugh." Associated with the Hudson River.

Hugh

(*alt. Hugo, Huw, Ugo*)

Old German, meaning "soul, mind, and intellect." Famous Hughs include actors Hugh Jackman, Hugh Laurie, and Hugh Grant.

Humbert

Old German, meaning "famous giant." Became well known due to the paedophile protagonist of Vladimir Nabokov's *Lolita*.

Humphrey

Old German, meaning "peaceful warrior." Actor Humphrey Bogart is best known for his role in *Casablanca*.

Hunter

English, from the word "hunter." Name of singer Hunter Hayes.

Hurley

Gaelic, meaning "sea tide."

Huxley

Old English, meaning "Hugh's meadow."

I Boys' names

Iago

Spanish, meaning "he who supplants." Also the name of the villain in Shakespeare's *Othello*.

Ian

(alt. Iain, Ion)

Gaelic, variant of John, meaning "God is gracious." Novelist Ian Fleming wrote the "James Bond" novels.

Ianto

Welsh, meaning "gift of God."

Ibrahim

Arabic, meaning "father of many." An Arabic name for the father of Islam, Abraham.

Ichabod

Hebrew, meaning "glory is good." Also the name of the protagonist in *The Legend of Sleepy Hollow*.

Ichiro

Japanese, meaning "firstborn son."

Idris

Welsh, meaning "fiery leader." Actor Idris Elba is known for his roles in *Luther* and *Mandela: Long Walk to Freedom*.

Ifan

Welsh variant of John, meaning "God is gracious."

Ignacio

Latin, meaning "ardent" or "burning."

Ignatz

German, meaning "fiery."

Igor

Russian, meaning "Ing's soldier."

Ikaika

Hawaiian, meaning "strong."

Ike

Hebrew, short for Isaac, meaning "laughter." Famous Ikes include singer Ike Turner and former US President Dwight D. Eisenhower (known as Ike).

Ilan

Hebrew, meaning "tree."

Ilias

Greek variant of Elijah, Hebrew, meaning "the Lord is my God."

Indiana

Latin, meaning "from India." Also the name of a US state.

Indigo

English, describing a deep blue color derived from a plant.

Indio

Spanish, meaning "indigenous people."

Ingo

Danish, meaning "meadow."

Inigo

Spanish, meaning "fiery." Inigo Montoya is a character in *The Princess Bride*.

Ioannis

Greek, meaning "the Lord is gracious."

Ira

Hebrew, meaning "full grown and watchful."

Irvin
(alt. Irving, Irwin)

Gaelic, meaning "green and fresh water." Composer Irving Berlin is known for songs such as "White Christmas."

Isaac
(alt. Isaak)

Hebrew, meaning "laughter." Isaac was the son of Abraham and Sarah in the Bible and the Qur'an.

Isadore
(alt. Isidore, Isidro)

Greek, meaning "gift of Isis."

Isai
(alt. Isaiah, Isaias, Izaiah)

Arabic, meaning "protection and security."

Iser

Yiddish, meaning "God wrestler."

Ishmael
(alt. Ismael)

Hebrew, meaning "God listens." The narrator and protagonist of *Moby-Dick*, by Herman Melville.

Israel

Hebrew, meaning "God perseveres." Also the name of the country.

Istvan

Hungarian variant of Stephen, meaning "crowned."

Itai

Hebrew, meaning "the Lord is with me."

Ivan

A Slavic version of John, meaning "God is gracious." Several Russian tsars bore the name, including the infamous Ivan the Terrible. Ivan Rodriguez was a Major League Baseball player for many years.

Ivanhoe

Russian, meaning "God is gracious." Also title of the novel by Walter Scott.

Ivey

English, variant of Ivy.

Ivo

French, from the word "yves," meaning "yew tree."

Ivor

Scandinavian, meaning "yew." Associated with the Ivor Novello songwriting awards.

Ivory

English, from the word "ivory."

J

Boys' names

Jabari
Swahili, meaning "valiant."

Jabez
Hebrew, meaning "borne in pain."

Jace
(alt. Jaece, Jase, Jayce)
Hebrew, meaning "healer."

Jacek
(alt. Jacirto)
Polish, meaning "hyacinth." Derived from the Greek name Hyakinthos, which comes from a myth about a beautiful boy.

Jack
(alt. Jackie, Jacky, Jacques, Jaquez)
From the Hebrew John, meaning "God is gracious." Famous Jacks include actors Jack Black, Jack Nicholson, and Jack Lemmon.

Jackson
(alt. Jaxon)
English, meaning "son of Jack." Artist Jackson Pollock is known for his large, paint-splashed paintings.

Jacob
(alt. Jaco, Jacobo, Jago)
Hebrew, meaning "he who supplants." A main character in the "Twilight" series.

Jaden
(alt. Jadyn, Jaeden, Jaiden, Jaidyn, Jayden, Jaydin)
Hebrew, meaning "Jehovah has heard." Will Smith's son is Jaden Smith.

Jafar
Arabic, meaning "stream." The name of the villain in Disney's *Aladdin*.

Jagger

Old English, meaning "one who cuts." Made famous by Rolling Stones singer Mick Jagger.

Jaheem

(alt. Jaheim)

Hebrew, meaning "raised up."

Jahir

Hindi, meaning "jewel."

Jaime

Variant for James, meaning "he who supplants." "J'aime" is also French for "I love."

Jair

(alt. Jairo)

Hebrew, meaning "God enlightens."

Jake

Shortened form of Jacob, meaning "he who supplants." Famous Jakes include actor Jake Gyllenhaal and pitcher Jake Peavy.

Jalen

American English, meaning "healer" or "tranquil." Derives from the Greek spelling of Galen.

Jali

Gujarati, meaning "latticed screen."

Jalon

Greek, meaning "healer" or "tranquil."

Jamaal

(alt. Jamal, Jamar, Jamarcus, Jamari, Jamarion, Jamir)

Arabic, meaning "handsome." Jamar is a modern variant of the name.

James

(abbrev. Jamie, Jaimie, Jim, Jimmy)

English, meaning "he who supplants." Famous Jameses include actors James Franco, James Coburn, and Jim Carey and fictional characters James Bond and James T. Kirk.

Jameson

(alt. Jamison)

English, meaning "son of James." Associated with Jameson Irish Whiskey.

Jamil

Arabic, meaning "handsome."

Jamin

Hebrew, meaning "son of the right hand."

Jan

(alt. Janko, János)

Slavic, from John, meaning "the Lord is gracious." Also a term of endearment in Arabic, meaning "dear."

Janus

Latin, meaning "gateway." Roman god of doors, beginnings and endings.

Japheth
(alt. Japhet)
Hebrew, meaning "comely." One of the sons of Noah.

Jared
(alt. Jarem, Jaren, Jaret, Jarod, Jarrod)
Hebrew, meaning "descending." Actor Jared Leto appeared in *Dallas Buyers' Club*.

Jarlath
Gaelic, from Iarlaith, from St. Iarlaithe mac Loga.

Jarom
Greek, meaning "to raise and exalt." One of the prophets in the Book of Mormon.

Jarrell
Variant of Gerald, meaning "spear ruler."

Jarrett
Old English, meaning "spearbrave."

Jarvis
Old German, meaning "with honor."

Jason
(alt. Jayce)
Greek, meaning "healer." Famous Jasons include actors Jason Sudeikis and Jason Bateman, and singer Jason Derulo.

Jasper
Greek, meaning "treasure holder" or "speckled stone." Jasper as a stone has been used for jewelry for thousands of years.

Javen
Arabic, meaning "youth." One of Noah's grandsons in the Bible.

Javier
Spanish, meaning "bright." Actor Javier Bardem appeared in *Skyfall*.

Jay
Latin, meaning "jaybird." Associated with rapper Jay-Z.

Jaylan
(alt. Jaylen, Jalon)
Greek, meaning "healer."

Jeevan
Indian, meaning "life."

Jefferson
English, meaning "son of Jeffrey." Thomas Jefferson was the third president of the United States.

Jeffrey
(abbrev. Jeff)
Old German, meaning "peace." Famous Jeffs include actors Jeff Bridges and Jeff Daniels.

Jensen
(alt. Jenson)

Scandinavian, meaning "son of Jan." Famous Jensens include actor Jensen Ackles and Formula 1 driver Jenson Button.

Jeremy
(alt. Jem)

Hebrew, meaning "the Lord exalts." Famous Jeremys include Jeremy Renner and Jeremy Irons.

Jeriah

Hebrew, meaning "Jehovah has seen."

Jericho

Arabic, meaning "city of the moon." Site of the epic biblical Battle of Jericho.

Jermaine

Latin, meaning "brotherly." Jermaine Jackson was one of the original members of the Jackson Five.

Jerome

Greek, meaning "sacred name."

Jerry

English, from Gerald, meaning "spear ruler." Famous Jerrys include presenter Jerry Singer, comedian Jerry Seinfeld, and the film *Jerry Maguire*.

Jesse

Hebrew, meaning "the Lord exists." Famous Jesses include outlaw Jesse James.

Jesus

Hebrew, meaning "the Lord is Salvation" and the Son of God.

Jet
(alt. Jett)

English, meaning "black gemstone."

Jethro

Hebrew, meaning "eminent." Famous Jethros include the band Jethro Tull, and the father-in-law of Moses in the Bible.

Jiri
(alt. Jiro)

Czech, meaning "farmer."

Joachim

Hebrew, meaning "established by God." The name of the Virgin Mary's father in the Bible.

Joah
(alt. João)

Hebrew, meaning "God is gracious."

Joaquin

Hebrew, meaning "established by God." Academy Award-winner Joaquin Phoenix changed his name to "Leaf" as a child to match his siblings River and Rain.

Joel

Hebrew, meaning "Jehovah is the Lord." Famous Joels include comedian Joel McHale and singer Joel Madden.

John
(alt. Jon, Johnny)

Hebrew, meaning "God is gracious." Famous Johns include musicians John Lennon and John Legend, and comedian Jon Stewart. Actor Johnny Depp and singer Johnny Cash are both also Johns by birth.

Jolyon

English, meaning "young."

Jonah
(alt. Jonas)

Hebrew, meaning "dove." A character in the Bible who was swallowed by a whale.

Jonathan
(alt. Johnathan, Johnathon, Jonathon; abbrev. Jon, Johnny, Jonny, Jonty)

Hebrew, meaning "God is gracious." Famous Jonathans include actors Jonathan Taylor Thomas and Jonathan Rhys Meyers, and author Jonathan Swift.

Jordan
(alt. Jory, Judd)

Hebrew, meaning "downflowing." Michael Jordan is a legendary basketball player.

Jorge

From George, meaning "farmer." Actor Jorge Garcia is known for his role as Hurley in *Lost*.

José

Spanish variant of Joseph, meaning "God increases." Associated with Jose Cuervo tequila.

Joseph
(abbrev. Joe, Joey, Joss)

Hebrew, meaning "Jehovah increases." Famous Josephs include actor Joseph Gordon-Levitt and baseball legend Joe DiMaggio.

Joshua
(alt. Joshué; abbrev. Josh)

Hebrew, meaning "Jehovah is salvation." The leader of the Israelites after Moses' death in the Bible. Actor Josh Hutcherson is known for his role in the "Hunger Games" trilogy.

Josiah

Hebrew, meaning "God helps." One of the kings of Judah in the Bible.

Jovan

Latin, meaning "the supreme God."

Joweese

Native American, meaning "chirping bird." More commonly used for girls originally, it has now become a boys' name.

Joyce

Latin, meaning "joy." Used for boys and girls.

Juan

Spanish variant of John, meaning "God is gracious." Juan Pablo Galavis was a notorious contestant on *The Bachelor*.

Jubal

Hebrew, meaning "ram's horn."

Jude

Hebrew, meaning "praise" or "thanks." Associated with the Beatles' song "Hey Jude."

Judson

Variant of Jude, meaning "praise" or "thanks."

Julian

(alt. Julien, Julio; abbrev. Jules)

Greek, meaning "belonging to Julius." The original calendar in the Roman Empire was the Julian calendar.

Julius

Latin, meaning "youthful." Julius Caesar was a Roman emperor.

Junior

Latin, meaning "the younger one." Can also be used as a suffix to names to denote a name that has been passed down generations—for example James Earl Carter, Sr. was the father of US President James Earl Carter, Jr.

Junius

Latin, meaning "young."

Jupiter

Latin, meaning "the supreme God." Jupiter was king of the Roman gods and the god of thunder.

Juraj

Hebrew, meaning "God is my judge."

Jurgen

German form of George, meaning "farmer."

Justice

English, from the word "justice," meaning a set of moral values, ethics, and law.

Justin

(alt. Justus)

Latin, meaning "just and upright." Famous Justins include singers Justin Timberlake and Justin Bieber.

Juwan

Hebrew, meaning "the Lord is gracious."

Boys' names

Kabelo
African, meaning "gift."

Kade
Scottish, meaning "from the wetlands."

Kadeem
Arabic, meaning "one who serves." Actor Kadeem Hardison is known for his role in *A Different World*.

Kaden
(alt. Kadin, Kaeden, Kaedin, Kaiden)
Arabic, meaning "companion."

Kadir
Arabic, meaning "capable and competent."

Kafka
Czech, meaning "bird-like." Name of the influential author Franz Kafka.

Kahekili
Hawaiian, meaning "the thunder." Also the name of several kings of Maui.

Kai
Greek, meaning "keeper of the keys." Kai also means "dog" in Cornish, "ocean water" in Hawaiian, and "food" in Maori.

Kaito
Japanese, meaning "ocean and sake dipper." One of the most popular names for boys in Japan.

Kalani
Hawaiian, meaning "sky."

Kale
German, meaning "free man."

Kaleb
Hebrew, meaning "dog" or "aggressive." Also an alternate spelling for Caleb.

Kalen
(alt. Kaelen, Kalan)
Gaelic, meaning "uncertain."

Kaleo
Hawaiian, meaning "the voice."
Kaleo Kanahele is a silver medal-winning paralympian in volleyball.

Kamari
Indian, meaning "the enemy of desire."

Kamil
Arabic, meaning "perfection." Also a Polish and Slovakian name meaning "religious service attender."

Kane
Gaelic, meaning "little battler." The title character of the film Citizen Kane.

Kani
Hawaiian, meaning "sound."

Kanye
Town in Botswana. Made popular by rapper Kanye West.

Kareem
(alt. Karim)
Arabic, meaning "generous." Kareem Abdul-Jabur is a legendary basketball player.

Karl
(alt. Karlson)
Old German, meaning "free man." Actor Karl Urban is known for his roles in The Lord of the Rings and Star Trek.

Kavon
Gaelic, meaning "handsome."

Kayden
Arabic, meaning "companion."

Kazimierz
Polish, meaning "declares peace."

Kazuki
Japanese, meaning "radiant hope."

Kazuo
Japanese, meaning "harmonious man." Depending on the characters/spellings used, Kazuo can also mean "first son" or "first in leadership."

Keagan
(alt. Keegan, Kegan)
Gaelic, meaning "small flame."

Keane
Gaelic, meaning "fighter."

Keanu
Hawaiian, meaning "breeze." Actor Keanu Reeves is known for his roles in Speed and "The Matrix" trilogy.

Keary

Gaelic, meaning "black-haired."

Keaton

English, meaning "place of hawks."

Keeler

Gaelic, meaning "beautiful and graceful."

Keenan

(alt. Kenan, Keenen)

Gaelic, meaning "little ancient one." Keenen Ivory Wayans is one of the Wayans comedy brothers.

Keiji

Japanese, meaning "govern with discretion."

Keir

Gaelic, meaning "dark-haired" or "dark-skinned."

Keith

Gaelic, meaning "woodland." Keith Richards is one of the legendary members of the Rolling Stones.

Kekoa

(alt. Koa)

Hawaiian, meaning "brave one" or "soldier."

Kelby

Old English, meaning "farmhouse near the stream."

Kell

(alt. Kellan, Kellen, Kelley, Kelly, Kiel)

Norse, meaning "spring." Associated with the ancient Book of Kells.

Kelsey

Old English, meaning "victorious ship." Actor Kelsey Grammer is known for his roles in *Cheers* and *Frasier*.

Kelton

Old English, meaning "town of the keels."

Kelvin

Old English, meaning "friend of ships." A kelvin is a unit of temperature measurement.

Kendal

Old English, meaning "the Kent river valley."

Kendon

Old English, meaning "brave guard."

Kendrick

Gaelic, meaning "royal ruler."

Kenelm

Old English, meaning "bold."

Kenji

Japanese, meaning "intelligent second son." Also the name of a period in Japanese history in the 13th century.

Kennedy

Gaelic, meaning "helmet head."
The Kennedy family is a prominent
American Catholic dynasty, whose
members included the 35th
President of the United States, John
F. Kennedy.

Kenneth

(alt. Kenne; abbrev. Ken)

Gaelic, meaning "born of fire."
Kenneth Branagh is an actor of stage
and screen, including in the *Harry
Potter* films.

Kennison

English, meaning "son of Kenneth."

Kent

English, meaning "rim or border."
Associated with Clark Kent, aka
Superman.

Kenton

English, meaning "town of Ken."

Kenya

(alt. Kenyatta, Kenyon)

From the country and mountain in
Africa.

Kenzo

Japanese, meaning "wise." Kenzo is
the name of a fashion brand.

Keola

Hawaiian, meaning "life."

Keon

(alt. Keoni)

Persian, meaning "King of Kings."
In Hawaiian, the name also means
"God is gracious."

Kepler

German, meaning "hat maker."

Kermit

(alt. Kerwin)

Gaelic, meaning "without
envy." Associated with Kermit
the Frog.

Kerr

English, meaning "wetland." Kerr
Smith is an American actor.

Keshav

Indian, meaning "beautiful haired."
One of the names for Vishnu in the
Hindu religion.

Kevin

Gaelic, meaning "handsome
beloved." Famous Kevins include
actors Kevin Bacon and Kevin
Kline.

Khalid

(alt. Khalif)

Arabic, meaning "immortal." Actor
Khalid Abdalla is known for his
roles in *United 93* and *The Kite
Runner*.

Khalil

Arabic, meaning "friend." Khalil Gibran is an influential poet, writer, and philosopher, frequently quoted at weddings.

Kian
(alt. Keyon, Kyan)

Persian, meaning "king or realm." In Ireland, the same spelling also means "ancient."

Kiefer

German, meaning "barrel maker." 24 star Kiefer Sutherland's full name is Kiefer William Frederick Dempsey George Rufus Sutherland.

Kieran
(alt. Kieron, Kyron)

Gaelic, meaning "black." Actor Kieran Culkin is known for his role in Scott Pilgrim vs. the World.

Kijana

Swahili, meaning "youth."

Kilby

English, from the town of the same name.

Kilian

Irish, meaning "bright-headed."

Kimani

African, meaning "beautiful and sweet."

King

English, meaning "male ruler of state."

Kingsley

English, meaning "the king's meadow." Kingsley Shacklebolt is a character in the Harry Potter series.

Kirby

German, meaning "settlement by a church." Also the name of a small, pink, bubble-like video game character.

Kirk

Old German, meaning "church." Famous Kirks include Kirk Douglas and Captain James T. Kirk from Star Trek.

Klaus

German, meaning "victorious."

Kobe
(alt. Koda, Kody)

Japanese, meaning "a Japanese city." Legendary player Kobe Bryant recently retired from professional basketball.

Kofi

Ghanaian, meaning "born on Friday." Kofi Annan was the secretary general of the UN until 2006.

Kohana

Japanese, meaning "little flower."

Kojo

Ghanaian, meaning "Monday."

Korben

(alt. Korbin)

Gaelic, meaning "a steep hill." Korben Dallas is a character in *The Fifth Element*.

Kramer

German, meaning "shopkeeper." Kramer is a character from *Seinfeld*.

Kurt

German, meaning "courageous advice." Famous Kurts include *Glee* character Kurt, actor Kurt Russell, and the late Nirvana singer Kurt Cobain.

Names of poets

Alfred (Lord Tennyson)

Allen (Ginsberg)

Dylan (Thomas)

Geoffrey (Chaucer)

Langston (Hughes)

Ralph (Waldo Emerson)

Robert (Burns)

Seamus (Heaney)

Walt (Whitman)

William (Wordsworth)

Kurtis

French, meaning "courtier."

Kwame

Ghanaian, meaning "born on Saturday."

Kyden

English, meaning "narrow little fire."

Kyle

(alt. Kylan, Kyleb, Kyler)

Gaelic, meaning "narrow and straight." Actor Kyle Massey is known for his roles on The Disney Channel.

Kyllion

Irish, meaning "war."

Kylo

American English, meaning "villain". Made famous by *Star Wars* antagonist Kylo Ren.

Kyree

From Cree, a Canadian tribe.

Kyros

Greek, meaning "legitimate power."

L Boys' names

Laban

Hebrew, meaning "white." Laban is the brother of Rebekah in the Bible.

Lachlan

Gaelic, meaning "from the land of lakes."

Lacy

Old French, after the place in France. Masculine form of Lacey.

Lalit

Hindi, meaning "beautiful."

Lamar
(alt. Lemar)

Old German, meaning "water." Lamar Odom is known for his marriage to Khloe Kardashian and his skills as a basketball player.

Lambert

Scandinavian, meaning "land brilliant."

Lambros

Greek, meaning "brilliant and radiant."

Lamont

Old Norse, meaning "law man."

Lance

French, meaning "land." Lance Armstrong is a disgraced former racing cyclist.

Lancelot

Variant of Lance, meaning "land." The name of one of the Knights of the Round Table.

Landen
(alt. Lando, Landon, Landyn, Langdon)

English, meaning "long hill."

Lane
(alt. Layne)

English, from the word "lane."

Lannie
(alt. Lanny)

German, meaning "precious." Also a nickname for Roland or Orlando.

Larkin

Gaelic, meaning "rough" or "fierce." Philip Larkin was a famous poet.

Laron

French, meaning "thief."

Lasse

Finnish, meaning "girl." (Still, ironically, a boy's name.) Lasse Holstrom is a film director and Lasse Viren one of the all-time great long distance runners.

Laszlo

Hungarian, meaning "glorious rule."

Lathyn

Latin, meaning "fighter."

Latif

Arabic, meaning "gentle."

Laurel

Latin, meaning "bay." One of the founders of Jamaican ska music was Laurel Aitken. Used for both boys and, more commonly, girls.

Laurent

French, from Laurence, meaning "man from Laurentum." The founder of YSL was Yves Saint Laurent.

Lawrence
(alt. Lars, Lawrence; abbrev. Larry)

Latin, meaning "man from Laurentum." Actor Laurence Olivier is a stage legend also known for his roles in dozens of Hollywood movies. Larry King is a longstanding live TV presenter.

Lawson

Old English, meaning "son of Lawrence."

Lazarus

Hebrew, meaning "God is my help."

Leandro

Latin, meaning "lion man."

Lear

German, meaning "of the meadow." The title character in Shakespeare's play *King Lear*.

Lee
(alt. Leigh)

Old English, meaning "meadow" or "valley." Famous Lees include actor Lee Marvin and JFK assassin Lee Harvey Oswald.

Leib

Yiddish, meaning "lion."

Leif
(alt. Leiv, Lief, Liev)

Scandinavian, meaning "heir." Actor Liev Schreiber is known for his roles in *X-Men Origins: Wolverine*, and the "Scream" trilogy.

Leith

From the Scottish town of the same name.

Lennox
(alt. Lenny)

Gaelic, meaning "with many elm trees." Famous Lennoxes include boxer Lennox Lewis.

Leo

Latin, meaning "lion." Also the name of the star sign.

Leon

Latin, meaning "lion." Associated with the band Kings of Leon.

Leonard

Old German, meaning "lion strength." Actor Leonard Nimoy was known for his role in *Star Trek*.

Leonardo

Italian, meaning "bold lion." Artist Leonardo da Vinci painted the *Mona Lisa*.

Leopold

German, meaning "brave people."

Leroy

French, meaning "king." The title character of the song "Bad Bad Leroy Brown."

Lesley
(alt. Leslie; abbrev. Les)

Scottish, meaning "holly garden." Used for both boys and girls.

Lester

English, meaning "from Leicester."

Lewis

French, meaning "renowned fighter." Famous Lewises include comedian Lewis Black and author Lewis Carroll.

Lexar
(alt. Lex, Lexer)

Shortened form of Alexander, meaning "man's defender."

Liam

German, meaning "helmet." Famous Liams include actor Liam Neeson and One Direction member Liam Payne.

Lincoln

English, meaning "lake colony." Abraham Lincoln was the 16th President of the United States.

Lindsay
(alt. Lindsey)

Scottish, meaning "linden tree." Singer Lindsey Buckingham is a founding member of Fleetwood Mac. Can be used for boys and girls.

Linus

Latin, meaning "lion." A character in the *Peanuts* cartoon.

Lionel

English, meaning "lion." Famous Lionels include singer Lionel Richie, and composer Lionel Bart.

Llewellyn

Welsh, meaning "like a lion."

Lloyd

Welsh, meaning "gray-haired and sacred." Andrew Lloyd Webber is the composer of *Cats* and other musicals.

Logan

Gaelic, meaning "hollow." Associated with sci-fi novel *Logan's Run*.

Lonnie

English, meaning "lion strength."

Lorcan

Gaelic, meaning "little fierce one."

Louis

(alt. Lou, Louie, Luigi, Luis)

French, meaning "famous warrior." Famous Louises include fifth in line to the British throne Prince Louis and designer Louis Vuitton.

Lucas

(alt. Lukas, Luca)

English, meaning "man from Luciana." George Lucas is the legendary *Star Wars* producer.

Lucian

(alt. Lucio)

Latin, meaning "light."

Ludwig

German, meaning "famous fighter." Ludwig van Beethoven was a hugely influential composer.

Luke

(alt. Luc, Luka)

Latin, meaning "from Lucanus" (in southern Italy). Famous Lukes include the Gospel of Luke from the Bible, *Star Wars* character Luke Skywalker, and actor Luke Perry.

Lupe

Latin, meaning "wolf." Lupe Fiasco is a rapper.

Luther

German, meaning "soldier of the people." Superman's arch-enemy is supervillain Lex Luther.

Lyle

French, meaning "the island." Lyle Lovett is a country singer-songwriter and actor.

Lyn

(alt. Lyndon)

Spanish, meaning "pretty." Used for both boys and girls.

M Boys' names

Mac
(alt. Mack, Mackie)
Scottish, meaning "son of."

Macaulay
Scottish, meaning "son of the phantom." Name of the actor Macaulay Culkin.

Mace
English, meaning "heavy staff" or "club." Also a shortened form of Mason.

Mackenzie
Scottish, meaning "the fair one." Actor Mackenzie Crook is known for his roles in Pirates of the Caribbean and Game of Thrones.

Mackland
Scottish, meaning "land of Mac."

Macon
French, from the name of towns in France and Georgia.

Macsen
Scottish, meaning "son of Mac."

Madden
(alt. Mads)
Irish, meaning "descendant of the hound." Associated with the Madden NFL gaming series.

Maddox
(alt. Maddux)
English, meaning "good" or "generous." Derived from Madoc, who was a legendary Welsh prince. Name chosen by Angelina Jolie for her first adopted child, now Maddox Jolie-Pitt.

Madison
(alt. Madsen)

Irish, meaning "son of Madden." James Madison was the fourth President of the United States.

Magnus
(alt. Manus)

Latin, meaning "great." Popular name in Scandinavia.

Maguire

Gaelic, meaning "son of the beige one." The title character of the movie *Jerry Maguire*.

Mahesh

Hindi, meaning "great ruler." One of the names for Lord Shiva in the Hindu faith.

Mahir

Arabic, meaning "skillful."

Mahlon

Hebrew, meaning "sickness."

Mahmoud

Arabic, meaning "praiseworthy." Mahmoud Ahmadinejad was the president of Iran until 2013.

Mahoney

Irish, meaning "bear."

Major

English, from the word "major." Reported as one of the fastest climbing boys' names.

Makal

From Michael, meaning "close to God."

Makani

Hawaiian, meaning "wind."

Makis

Hebrew, meaning "gift from God."

Mako

Hebrew, meaning "God is with us."

Malachi
(alt. Malachy)

Irish, meaning "messenger of God." The name of a Jewish prophet in the Bible.

Malcolm

English, meaning "Columba's servant." Well-known Malcolms include activist Malcolm X, and sitcom *Malcolm in the Middle*.

Mali

Arabic, meaning "full and rich." Also the name of a West African republic.

Manfred

Old German, meaning "man of peace." Associated with the band Manfred Mann.

Manish
(alt. Manesh)

English, meaning "manly."

Manley

English, meaning "manly and brave."

Mannix

Gaelic, meaning "little monk."
Associated with the show *Mannix.*

Manoi
(alt. Manos)

Japanese, meaning "love springing from intellect."

Manuel

Hebrew, meaning "God is with us."

Manus

Gaelic, meaning "great." Popular during the Viking period.

Manzi

Italian, meaning "steer."

Marcel
(alt. Marcelino, Marcello)

French, meaning "little warrior."
Marcel Marceau was perhaps the most famous mime of all time.

Mariano

Latin, meaning "from the god Mars."
Also a tribute to the Virgin Mary.

Mario
(alt. Marius)

Latin, meaning "manly." Famous Marios include presenter Mario Lopez, and Nintendo character Mario.

Mark
(alt. Marc, Marco, Marcus, Marek, Markus)

English, meaning "from the god Mars." Famous Marks include the Gospel of Mark in the Bible, and actors Mark Hamill and Mark Wahlberg.

Marley
(alt. Marlin, Marlow)

Old English, meaning "meadow near the lake." Famous Marleys include singer Bob Marley, and the infamous Labrador dog Marley.

Marlon

English origin, meaning "little hawk."
Actor Marlon Brando is a famous bearer of this name.

Marshall

Old French, meaning "caretaker of horses."

Martin
(alt. Marty)

Latin, meaning "dedicated to Mars."
Famous Martins include actors Martin Freeman and Martin Sheen, and director Martin Scorsese.

Marvel

English, from the word "marvel."
Associated with Marvel comic books.

Marvin

Welsh, meaning "sea friend." Famous Marvins include singer Marvin Gaye, composer Marvin Hamlish, and character Marvin the Martian.

Mason

English, from the word for someone who works with either stone or brick.

Mathias

(alt. Matthias)

Hebrew, meaning "gift of God." Matthias was the apostle chosen to replace Judas in the Bible.

Matthew

(alt. Mathieu; abbrev. Matt)

Hebrew, meaning "gift of the Lord." Famous Matthews include the Gospel of Matthew from the Bible, and actors Matthew McConaughey and Matthew Perry.

Maurice

(alt. Mauricio)

Latin, meaning "dark skinned" or "Moorish." Famous Maurices include children's author Maurice Sendak.

Maverick

American English, meaning "nonconformist leader." Made popular by the movie *Top Gun*.

Maximillian

(alt. Max, Maxie, Maxim, Maximilian)

Latin, meaning "greatest." Also the name of several Roman emperors. More common now in the abbreviated form Max, as with actor Max Greenfield.

Maximino

Latin, meaning "little Max."

Maxwell

Latin, meaning "Maccus' stream." Actor Maxwell Caulfield is known for his role in *Dynasty*.

Maynard

Old German, meaning "brave." A character from *Desperate Housewives*.

McArthur

Scottish, meaning "son of Arthur." Associated with General Douglas MacArthur.

McCoy

Scottish, meaning "son of Coy."

Mckenna

(alt. Mackenna)

Irish Gaelic, meaning "son of the handsome one." Also used as a girl's name.

Mearl

English, meaning "my earl."

Mederic

French, meaning "doctor."

Mekhi

African, meaning "who is God?"
Actor Mekhi Phifer is known for his
roles in *ER* and *8 Mile*.

Mel

Gaelic, meaning "smooth brow."
Famous Mels include actor Mel
Gibson. Also an abbreviation for
Melvin.

Melbourne

From the city in Victoria, Australia.

Melchior

Persian, meaning "king of the city."
The name of one of the Three Kings
in the Bible.

Melton

English, meaning "town of Mel."

Melva

Hawaiian, meaning "plumeria."

Melville

Scottish, meaning "town of Mel."
Herman Melville is the author of
Moby-Dick.

Melvin

(alt. Melvyn; abbrev. Mel)

English, meaning "smooth brow."
Actor Melvyn Douglas was known for
his roles in *Hud* and *Being There*.

Memphis

Greek, meaning "established and
beautiful." Also the name of the
Tennessee city.

Mercer

English, from the word "mercer."

Merl

French, meaning "blackbird."

Merlin

Welsh, meaning "sea fortress." Merlin
is perhaps the most famous wizard
of all, appearing in stories from the
medieval era.

Merrick

Welsh, meaning "Moorish."

Merrill

Gaelic, meaning "shining sea."

Merritt

English, from the word "merit."

Merton

Old English, meaning "town by the
lake."

Meyer

Hebrew, meaning "bright farmer."

Michael

*(alt. Michel, Michele, Miguel; abbrev.
Mick, Mickey, Mike, Mikey)*

Hebrew, meaning "resembles
God." Famous Michaels include the
archangel, singers Michael Jackson
and Michael Bublé, and legendary
basketball player Michael Jordan.

Michalis
(alt. Miklos)

Greek form of Michael, meaning "resembles God."

Michelangelo

Italian, meaning "Michael's angel." Name of the famous Italian artist who painted the Sistine Chapel.

Milan

From the name of the Italian city. Also the name of Shakira's oldest son.

Miles
(alt. Milo, Milos, Myles)

English, from the word "miles." Famous Mileses include trumpeter Miles Davies, singer Miles Kane, and *Star Trek: Next Generation* character Miles O'Brien.

Milton

English, meaning "miller's town." Poet John Milton was the author of *Paradise Lost.*

Miro

Slavic, meaning "peace."

Misha

Russian, meaning "who is like God."

Mitchell
(abbrev. Mitch)

English, meaning "who is like God."

Modesto

Italian, meaning "modest." Also the name of a Californian town.

Moe

Hebrew, meaning "God's helmet." Moe is a character from *The Simpsons.*

Mohamed
(alt. Mohammad, Mohamet, Mohammed, Muhammad)

Arabic, meaning "praiseworthy." Acknowledged as the prophet and founder of Islam.

Monroe

Gaelic, meaning "mouth of the river Rotha." Marylin Monroe was a screen legend.

Monserrate

Latin, meaning "jagged mountain."

Montague
(abbrev. Monty)

French, meaning "pointed hill."

Montana

Latin, meaning "mountain." Also the name of the state.

Monte

Italian, meaning "mountain."

Montgomery
(abbrev. Monty)

Variant of Montague, meaning "pointed hill." Actor Montgomery Clift was known for his roles in From Here to Eternity and A Place in the Sun.

Moody
English, from the word "moody."

Mordecai
Hebrew, meaning "little man."

Morgan
Welsh, meaning "circling sea." Famous Morgans include actor Morgan Freeman and filmmaker Morgan Spurlock. Can be both a boys' and girls' name.

Moritz
Latin, meaning "dark skinned and Moorish." Also a German variation of Maurice.

Moroccan
Arabic, meaning "from Morocco." Popularized by Mariah Carey's choice for her son.

Morpheus
Greek, meaning "shape." The Roman god of dreams in the epic poem Metamorphoses.

Morris
Welsh, meaning "dark-skinned and Moorish."

Morrison
English, meaning "son of Morris." Associated with singer and guitarist Jim Morrison.

Mortimer
French, meaning "dead sea."

Morton
Old English, meaning "moor town."

Moses
(alt. Moshe, Moshon)

Hebrew, meaning "savior." A key figure in the Bible.

Moss
English, from the word "moss."

Mungo
Gaelic, meaning "most dear." Lake Mungo is in Australia.

Murphy
Irish, meaning "sea warrior." Murphy's Law states if something can go wrong, it will.

Murray
Gaelic, meaning "lord and master."

Mustafa
Arabic, meaning "chosen." Also a name for the prophet Muhammad in Islam.

Myron
Greek, meaning "myrrh."

N

Boys' names

Najee

Arabic, meaning "dear companion." Also the name of an influential jazz musician.

Nakia

Arabic, meaning "pure."

Nakul

Indian, meaning "mongoose." Choreographer Nakul Dev Mahajan has made a name for himself as a mainstream Bollywood choreographer.

Naphtali

Hebrew, meaning "wrestling." One of Joseph's brothers in the Bible.

Napoleon

Italian origin, meaning "man from Naples." Name of the French general who became Emperor of France.

Narciso

Latin, from the myth of Narcissus, who drowned after gazing at his own reflection.

Nash

English, meaning "at the ash tree." Singer songwriter Graham Nash is known for his involvement with Crosby, Stills & Nash.

Nasir

Arabic, meaning "helper."

Nathan

(alt. Nathaniel; abbrev. Nate)

Hebrew, meaning "God has given." The name of several characters in the Bible.

Naveen

Indian, meaning "new." Actor Naveen Andrews is known for his roles in Lost and The English Patient.

Ned

Originally a nickname for Edward, meaning "wealthy guard." Now used frequently in its own right. Ned Flanders is a character from *The Simpsons*.

Neftali

Hebrew, meaning "struggling."

Nehemiah

Hebrew, meaning "comforter."

Neil

(alt. Neal, Niall)

Irish, meaning "champion." Famous Neils include astrophysicist Neil deGrasse Tyson, actor Neil Patrick Harris, and singer Neil Young.

Neilson

Irish, meaning "son of Neil."

Nelson

Variant of Neil, meaning "champion." Famous Nelsons include Nelson Mandela and Lord Horatio Nelson.

Nemo

Latin, meaning "nobody." Made popular after the Disney/Pixar film *Finding Nemo*.

Neo

Latin, meaning "new." Neo is a character in "The Matrix" trilogy.

Nephi

Greek, meaning "cloud."

Nessim

Arabic, meaning "breeze."

Nestor

Greek, meaning "traveler." Also the name of a king in ancient Greek mythology.

Neville

Old French, meaning "new village." Neville Longbottom is a character in the *Harry Potter* series.

Newton

English, meaning "new town." Scientist Sir Isaac Newton is celebrated as the discoverer of gravity.

Nicholas

(alt. Nicklas, Nicolas, Niklas, Nikola; abbrev. Nick, Nicky, Nicoi)

Greek, meaning "victorious." Famous Nicholases include St. Nicholas (the original Santa Claus), actor Nicolas Cage, and alchemist Nicholas Flamel.

Nigel

Gaelic, meaning "champion." Producer Nigel Lythgoe is known for his work on *So You Think You Can Dance*.

Nikhil

Sanskrit, meaning "whole" or "entire."

Nikita

Greek, meaning "unconquered." Used for both boys and girls.

Nimrod

Hebrew, meaning "we will rebel." A prominent character in the Bible.

Nissim

Hebrew, meaning "wonderful things."

Noah

Hebrew, meaning "peaceful." A prominent character in the Bible, the subject of the movie *Noah*.

Noel

French, meaning "Christmas." Famous Noels include comedian and actor Noel Coward.

Nolan

Gaelic, meaning "champion."

Norbert

Old German, meaning "northern brightness."

Norman
(abbrev. Norm)

Old German, meaning "northerner." The Norman people of the Middle Ages originated from Normandy in France.

Normand

French, meaning "from Normandy."

Norris

Old French, meaning "northerner."

Norton

English, meaning "northern town."

Norval

French, meaning "northern town."

Norwood

English, meaning "northern forest."

Nova

Latin, meaning "new." Also the name of a vast nuclear explosion in a white dwarf star.

Nuno

Latin, meaning "ninth."

Nunzio

Italian, meaning "messenger."

Boys' names

Oakley

English, meaning "from the oak meadow." The name of a brand of clothing.

Obadiah

Hebrew, meaning "God's worker." Used throughout the Bible to indicate a servant of God.

Obama

African, meaning "crooked." Surname of the 44th president of the United States.

Obed

Hebrew, meaning "servant of God."

Oberon
(abbrev. Obi, Obie)

Old German, meaning "royal bear." The Fairy King in Shakespeare's *A Midsummer Night's Dream*.

Octave
(alt. Octavian, Octavio)

Latin, meaning "eight." An octave is a series of eight notes in a musical scale.

Oda
(alt. Odell, Odie, Odis)

Hebrew, meaning "praise God."

Ogden

Old English, meaning "oak valley."

Oisin

Celtic, meaning "fawn." From an ancient Irish poet.

Ola

Norse, meaning "precious." Ola Nordmann is a personification of Norway, in the same way Uncle Sam represents the USA.

Olaf
(alt. Olan)

Old Norse, meaning "ancestor." The name of the animated snowman in Disney's *Frozen*.

Oleander

Hawaiian, meaning "joyous."

Oleg
(alt. Olen)

Russian, meaning "holy."

Olin

Russian, meaning "rock."

Oliver
(alt. Olivier; abbrev. Ollie, Olly)

Latin, meaning "olive tree." Associated with the musical *Oliver!* and Disney's *Oliver and Company*.

Omar
(alt. Omari, Omarion)

Arabic, meaning "speaker." Actor Omar Epps is known for his roles in *House* and *Resurrection*.

Ora

Latin, meaning "hour."

Oran
(alt. Oren, Orrin)

Gaelic, meaning "light and pale."

Orange

English, from the word "orange," applied to both the fruit and the color.

Orion

From the ancient Greek legend of a massive hunter.

Orlando
(alt. Orlo)

Old German, meaning "old land." Famous Orlandos include actor Orlando Bloom, the Shakespearean character Orlando from *As You Like It*, and the city of Orlando in Florida.

Orpheus

Greek, meaning "beautiful voice." A legendary ancient Greek musician, poet, and prophet.

Orson

Latin, meaning "bear." Film director Orson Welles was known for the movies *Citizen Kane* and *Touch of Evil*.

Orville

Old French, meaning "gold town." Associated with popcorn brand Orville Redenbacher.

Osaka

From the Japanese city.

Osborne
(alt. Osbourne)

Norse, meaning "bear god." Associated with Sharon and Ozzy Osbourne's family.

Oscar

Old English, meaning "spear of the gods." The Oscars is the nickname for the Academy Awards.

Oswald

German, meaning "God's power." Oswald the Lucky Rabbit was Walt Disney's first creation.

Otha
(alt. Otho)

German, meaning "wealth."

Othello

Old German, meaning "wealth." From the Shakespearean character and play.

Otis

German, meaning "wealth." Otis Redding was a legendary singer and several US sports stars share the same given name.

Otten

German, meaning "son of Otto."

Otto

German, meaning "wealthy." Anne Frank's father was called Otto Frank.

Owain

Welsh, meaning "youth."

Owen
(alt. Eoghan, Eoin)

Welsh, meaning "well born and noble" or "little warrior." Famous Owens include actor Owen Wilson. Eoghan and Eoin are the Irish variants.

Oz

Hebrew, meaning "strength." Associated with *The Wizard of Oz*.

P

Boys' names

Pablo

Spanish, meaning "little." Famous Pablos include artist Pablo Picasso.

Paco

Native American, meaning "eagle." Paco Rabanne is a Spanish fashion designer and brand name. His real first name is Francisco.

Padma

Sanskrit, meaning "lotus."

Padraig
(alt. Podrick)

Irish, meaning "noble." Podrick Payne is a character in *Game of Thrones*.

Panos

Greek, meaning "all holy."

Paolo

Italian, meaning "little."

Paresh

Sanskrit, meaning "supreme standard."

Parker

Old English, meaning "park keeper."

Pascal

Latin, meaning "Easter child." The more common female equivalent is Pascale.

Patrick
(alt. Patrice; abbrev. Paddy, Pat)

Irish, meaning "noble." St. Patrick is the patron saint of Ireland.

Patten
(alt. Patton)

English, meaning "noble." Patton Oswalt is a comedian.

Paul

Hebrew, meaning "small." Paul was one of Jesus's main disciples.

Pavel
Latin, meaning "small."

Pax
Latin, meaning "peace."

Paxton
English, meaning "town of peace."

Payne
Latin, meaning "peasant."

Payton
Latin, meaning "peasant's town."

Pedro
Spanish form of Peter, meaning "rock."

Penn
English, meaning "hill." Penn Jillette is a magician and one half of Penn and Teller.

Percival
(alt. Percy)
French, meaning "pierce the valley." The name of one of the Knights of the Round Table.

Perez
Hebrew, meaning "breach." Famous Perezes include Perez Morton, the lawyer and revolutionary Boston patriot, and professional gossiper Perez Hilton.

Pericles
Greek, meaning "far-famed." Pericles was an influential ancient Greek general and statesman.

Perrin
Greek, meaning "rock."

Perry
English, meaning "rock." Associated with the series *Perry Mason*.

Pervis
English, meaning "purveyor."

Peter
(alt. Pedro, Petros, Pierre, Piers; abbrev. Pete)
Greek, meaning "rock." St. Peter was one of Jesus's disciples in the Bible.

Peyton
Old English, meaning "fighting man's estate." Peyton Manning recently retired from professional football.

Philip
(alt. Phillip; abbrev. Phil, Pip)
Greek, meaning "lover of horses." Famous Philips include husband of the Queen, Prince Philip, Philip the Apostle, and author Philip Pullman.

Philo
Greek, meaning "love."

Phineas
(alt. Pinchas)

Hebrew, meaning "oracle." A character in the cartoon *Phineas and Ferb*.

Phoenix

Greek, meaning "dark red." In ancient Greek mythology, a phoenix is a bird that has the power to regenerate itself from its ashes.

Pierce
(alt. Pierson)

Meaning "son of Piers."

Placido

Latin, meaning "placid." Placido Domingo is a famous tenor opera singer.

Pradeep

Hindi, meaning "light."

Pranav

Sanskrit, meaning "spiritual leader."

Presley

Old English, meaning "priest's meadow." Made famous by legendary singer Elvis Presley.

Preston

Old English, meaning "priest's town." Preston Burke is a character from *Grey's Anatomy*.

Primo

Italian, meaning "first." Also a slang term for "excellent."

Primus

Latin, meaning "first." Often used as a name for villains in Marvel comic books.

Prince

English, from the word "prince." Associated with singer and guitarist Prince.

Prospero

Latin, meaning "prosperous." Prospero is the protagonist in Shakespeare's play *The Tempest*.

Pryce
(alt. Prize)

Old French, meaning "prize."

Pryor

English, meaning "first." Famous Pryors include legendary comedian Richard Pryor.

Ptolemy

Greek, meaning "aggressive" or "warlike."

Boys' names

Qabil
(alt. Quabil, Quadim)
Arabic, meaning "able."

Quadir
Arabic, meaning "powerful."

Quaid
Irish, meaning "fourth."

Quemby
Norse, meaning "from the woman's estate."

Quentin
(alt. Quinten, Quintin, Quinton, Quintus)
Latin, meaning "fifth." Director Quentin Tarantino is known for his movies including *Kill Bill* and *Django Unchained*.

Quillan
Gaelic, meaning "sword."

Quillon
Gaelic, meaning "club."

Quincy
Old French, meaning "estate of the fifth son." Quincy Jones is a music mogul.

Quinlan
Gaelic, meaning "fit, shapely, and strong."

Quinn
Gaelic, meaning "counsel." Quinn is a character from *Glee*.

R

Boys' names

Radames

Slavic, meaning "famous joy." A character in the Verdi opera *Aida*.

Raekwon

Hebrew, meaning "God has healed." Associated with Raekwon of Wu-Tang Clan.

Rafael

(alt. Rafe, Rafer, Raffi, Raphael)

Hebrew, meaning "God has healed." One of the archangels in the Bible.

Ragnar

Old Norse, meaning "judgment warrior." Ragnar Lodbrok was a legendary Norse ruler from the Viking era.

Raheem

(alt. Rahim)

Arabic, meaning "merciful and kind."

Rahm

Hebrew, meaning "mercy."

Rahul

(alt. Raoul, Raul)

Indian, meaning "efficient." Rahul was the Buddha's son.

Raiden

(alt. Rainen)

From the Japanese god of thunder.

Rainer

Old German, meaning "deciding warrior."

Raj

Sanskrit, meaning "kingdom," and Polish, meaning "heaven."

Rajesh

(alt. Ramesh)

Indian, meaning "ruler of kings."

Raleigh

Old English, meaning "deer's meadow." Made famous by the explorer Sir Walter Raleigh.

Ralph

Old English, meaning "wolf." Famous Ralphs include actor Ralph Fiennes, fashion brand Ralph Lauren, and character Ralph from *The Simpsons*.

Ram

English, from the word for a male sheep.

Ramiro

Germanic, meaning "powerful in battle." Popular name for baby boys in Argentina.

Ramsey
(alt. Ramsay)

Old English, meaning "wild garlic island." Gordon Ramsay is a celebrity chef.

Randall
(alt. Randal, Randolph, Randy)

Old German, meaning "wolf shield." Can be traced back to the poem "Lord Randall" in 1882.

Raniel

English, meaning "God is my happiness."

Ranjit

Indian, meaning "influenced by charm."

Rannoch

Gaelic, meaning "fern." Also the name of an area in the Scottish Highlands.

Rashad

Arabic, meaning "good judgment."

Rashid
(alt. Rasheed)

Indian, meaning "rightly guided." Ar-Rashid, meaning "The Guide," is one of Allah's names in the Islamic tradition.

Rasmus

Greek, meaning "beloved."

Raven

English, from the word for the large, black bird.

Ravi

Hindi, meaning "sun."

Ray

English, from the word "ray." Famous Rays include singer Ray Charles. Other well-known Rays were actually given the name Raymond.

Raymond
(alt. Rayner; abbrev. Ray)

English, meaning "advisor." Title character of the sitcom *Everybody Loves Raymond*. Actors Ray Winstone and Ray Liotta are both Raymonds.

Raz

Israeli, meaning "secret" or "mystery."

Reagan
(abbrev. Reggie)

Irish, meaning "little king." Ronald Reagan was the 40th President of the United States.

Reginald
(abbrev. Reg, Reggie)

Latin, meaning "regal." Singer Sir Elton John's birth name was Reginald Kenneth Dwight.

Regis

Latin, meaning "of the king."

Reid

Old English, meaning "by the reeds."

Reilly
(alt. Riley)

Irish, meaning "courageous."

Remus

Latin, meaning "swift." Famous Remuses include Romulus and Remus of the ancient Roman myth, and the *Harry Potter* character Remus Lupin.

Rémy

French, meaning "from Rheims."

Renatus
(alt. Renat, Renate, Renato, Rene)

Latin, meaning "rebirth."

Reno

Latin, meaning "renewed." Also the name of the city in Nevada.

Reuben

Spanish, meaning "a son." The name of a sandwich containing corned beef, Swiss cheese, and sauerkraut.

Reuel

Hebrew, meaning "friend of God."

Rex

Latin, meaning "king." The kings of ancient Rome were called Rex, before it became a republic.

Rey

Spanish, meaning "king," and Telugu, meaning "friend."

Reynold

Latin, meaning "king's advisor."

Rhodes

German, meaning "where the roses grow." Also the name of the Greek island.

Rhodri

Welsh, meaning "ruler of the circle."

Rhys
(alt. Reece, Riece)

Welsh, meaning "enthusiasm."
Famous Rhyses include actors
Jonathan Rhys Meyers and Rhys Ifans.

Richard
*(alt. Ricardo, Rikardo; abbrev. Dick,
Dickie, Richie, Rick, Ricki, Ricky,
Ritchie)*

Old German, meaning "powerful
leader." Famous Richards include
37th President of the United States
Richard Nixon, comedian Richard
Pryor, and actor Richard Gere.

Ridley

English, meaning "cleared wood."
Director Sir Ridley Scott is known
for the films *Gladiator* and *Thelma &
Louise.*

Rigby

English, from the place in Lancashire.
Often associated with the Beatles'
song "Eleanor Rigby."

Riky

Irish Gaelic, meaning "courageous."

Ringo

English, meaning "ring." Ringo Starr
was the drummer with the Beatles.

Rio

Spanish, meaning "river." *Rio* is a
song by Duran Duran and associated
with the movie *Rio.*

Riordan

Gaelic, meaning "bard."

Rishi

Sanskrit, meaning "scribe."

Roald

Scandinavian, meaning "ruler."
Roald Dahl is the author of *Charlie
and the Chocolate Factory* and other
children's books.

Robert
*(alt. Roberto; abbrev. Bob, Bobby,
Dobby, Rob, Robbie)*

Old German, meaning "bright fame."
Famous Roberts include actors
Robert de Niro and Robert Pattinson,
and legendary singers Bob Dylan and
Bob Marley.

Robin

English, from the word for the small,
flame-breasted bird. Famous Robins
include comedian Robin Williams,
singer Robin Thicke, and outlaw
legend Robin Hood.

Robinson

English, meaning "son of Robin."
The eponymous hero of the novel
Robinson Crusoe.

Rocco
(alt. Rocky)

Italian, meaning "rest." Also the
name of Madonna's son.

Roderick

(abbrev. Rod, Roddy)

German, meaning "famous power." A character from *The Following*.

Rodney

(abbrev. Rod, Roddy)

Old German, meaning "island near the clearing."

Rodrigo

Spanish form of Roderick, meaning "famous power." Famous Rodrigos include Spanish composer Joaquin Rodrigo.

Roger

Old German, meaning "spear man." Famous Rogers include athlete Roger Bannister, The Who singer Roger Daltrey, and tennis pro Roger Federer.

Roland

(alt. Rowland)

Old German, meaning "renowned land."

Rolf

Old German, meaning "wolf."

Rollie

(alt. Rollo)

Old German, meaning "renowned land."

Roman

Latin, meaning "from Rome." Associated with the Roman people.

Romeo

Latin, meaning "pilgrim to Rome." Made famous by Shakespeare's play *Romeo and Juliet*. Also the name of David and Victoria Beckham's second son.

Ronald

(alt. Ron, Ronnie)

Norse, meaning "mountain of strength." Ron Weasley is a character in the *Harry Potter* series.

Ronan

Gaelic, meaning "little seal."

Rory

English, meaning "red king." Rory Calhoun was an actor. Golfer Rory McIlroy has won the US Open.

Ross

(alt. Russ)

Scottish, meaning "cape."

Rowan

(alt. Roan)

Gaelic, meaning "little red one." Rowan Atkinson is a comedian and comic actor, and also the voice of Zazu in *The Lion King*.

Roy

Gaelic, meaning "red." Famous Roys include singer Roy Orbison.

Ruben

Hebrew, meaning "son."

Rudolph
(alt. Rudy)

Old German, meaning "famous wolf." The name of Santa's legendary reindeer.

Rufus

Latin, meaning "red-haired." Actor Rufus Sewell is known for his role in A Knight's Tale.

Rupert

Variant of Robert, meaning "bright fame." Actor Rupert Grint is known for his role in the Harry Potter series.

Russell

Old French, meaning "little red one." Comedian Russell Brand is known for his role in Arthur.

Rusty

English, meaning "ruddy."

Ryan

Gaelic, meaning "little king." Famous Ryans include actor Ryan Gosling and comedian Ryan Stiles.

Ryder

English, meaning "horseman."

Rye

English, from the word "rye."

Ryker

From Richard, meaning "powerful leader." Ryker's Island is a fictional prison facility in Marvel Comics stories.

Rylan

English, meaning "land where rye is grown."

Ryley

Old English, meaning "rye clearing."

S

Boys' names

Saber
(alt. Sabre)

French, meaning "sword."

Sagar
African, meaning "ruler of the water."

Sage
English, meaning "wise." Can also refer to the herb.

Sakari
Native American, meaning "sweet."

Salim
(alt. Saleem)

Arabic, meaning "secure." The Salim Khan family are a Bollywood dynasty.

Salvador
Spanish, meaning "savior." Famous Salvadors include artist Salvador Dali.

Salvatore
Italian, meaning "savior." There have been dozens of the Italian, Sicilian, or New York mafia called Salvatore.

Samir
Arabic, meaning "pleasant companion."

Samson
Hebrew, meaning "son of Sam." The character Samson from the Bible had extraordinary strength.

Samuel
(alt. Sam, Sama, Sammie, Sammy)

Hebrew, meaning "God is heard." Famous Samuels include a prophet from the Bible, actor Samuel L. Jackson, and author Samuel Langhorne Clemens (known as Mark Twain).

Sandeep
(alt. Sundeep)

Hindi, meaning "lighting the way."

Sanjay

Hindi, meaning "victory." Sanjay Gupta is a well-known TV doctor.

Santana

Spanish, meaning "saint." Associated with guitarist Carlos Santana.

Santiago

Spanish, meaning "Saint James." Also the name of the capital city of Chile.

Santino

Spanish, meaning "little Saint James."

Santo
(alt. Santos)

Latin, meaning "saint."

Sasha
(alt. Sacha, Sascha)

Russian, derived from Alexander, meaning "defending men." Sasha can be used for boys or girls. In the US, female Sashas are significantly more common.

Sawyer

English, meaning "one who saws wood." Associated with the novel Tom Sawyer.

Scott
(alt. Scottie)

English, meaning "from Scotland." Scott Dixon is an IndyCar champion, and cartoonist Scott Adams created Dilbert.

Seamus

Irish variant of James, meaning "he who supplants." Seamus Heaney is a Nobel prize-winning poet.

Sean
(alt. Shaun, Shawn)

Variant of John, meaning "God is gracious." Famous Seans include actors Sean Penn and Sean Connery.

Sebastian
(alt. Sébastien; abbrev. Seb)

Greek, meaning "revered." The name of the crab character in Disney's The Little Mermaid.

Old name, new fashion

Augustus	Norris
Bertrand	Percival
Edgar	Reginald
Felix	Sebastian
Gilbert	Theodore
Hector	Winston
Jasper	

Sergio
(alt. Serge)
Latin, meaning "servant."

Seth
Hebrew, meaning "appointed." Famous Seths include actors Seth MacFarlane and Seth Greene.

Severus
Latin, meaning "severe." Severus Snape is a character in the *Harry Potter* series.

Seymour
English, from the place name in northern France. Famous Seymours include Principal Seymour Skinner of *The Simpsons*, and actor Philip Seymour Hoffman.

Shane
Variant of Sean, meaning "God is gracious." Famous Shanes include actors Shane West and Shane Harper.

Sharif
Arabic, meaning "honored." Also a name for descendants of one of Muhammad's grandchildren.

Shea
Gaelic, meaning "admirable."

Shelby
Norse, meaning "willow." Associated with the Mustang car.

Sherlock
English, meaning "fair-haired." The name of the lead character in Sir Arthur Conan Doyle's "Sherlock Holmes" novels.

Sherman
Old English, meaning "shear man."

Shmuel
Hebrew, meaning "his name is God."

Shola
Arabic, meaning "energetic."

Sidney
(alt. Sid, Sydney)
English, meaning "wide meadow." Actor Sidney Poitier is known for his roles in *Guess Who's Coming to Dinner* and *In The Heat of the Night*.

Sigmund
Old German, meaning "victorious hand." Associated with neurologist Sigmund Freud.

Silvanus
(alt. Silvio)
Latin, meaning "woods." An ancient Roman deity of woods and fields.

Simba
(alt. Sim)
Swahili, meaning "lion." Associated with the character from Disney's *The Lion King*.

Simon
(alt. Simeon)

Hebrew, meaning "to hear." Famous Simons include music producer Simon Cowell and actor Simon Pegg.

Sinbad

Persian, meaning "Lord of Sages." Literary merchant adventurer.

Sindri

Norse, meaning "dwarf."

Sipho

African, meaning "the unknown one."

Sire

English, from the word used to address reigning kings or nobility.

Sirius

Hebrew, meaning "brightest star." Sirius Black is a character from the *Harry Potter* series.

Skipper

English, meaning "ship captain."

Skyler

Dutch, meaning "guarded" or "scholar."

Solomon

Hebrew, meaning "peace." One of the most important kings in the Bible and the Torah.

Sonny

American English, meaning "son." Singer Sonny Bono was half of Sonny and Cher.

Soren

Scandinavian, meaning "brightest star."

Spencer

English, meaning "guardian." Famous Spencers include actor Spencer Tracy and reality TV star Spencer Pratt.

Spike

English, from the word "spike." Director Spike Lee is known for *Do the Right Thing* and *4 Little Girls*.

Stanford

English, meaning "stone ford." Made famous by Stanford University.

Stanley
(alt. Stan)

English, meaning "stony meadow." Famous Stanleys include director Stanley Kubrick, actor Stanley Tucci, and comic book writer Stan Lee.

Stavros

Greek, meaning "cross."

Stellan

Latin, meaning "starred."

Steno

German, meaning "stone."

Stephen
(alt. Stefan, Stefano, Steffan, Steven; abbrev. Steve, Stevie)

English, meaning "crowned." Famous Stephens include author Stephen King, physicist Stephen Hawking, and actor Stephen Fry.

Stewart
(alt. Stuart)

English, meaning "steward." Stewart Copeland was the American drummer in The Police.

Stoney
English, meaning "stone like."

Storm
English, from the word "storm."

Sven
Norse, meaning "boy." The name of the reindeer in Disney's *Frozen*.

Syed
(alt. Sayyid)

Arabic, meaning "lucky." Associated with the character from *Lost*.

Sylvester
Latin, meaning "wooded." The name of the cartoon cat.

T Boys' names

Tacitus

Latin, meaning "silent, calm." Also the name of an ancient Roman historian.

Tad

English, from the word "tadpole."

Taj

Indian, meaning "crown." Made famous by the Indian palace the Taj Mahal.

Takashi

Japanese, meaning "praiseworthy."

Takoda

Sioux, meaning "friend to everyone."

Talbot
(alt. Tal)

English, meaning "command of the valley." Aristocratic name.

Tamir

Arabic, meaning "tall and wealthy."

Tanner

Old English, meaning "leather-maker."

Taras
(alt. Tarez)

Scottish, meaning "crag." Taras was the son of Poseidon in ancient Greek mythology.

Tarek
(alt. Tarik)

Arabic, meaning "to strike."

Tarian

Welsh, meaning "shield."

Tariq

Arabic, meaning "morning star."

Tarquin

Latin, from the Roman clan name. Tarquin Hall is a poet.

Tarun

Hindi, meaning "young."

Tatanka

Hebrew, meaning "bull." Legendary Native American leader Sitting Bull's Western name was Tatanka Lyotake.

Tate

English, meaning "cheerful." Actor Tate Donovan is known for his role in *Damages*.

Taurean

English, meaning "bull-like." Also used to describe people born under the Taurus star sign.

Tavares

English, meaning "descendant of the hermit."

Tave

(alt. Tavian, Tavis, Tavish)

French, from Gustave, meaning "royal staff," and in Nordic cultures it can mean "guarantor."

Taylor

(alt. Tay)

English, meaning "tailor." Famous Taylors include actor Taylor Lautner and singer Taylor Hanson.

Tennessee

Native American, meaning "river town." Also the name of the state.

Terence

(alt. Terrill, Terry)

English, meaning "tender." Actor Terence Stamp is known for his roles in *Billy Budd* and *The Collector*.

Tex

English, meaning "Texan."

Thane

(alt. Thayer)

Scottish, meaning "landholder." Actor Thane Bettany is the father of actor Paul Bettany.

Thatcher

(alt. Thaxter)

Old English, meaning "roof thatcher."

Thelonious

Latin, meaning "ruler of the people." Thelonious Monk was an influential jazz pianist and composer.

Theodore

(abbrev. Theo)

Greek, meaning "God's gift." Theodore Roosevelt was the 26th President of the United States.

Theophile

Latin, meaning "beloved of God," also "one who loves God."

Theron

Greek, meaning "hunter."

Thierry

French variant of Terence, meaning "tender." Made famous by soccer star Thierry Henry.

Thomas

(alt. Thom, Tom, Tomlin, Tommy)

Aramaic, meaning "twin." Famous Thomases include inventor Thomas Edison and children's character Thomas the Tank Engine.

Thomson

(alt. Thomsen)

English, meaning "son of Thomas." "Thomsen" means "twin" in Aramaic.

Thor

Norse, meaning "thunder." Thor was a hammer-wielding deity in Norse mythology.

Tiago

From Santiago, meaning "Saint James." Also used as a shortened form of Santiago.

Tiberius

English, meaning "from the river Tiber."

Tibor

Latin, from the river Tiber, or Hungarian for "a short meeting."

Tieman

(alt. Tiemann)

Gaelic, meaning "lord."

Tilden

(alt. Till)

English, meaning "fertile valley."

Timothy

(alt. Tim, Timmie, Timmy, Timon)

Greek, meaning "God's honor." Famous Timothys include actors Timothy Dalton, Timothy Spall, and Christopher Timothy.

Tito

(alt. Titus, Tizian)

Latin, meaning "defender." Associated with singer Tito Jackson, from the Jackson Five.

Tobias

(alt. Toby)

Hebrew, meaning "God is good."

Tod

(alt. Todd)

English, meaning "fox." Famous Tods include Todd Flanders in *The Simpsons* and Todd Alquist in *Breaking Bad*.

Tonneau

French, meaning "barrel."

Torey

Norse, meaning "Thor."

Torin

Gaelic, meaning "chief."

Torquil

Gaelic, meaning "helmet." In Scandinavia the name is also derived from Thor, after the god of thunder and lightning.

Toshi

Japanese, meaning "reflection."

Travis

French, meaning "crossover." Famous Travises include actor Travis Fimmel and drummer Travis Barker.

Trevor
(alt. Tvevin)

Welsh origin, meaning "great settlement." Comedian Trevor Noah currently hosts *The Daily Show*.

Trey
(alt. Tyree)

French, meaning "three." Sometimes used as a nickname for a third-born child.

Tristan
(alt. Tristram)

Celtic from the Celtic hero. Also one of the Knights of the Round Table.

Troy

Gaelic, meaning "descended from the soldier." Troy was a legendary city in ancient Greece.

Tudor

Variant of Theodore, meaning "God's gift." Also the name of the British dynasty which included Henry VIII and Elizabeth I.

Tyler

English, meaning "tile maker."

Tyrell

French, meaning "puller." Associated with House Tyrell from *Game of Thrones*.

Tyrone

Gaelic, meaning "Owen's county."

Tyson

English, meaning "son of Tyrone." Mike Tyson is widely regarded as one of the best heavyweight boxers of all time, as well as the most ferocious and controversial.

U

Boys' names

Uberto
(alt. Umberto)
Italian, variant of Hubert, meaning "bright or shining intellect."

Udo
German, meaning "power of the wolf."

Ulf
German, meaning "wolf." Also the name of a Danish Viking chief.

Ulrich
German, meaning "noble ruler."

Ultan
Irish, meaning "from Ulster."

Ulysses
Greek, meaning "wrathful." Made famous by the mythological voyager from ancient Greece.

Upton
English, meaning "high town."

Urho
Finnish, meaning "brave."

Uri
(alt. Uriah, Urias)
Hebrew, meaning "my light." Famous Uris include magician Uri Geller.

Uriel
Hebrew, meaning "angel of light." One of the archangels in the Bible.

Usher
English, from the word "usher." Associated with the R&B star Usher.

Uzi
Hebrew, meaning "my strength." A type of submachine gun.

Uzzi
(alt. Uzziah)
Hebrew, meaning "the Lord is my strength." Also the name of several characters in the Bible.

V

Boys' names

Vadim

Russian, meaning "scandal maker." Vadim the Bold was a legendary warrior in Eastern Europe during the ninth century.

Valdemar

German, meaning "renowned leader."

Valente

Latin, meaning "valiant."

Valentine

(alt. *Valentin, Valentino*; abbrev. *Val*)
English, from the word "valentine." St. Valentine's Day is named after Valentinus, who was said to have healed the broken heart of his jailer's daughter. One of the more popular dancers on *Dancing With The Stars* is Valentin Chmerkovskiy.

Valerio

Italian, meaning "to be strong."

Van

Dutch, meaning "son of." Famous Vans include the band Van Halen, singer Van Morrison, and the brand of shoe.

Vance

English, meaning "marshland." Vance Astrovik is the real name of the comic book hero Justice.

Vangelis

Greek, meaning "good news." Vangelis is a modern Greek composer.

Varro

Latin, meaning "strong."

Varun

Hindi, meaning "water god." Shortened form of Varuna, who is the Hindu god of all water.

Vasilis
(alt. Vasilly)
Greek, meaning "kingly."

Vaughan
Welsh, meaning "little."

Vernell
French, meaning "green and flourishing."

Verner
German, meaning "army defender." The German form of Werner, although Verner is a more common spelling in Europe.

Vernon
(alt. Vernie)
French, meaning "alder grove." Vernon Dursley is a character in the *Harry Potter* series.

Versilius
Latin, meaning "flier."

Vester
Latin, meaning "wooded." Associated with the guitar maker.

Victor
(alt. Vic, Viktor)
Latin, meaning "champion." Author Victor Hugo wrote *Les Miserables*.

Vidal
(alt. Vidar)
Spanish, meaning "life-giving." Vidal Sassoon is famed as a hairstylist.

Vijay
Hindi, meaning "conquering."

Vikram
Hindi, meaning "sun."

Ville
French, meaning "town."

Vincent
(abbrev. Vin, Vince, Vinnie)
English, meaning "victorious." Famous Vincents include actor Vince Vaughn, artist Vincent van Gogh, and soccer player turned actor Vinnie Jones.

Virgil
Latin, meaning "staff bearer." From the ancient Roman poet of the same name.

Vito
Spanish, meaning "life." Vito Corleone is a character from *The Godfather*.

Vittorio
Italian, meaning "victory."

Vitus
Latin, meaning "life." Associated with St. Vitus, or the condition Saint Vitus Dance.

Vivian

(alt. Vyvian; abbrev. Viv)

Latin, meaning "lively." Used as a name for boys and girls.

Vladimir

Slavic, meaning "prince." Famous Vladimirs include Russian President Vladimir Putin, and legendary warrior Vladimir the Impaler—also known as Dracula.

Volker

German, meaning "defender of the people."

"Bad boy" names

Ace	Conan
Arnie	Guy
Axel	Rhett
Bruce	Spike
Buzz	Tyson

Von

Norse, meaning "hope." In Germany, "von" also means "of" or "from," and is used to denote origin, such as Ulrich von Liechtenstein.

Boys' names

Wade

English, meaning "to move forward" or "to go." Wade Robson is a contemporary dance choreographer.

Waldemar

German, meaning "famous ruler."

Walden

English, meaning "valley of the Britons." Famed as the title of the book by Henry Thoreau.

Waldo

Old German, meaning "rule." "Where's Waldo" is a popular children's book character.

Walker

English, meaning "a fuller."

Wallace

English, meaning "foreigner" or "stranger." One of the duo *Wallace and Gromit*.

Wally

German, meaning "ruler of the army."

Walter

(alt. Walt)

German, meaning "ruler of the army." Famous Walters include *Breaking Bad*'s Walter White, and the movie *The Secret Life of Walter Mitty*.

Ward

English, meaning "guardian."

Wardell

Old English, meaning "watchman's hill."

Warner

German, meaning "army guard."
Made famous as the name of
the movie studio Warner
Brothers.

Warren

German, meaning "guard" or
"the game park." Warren Buffett
is a business tycoon and
philanthropist.

Warwick

Old English, meaning "buildings
near the weir." Associated with actor
Warwick Davis.

Washington

English, meaning "clever" or
"clever man's settlement." George
Washington was the first President of
the USA.

Wassily

Greek, meaning "royal" or "kingly."
Wassily Kandinsky was an abstract
artist.

Watson

English, meaning "son" or "son of
Walter." Dr. Watson is a character
from the "Sherlock Holmes"
stories.

Waverley
(alt. Waverly)

English, meaning "quaking aspen."

Waylon

English, meaning "land by the road."
Associated with country singer
Waylon Jennings.

Wayne

English, meaning "a cartwright."
Famous Waynes include comedian
Wayne Brady and rapper Lil Wayne.

Webster

English, meaning "weaver."

Weldon

English, meaning "from the hill of
well" or "hill with a well."

Wells

English, meaning "from the hill of
well" or "hill with a well."

Wendell
(alt. Wendel)

German, meaning "spring."

Werner

German, meaning "army guard."
Werner Heisenberg was a Nobel
prize winner and inspiration for
the alter ego of Walter White in
Breaking Bad.

Weston

English, meaning "from the west
town."

Wheeler

English, meaning "wheel maker."

Whitley

English, meaning "white wood."

Whitman

Old English, meaning "white man." Made famous by author and poet Walt Whitman.

Whitney

Old English, meaning "white island."

Wilber
(alt. Wilbur)

Old German, meaning "bright will." Wilbur Wright helped invent the first powered airplanes.

Wilder

English, meaning "wild and uncontrolled".

Wiley

Old English, meaning "beguiling" or "enchanting."

Wilford

Old English, meaning "the ford by the willows." Associated with actor Wilford Brimley.

Wilfred
(alt. Wilfredo, Wilfrid; abbrev. Wilf)

English, meaning "to will peace."

Wilhelm
(alt. Willem)

German, meaning "strong willed warrior." The "Wilhelm Scream" is a movie sound effect used in hundreds of movies.

Wilkes
(alt. Wilkie)

Old English, meaning "strong willed protector" or "strong and resolute protector." John Wilkes Booth was the assassin of President Lincoln.

William
(abbrev. Bill, Billy, Will, Willie, Willy)

English (Teutonic), meaning "strong protector" or "strong willed warrior." Famous Williams include William Shakespeare, Prince William of Great Britain, and rapper Will.i.am.

Willis

English, meaning "server of William." Actor Bruce Willis is known for his roles in *Die Hard* and *The Fifth Element*.

Willoughby

Old Norse and Old English, meaning "from the farm by the trees."

Wilmer

English (Teutonic), meaning "famously resolute." Actor Wilmer Valderrama is known for his role in *That 70s Show*.

Wilmot

English, meaning "resolute mind."

Wilson

English, meaning "son of William." Famous Wilsons include legendary R&B singer Wilson Pickett.

Wilton

Old Norse and English, meaning "from the farm by the brook/ streams."

Windell

(alt. Wendell)

German, meaning "wanderer" or "seeker." Actor Windell Middlebrooks is known for his role in *Scrubs*.

Windsor

Old English, meaning "river bank" or "landing place." The British Royal family is known as the House of Windsor.

Winfield

English, meaning "from the field of Wina."

Winslow

Old English, meaning "victory on the hill." Associated with the sitcom *Family Matters*.

Winston

English, meaning "from Wine's town." Sir Winston Chruchill was prime Minister of Great Britain during World War II.

Winter

Old English, meaning "to be born in the winter."

Winthrop

Old English, meaning "village of friends."

Winton

Old English, meaning "a friend's farm."

Wirrin

Aboriginal, meaning "a tea tree."

Wistan

Old English, meaning "battle stone" or "mark of the battle."

Wittan

Old English, meaning "farm in the woods" or "farm by the woods."

Wolf

(alt. Wolfe)

English, meaning "strong as a wolf." A wild animal in the dog family.

Wolfgang

Teutonic, meaning "the path of wolves." The composer Mozart's full name was Wolfgang Amadeus Mozart.

Wolfrom

Teutonic, meaning "raven wolf."

Wolter

Dutch, a form of Walter meaning "ruler of the army."

Woodburn

Old English, meaning "a stream in the woods."

Woodrow

English, meaning "from the row of houses by the wood." Woodrow Wilson was the 28th President of the United States.

Woodward

English, meaning "guardian of the forest."

Woody

American English, meaning "path in the woods." Famous Woodys include filmmaker Woody Allen and the character of Woody from the "Toy Story" series.

Worcester

Old English, meaning "from a Roman site." A tangy sauce of the same name.

Worth

American English, meaning "worth much" or "wealthy place" or "wealth and riches."

Wren

Old English, meaning "tiny bird."

Wright

Old English, meaning "to be a craftsman" or "from a carpenter." Wilbur and Orville Wright were the inventors of powered aircraft.

Wyatt

Teutonic, meaning "from wood" or "from the wide water." Famous Wyatts include director Rupert Wyatt, Wild West sheriff Wyatt Earp, and comedian Wyatt Cenac.

Wynn
(alt. Wyn)

Welsh, meaning "very blessed" or "the fair blessed one," and Old English, meaning "friend."

Boys' names

Xadrian

American English, a combination of X and Adrian, meaning "from Hadria."

Xanthus

Greek, meaning "golden haired."

Xavier

Latin, meaning "to the new house."

Xenon

Greek, meaning "the guest." One of the noble gases.

Xerxes

Persian, meaning "ruler of the people" or "respected king." Name of a king who attempted to invade the Greek mainland, but failed.

Xylander

Greek, meaning "man of the forest."

Y Boys' names

Yaal
Hebrew, meaning "ascending" or "one to ascend."

Yadid
Hebrew, meaning "the beloved one."

Yadon
Hebrew, meaning "against judgment." Associated with the Pokémon character.

Yahir
Spanish, meaning "handsome one."

Yair
Hebrew, meaning "the enlightening one" or "illuminating." The spelling Jair appears in the Bible.

Yakiya
Hebrew, meaning "pure" or "bright."

Yanis
(alt. Yannis)
Greek, a form of John meaning "gift of God."

Yarden
Hebrew, meaning "to flow downward."

Ye
Chinese, meaning "bright one" or "light."

Yehuda
Hebrew, meaning "to praise and exalt." Often translated as Judah, who was a son of Jacob in the Bible.

Yered
Hebrew, a form of Jared, meaning "descending."

Yerik

Russian, meaning "God-appointed one."

Yervant

Armenian, meaning "king of people."

Yitzak

(alt. Yitzaak)

Hebrew, meaning "laughter" or "one who laughs."

Ynyr

Welsh, meaning "to honor."

Yobachi

African, meaning "one who prays to God" or "prayed to God."

Yogi

Japanese, meaning "one who practices yoga" or "from yoga." Made famous by the cartoon character Yogi Bear.

Yona

Native American, meaning "bear," and Hebrew, meaning "dove." A name used to refer to ancient people who spoke Greek.

York

Celtic, meaning "yew tree" or "from the farm of the yew tree." Also an historic city in the UK.

Yosef

Hebrew, meaning "added by God" or "God shall add." Hebrew form of Joseph.

Yuri

Aboriginal, meaning "to hear"; Japanese, meaning "one to listen"; Russian, a form of George meaning "farmer."

Yves

French, meaning "miniature archer" or "small archer." Fashion brand YSL was founded by Yves Saint Laurent.

Z

Boys' names

Zachariah
(alt. Zac, Zach, Zachary)
Hebrew, meaning "remembered by the Lord" or "God has remembered." Famous Zachs include actors Zach Braff and Zach Galifianakis.

Zad
Persian, meaning "my son."

Zadok
Hebrew, meaning "righteous one." "Zadok the Priest" is a well known coronation anthem and has been sung at every crowning of a king or queen in the UK since 1727.

Zador
Hungarian, meaning "violent demeanor." Zador was the priest who anointed Solomon in the Bible.

Zafar
Arabic, meaning "triumphant."

Zaid
African, meaning "increase the growth" or "growth."

Zaide
Yiddish, meaning "the elder ones." Also the name of an unfinished opera by Mozart.

Zain
(alt. Zane)
Arabic, meaning "the handsome son." Actor Billy Zane is known for his roles in *Titanic* and *The Phantom*.

Zaire
African, meaning "river from Zaire." Zaire is the old name for Democratic Republic of the Congo.

Zarek

Persian, meaning "God protect our king." Associated with the Marvel comic book character.

Zayn

Arabic, meaning "masculine beauty." Made famous by singer Zayn Malik.

Zuma

Arabic, meaning "peace."

A name for all seasons

Spring	Summer	Fall	Winter
Alvern	Augustus	Aki	Aquilo
Attwell	Balder	Akiko	Caldwell
Avir	Cain	Demitrius	Colden
Bradwell	Dax	Dionysus	Crispin
Jarek	Leo	Forrest	Darke
Kell	Sky	George	Eirwen
Marcus	Somers	Goren	Gennaio
Rain	Sunny	Hunter	Jack
Tamiko	Theros	Red	Mistral
Weldon		Storm	Rain

Part Three

Girls' names A–Z

Baby names vary widely in spelling and pronunciation. To simplify things, this book usually lists each name only once: under the most common initial and spelling. If a name has a common alternate spelling with a different initial, it may also be listed under that letter.

Girls' names

A'mari

Variation of the Swahili or Muslim name Amira, meaning "princess."

Aanya

Sanskrit, meaning "the inexhaustible." Also variation of the Russian name Anya.

Aaryanna

Derivative of the Latin and Greek name Ariadne, meaning "the very holy one."

Abigail

(alt. Abagail, Abbigail, Abigale, Abigayle; abbrev. Abbey, Abbie, Abby, Abi)

Hebrew, meaning "my father's joy." A character in the Bible and the name of several Hawaiian princesses. The biblical Greek version of the name is Abigaia.

Abilene

(alt. Abelena, Abilee)

Latin and Spanish, meaning "hazelnut."

Abra

Female variation of Abraham. Also Sanskrit, meaning "clouds."

Abril

Spanish for the month of April; Latin, meaning "open."

Acacia

Greek, meaning "point" or "thorn." Also a species of flowering trees and shrubs.

Acadia

Greek, meaning "paradise." Originally, a French colony in Canada.

Ada
(alt. Adair, Adia)

Hebrew, meaning "adornment." Ada Lovelace is widely credited for being the world's first computer programmer, in the 19th century.

Adalee

German, meaning "noble." Also a contraction of Ada and Lee.

Adalia

Hebrew, meaning "God is my refuge." A genus of ladybug.

Addison
(alt. Addisyn, Addyson; abbrev. Addie, Addy, Adi)

English, meaning "son of Adam." Can be used for girls or boys.

Adelaide
(alt. Adalyn, Adalynn, Adelaida, Adeline, Adelina, Adelyn; abbrev. Addie, Addy, Adi)

Old German, meaning "noble kind." Popular after the rule of William IV and Queen Adelaide of England in the 19th century. Adeline Whitney was a children's author in that period.

Adele
(alt. Adela, Adelia, Adell, Adella, Adelle)

German, meaning "noble" or "nobility." Made famous by the singer Adele.

Aden
(alt. Addien)

Hebrew, meaning "decoration."

Aderyn

Welsh, meaning "bird." Also the name of several places in Wales.

Adesina

Yoruba, meaning "she paves the way." Usually given to a first-born daughter.

Adina
(alt. Adena)

Hebrew, meaning "high hopes" or "precious." Found in the Bible.

Adira

Hebrew, meaning "noble" or "powerful." Also the north Italian city.

Adley

English, meaning "son of Adam." Can be used for girls or boys.

Adrian

Italian, from the northern city of Adria. The name of an ancient Roman river. Can be used for girls, though more common for boys.

Adrienne
(alt. Adriane, Adriana, Adrianna, Adrianne)

Greek, meaning "from the city of Hadria," or Latin meaning "dark." A feminine form of Adrian.

Aegle

Greek, meaning "brightness" or "splendor." The name of several characters in ancient Greek mythology.

Aerin

Variant of Erin, meaning "peace-making." Taken from J. R. R. Tolkien's novels.

Aerith

Modern American, from the video game *Final Fantasy VII*.

Aero

(alt. Aeron)

Greek, meaning "flight."

Aerolynn

Combination of the Greek Aero, meaning "water," and the English Lynn, meaning "waterfall."

Africa

Celtic, meaning "pleasant," as well as the name of the continent.

Afsaneh

Iranian, meaning "a fairy tale."

Afsha

Persian, meaning "one who sprinkles light."

Afton

Originally a name of a river in Scotland.

Agatha

(abbrev. Aggie)

From St. Agatha, the patron saint of bells, meaning "good." Made famous by mystery novelist Agatha Christie.

Aglaia

Greek, meaning "brilliance." One of the three ancient Greek graces.

Agnes

Greek, meaning "virginal" or "pure." St. Agnes of Rome is the patron saint of girls.

Agrippina

Latin, meaning "born feet first." The name of several influential ancient Roman women.

Aida

Arabic, meaning "reward" or "present." The title of an opera by Giuseppe Verdi.

Aidanne

(alt. Aidan, Aidenn)

Gaelic, meaning "fire."

Ailbhe

Irish, meaning "noble" or "bright."

Aileen

(alt. Aelinn, Aleen, Aline, Alline)

Gaelic variant of Helen, meaning "light."

Ailith
(alt. Ailish)
Old English, meaning "seasoned warrior."

Ailsa
Scottish, meaning "pledge from God." Also the name of a Scottish island.

Aina
Scandinavian, meaning "forever."

Aine
(alt. Aino)
Celtic, meaning "happiness." The Celtic goddess of summer.

Ainsley
(alt. Ansley)
Scottish/Gaelic, meaning "one's own meadow." Ainsley Hayes is a character in West Wing. Can be used for girls or boys.

Aisha
(alt. Aeysha)
Arabic, meaning "woman"; Swahili, meaning "life." Aisha was one of the prophet Muhammad's wives.

Aishwarya
Arabic, meaning "woman." Aishwarya Rai Bachchan is a famous Bollywood actor.

Aislinn
(alt. Aislin, Aisling, Aislyn, Alene, Allene)
Irish Gaelic, meaning "dream." A tribute to aisling, which was an old poetic genre in Ireland.

Aiyanna
(alt. Aiyana)
Native American, meaning "forever flowering."

Aja
Hindi, meaning "goat."

Akela
(alt. Akilah)
Hawaiian, meaning "noble;" Hindi, meaning "alone." Akela is the wolf from The Jungle Book.

Akilina
Greek or Russian, meaning "eagle."

Akiva
Hebrew, meaning "protect and shelter."

Alaina
(alt. Alana, Alane, Alani, Alanna, Alayna, Aleena, Allannah, Allyn)
Feminine of Alan, originating from the Greek for "rock" or "comely." Also a spelling alternative for Eleanor.

Alana

(alt. Alanna, Allannah)

Gaelic, meaning "beauty"; Hawaiian, meaning "beautiful offering"; Old German, meaning "precious."

Alanis

(alt. Alarice)

Greek, meaning "rock" or "comely." Associated with singer Alanis Morissette.

Alba

Latin for "white." Also the Gaelic name for Scotland.

Alberta

(alt. Albertha, Albertine)

Feminine of Albert, from the Old German for "noble, bright, famous." Also a province in Canada.

Albina

Latin, meaning "white" or "fair." Name of an Etruscan goddess of the dawn.

Alda

German, meaning "old" or "prosperous." St. Alda was an Italian mystic in the 11th century.

Aldis

English, meaning "battle seasoned."

Aleta

(alt. Aletha)

Greek, meaning "footloose." Queen Aleta Ellis is a character from *The Legend of Prince Valiant.*

Alethea

(alt. Aletheia)

Greek, meaning "truth."

Alexandra

(alt. Alejandra, Alejandrina, Alejhandra, Aleksandra, Alessandra, Alexandrea, Alexandria, Aliandra; abbrev. Alex, Alexa, Alexi, Alexia, Alexina, Ali, Allie, Ally, Lexi, Lexie, Sandra, Sandy, Sasha, Sascha, Shura, Sondra, Xandra, Zandra)

Feminine of Alexander, from the Greek interpretation of "man's defender." Also one of the ancient Greek goddess Hera's names. Perhaps the name with the most short forms, from many languages, which are often used as names in their own right.

Alexis

(alt. Alexus, Alexys)

Greek, meaning "helper." Alexis was an ancient Greek poet of comedy.

Aleydis

Variant of Alice, meaning "nobility." Alternative name for St. Alice of Scharbeek, the patron saint of the blind and paralyzed.

Alfreda

Old English, meaning "elf power." The modern spelling of AElfthryth of Crowland.

Alibeth

Variant of Elizabeth, meaning "pledged to God." Popular name during the Middle Ages.

Alice

(alt. Alika, Aliki, Alize, Alyce, Alys, Alyse)

English, meaning "noble" or "nobility." Made famous by the novel Alice in Wonderland.

Alicia

(alt. Ahlicia, Alecia, Alesha, Alesia, Alessia, Alizia, Alisha, Alycia, Alysha, Alysia)

Latin, originally derived from Alice, meaning "nobility." Famous Alicias include singer Alicia Keys, actor Alicia Silverstone, and the birth name of singer Pink.

Alida

(alt. Aleida)

Latin, meaning "small-winged one."

Alima

Arabic, meaning "cultured."

Alina

(alt. Alena, Aleana)

Slavic form of Helen, meaning "light."

Alison

(alt. Allison, Allisyn, Allyson, Alyson; abbrev. Ali, Allie, Ally)

Variant of Alice, meaning "nobility." Originally the name was Alis in the Middle Ages, with the suffix "on," which means "little."

Alivia

Variant of Olivia, meaning "olive tree."

Aliya

(alt. Aaliyah, Aleah, Alia, Aliah, Aliyah)

Arabic, meaning "exalted" or "sublime." Aliya bint Ali was the last queen consort of Iraq.

Alla

Variant of Ella or Alexandra. Also a possible reference to Allah.

Allegra

Italian, meaning "joyous."

Allura

French, from the word for entice, meaning "the power of attraction."

Alma

Latin for "giving nurture"; Italian for "soul"; and Arabic for "learned." Also commonly written as Alma Mater, meaning "nourishing mother" or "fostering mother."

Almeda

(alt. Almeta)

Latin, meaning "ambitious."

Almera

(alt. Almira)

Feminine of Elmer, from the Arabic for "aristocratic"; Old English meaning "noble."

Alohi

Variant of the Hawaiian greeting Aloha, meaning "love and affection."

Alona
(alt. Alora)

Hebrew, meaning "oak tree."

Alpha

The first letter of the Greek alphabet, usually given to a firstborn daughter.

Alta

Latin, meaning "elevated."

Altagracia

Spanish, meaning "grace." Alta Gracia is also a city in Argentina.

Althaea
(alt. Altea, Altha, Althea)

Greek, meaning "healing power." Althaea was a prominent character in ancient Greek mythology.

Alva

Spanish, meaning "blonde" or "fair-skinned." In Norway and Sweden it is considered the female form of Alf, which means "elf."

Alvena
(alt. Alvina)

Old English, meaning "elf friend." In Old German it is the female form of Adelwin, meaning "noble friend."

Alvia
(alt. Alyvia)

Variant of Olivia, meaning "olive tree," or Elvira, from the ancient Spanish city.

Alyssa
(alt. Alisa, Alissa, Allyssa, Alysa)

Greek, meaning "rational." Associated with the alyssum flower.

Amadea

Feminine of Amadeus, meaning "God's love."

Amalia

German, meaning "work"; Hebrew, meaning "labor of love."

Amana

Hebrew, meaning "loyal and true." Also a genus of tulips.

Amanda
(alt. Amandine; abbrev. Mandy)

Latin, meaning "much loved." Famous Amandas include actors Amanda Bynes and Amanda Seyfried.

Amara
(alt. Amani)

Greek, meaning "lovely forever." Actor Amara Miller is known for her role in The Descendants.

Amarantha

Contraction of Amanda and Samantha, meaning "much loved listener."

Amari

(alt. Amaris, Amasa, Amata, Amaya)
Hebrew, meaning "pledged by God."

Amaryllis

(alt. Ameris)
Greek, meaning "fresh." Also a flower by the same name.

Amber

French, from the semiprecious stone of the same name. Famous Ambers include actor Amber Heard and model Amber Rose.

Amberly

Contraction of Amber and Leigh, meaning "stone" and "meadow."

Amberlynn

Contraction of Amber and Lynn, meaning "stone" and "waterfall."

Amelia

(alt. Aemilia, Amelie)
Greek, meaning "industrious." Famous Amelias include flying legend Amelia Earhart and two Princess Amelias of Great Britain. Amelie is the French variant and the title of a movie.

America

From the country and continents of the same name. Associated with *Ugly Betty* actor America Ferrera.

Amethyst

Greek, from the precious, mulberry-colored stone of the same name.

Amina

Arabic, meaning "honest and trustworthy."

Aminta

Greek, meaning "defender."

Amira

(alt. Amiya, Amiyah)
Arabic, meaning "a high-born girl"; Hebrew, meaning "rich princess."

Amity

Latin, meaning "friendship and harmony." Also a name of a faction in the "Divergent" series.

Amory

Variant of the Spanish name Amor, meaning "love."

Amy

(alt. Aimee, Amee, Ami, Amie, Ammie, Amya)
Latin, meaning "beloved." Famous Amys include actor Amy Adams and singer Amy Winehouse. Aimee is the French form used by actor Aimee Garcia, singer Aimee Mann, and Aimee Osbourne of the Osbourne family.

Ana-Lisa

Contraction of Anna and Lisa, meaning "grace" or "consecrated to God."

Anafa

Hebrew, meaning "heron."

Ananda

Hindi, meaning "bliss." One of Buddha's disciples.

Anastasia

(alt. Athanasia)

Greek, meaning "resurrection." Grand Duchess Anastasia of Russia was killed in 1918, following the Russian revolution.

Anat

Jewish, meaning "water spring." Anat is an important Semitic goddess.

Anatolia

Greek, meaning "east sunrise." From the eastern Greek town of the same name.

Andrea

(alt. Andreia, Andria, Andrine, Andrina)

Feminine of Andrew, from the Greek term for "a man's woman." Famous Andreas include writers Andrea Levy and Andrea Dworkin.

Andromeda

Greek, meaning "leader of men." From the heroine of an ancient Greek legend.

Anemone

Greek, meaning "breath." Also a flowering plant.

Angela

(alt. Angel, Angeles, Angelia, Angelle, Angie)

Greek, meaning "messenger from God" or "angel." Famous Angelas include actors Angela Lansbury and Angela Bassett.

Angelica

(alt. Angelina, Angeline, Angelique, Angelise, Angelita, Anjelica, Anjelina)

Latin, meaning "angelic." Famous Angelicas include actor Anjelica Huston and *Rugrats* character Angelica Pickles.

Anise

(alt. Anisa, Anissa)

French, from the licorice-flavored plant of the same name.

Aniston

English, meaning "town of Agnes."

Anita

(alt. Anitra)

Derived from Ann, Hannah, or Anahita (the Iranian water goddess), depending on the language. Famous Anitas include singer Anita Baker and *West Side Story* character Anita.

Anna

(alt. Ana)

Derived from Hannah, meaning "grace." A prophetess in the Bible.

Annabel
(alt. Anabel, Anabelle, Annabell, Annabella, Annabelle, Amabel)

Contraction of Anna and Belle, meaning "grace" and "beauty."

Annalise
(alt. Annalee, Annalisa, Anneli, Annelie, Annelise)

Contraction of Anna and Lise, meaning "grace" and "pledged to God."

Anne
(alt. Ann)

Originally a French form of Anna, meaning "grace," but used in England for many hundreds of years. Famous Annes include actor Anne Hathaway and two of the wives of Henry VIII.

Annemarie
(alt. Annamae, Annamarie, Annelle, Annmarie)

Contraction of Anna and Mary, meaning "grace" and "star of the sea." The name of actor Anne-Marie Duff.

Annette
(alt. Annetta)

Hebrew, derived from Hannah, meaning "grace." Associated with actors Annette Funicello and Annette Bening.

Annis
Greek, meaning "finished or completed." The Black Annis is a blue-faced witch in English mythology.

Annora
Latin, meaning "honor."

Anoushka
(alt. Anousha)

Russian variation of Ann, meaning "grace."

Anthea
(alt. Anthi)

Greek, meaning "flower-like." Also another name for the ancient Greek goddess Hera.

Antigone
In ancient Greek mythology, Antigone was the daughter of Oedipus.

Antoinette
(alt. Antonetta, Antonette, Antonietta; abbrev. Toni)

Female form of Anthony, meaning "invaluable grace." French queen consort Marie Antoinette was executed during the French Revolution.

Antonia
(alt. Antonella, Antonina)

Latin, meaning "invaluable." A very popular name in ancient Rome.

Anwen

Welsh, meaning "very fair."

Anya

(alt. Aanya, Aniya, Aniyah, Aniylah, Anja)

Russian, meaning "grace."

Aoife

Gaelic, meaning "beautiful joy." Associated with goddess Esuvia.

Apollonia

Feminine of Apollo, the Greek god of the sun. St. Apollonia is the patron saint of dentistry.

Apple

From the name of the fruit. Famous Apples include technology company Apple Inc., and Gwyneth Paltrow's daughter.

April

(alt. Avril)

Latin, meaning "opening up." Also the fourth month, which has associations with the goddess Venus.

Aquilina

(alt. Aqua, Aquila)

Spanish, meaning "like an eagle." Associated with St. Aquilina.

Ara

Arabic, meaning "brings rain." Also a star constellation. Can be used for girls or boys.

Arabella

(alt. Arabelle; abbrev. Bel, Bella)

Latin, meaning "answered prayer." The name of an opera by Richard Strauss.

Araceli

(alt. Aracely)

Spanish, meaning "altar of Heaven."

Araminta

Contraction of Arabella and Aminta, meaning "answered prayer" and "defender."

Arcadia

Greek, meaning "paradise." The daughter of ancient Roman Emperor Arcadius.

Ardelle

(alt. Ardell, Ardella)

Latin, meaning "burning with enthusiasm." Ardelle Kloss is a figure skater.

Arden

(alt. Ardis, Ardith)

Latin, meaning "burning with enthusiasm." Made famous by the cosmetics company Elizabeth Arden.

Arella

(alt. Areli, Arely)

Hebrew, meaning "angel."

Aretha

Greek, meaning "woman of virtue." Aretha Franklin is a soul singer.

Aria
(alt. Ariah, Arya)
Italian, meaning "melody." Arya Stark is a character in *Game of Thrones*.

Ariadne
Both Greek and Latin, meaning "the very holy one." In ancient Greek mythology, Ariadne was the daughter of King Minos.

Ariana
(alt. Ariane, Arianna, Arienne)
Welsh, meaning "silver."

Ariel
(alt. Ariela, Ariella, Arielle)
Hebrew, meaning "lioness of God." Ariel is the main character in Disney's *The Little Mermaid*.

Arlene
(alt. Arleen, Arline; abbrev. Arlie, Arly)
Gaelic, meaning "pledge." Associated with actor Arlene Dahl.

Armida
Latin, meaning "little armed one." Taken from the character of Armida in *Gerusalemme liberata* by Italian poet Torquato Tasso.

Artemisia
(alt. Artemis, Arti, Artie)
Greek/Spanish, meaning "perfect." Artemisia was a legendary female ancient Persian naval commander.

Arwen
Welsh, meaning "fair" or "fine." Arwen is a key Elven figure in *The Lord of the Rings*.

Ashanti
Geographical area in Africa. Also the name of the popular R&B singer Ashanti.

Ashby
English, meaning "ash tree farm."

Ashley
(alt. Ashlee, Ashleigh, Ashli, Ashlie, Ashly)
English, meaning "ash tree meadow." Famous Ashleys include actor Ashley Judd, and singers Ashley Tisdale and Ashlee Simpson. Can be used for girls or boys.

Ashlynn
(alt. Ashlyn)
Irish Gaelic, meaning "dream."

Ashton
(alt. Ashtyn)
Old English, meaning "ash tree town." Can be used for girls or boys.

Asia
Name of the continent. Also a name for an Oceanid in ancient Greek mythology.

Asma
(alt. Asmara)
Arabic, meaning "highstanding."

Aspen
(alt. Aspynn)

Name of the tree. Also the Colorado city famous for its ski resort.

Assumpta
(alt. Asumpta, Assunta)

Italian, meaning "raised up."

Asta
(alt. Asteria, Astor, Astoria)

Greek or Latin, meaning "starlike."

Astrid

Old Norse, meaning "beautiful like a God." Astrid Lundgren is the author of *Pippi Longstocking*.

Atara

Hebrew, meaning "diadem" or "crown." Also a genus of butterfly.

Athena
(alt. Athenais)

Greek, meaning "wise." Athena was the ancient Greek goddess of wisdom, mathematics, and arts and crafts.

Aubrey
(alt. Aubree, Aubriana, Aubrie)

French, meaning "elf ruler."

Audrey
(alt. Audra, Audrie, Audrina, Audry)

English, meaning "noble strength." St. Etheldreda was known as St. Audrey, and was a seventh-century English princess. Made famous by reality star Audrina Patridge.

Augusta
(alt. August, Augustine)

Latin, meaning "worthy of respect."

Aura
(alt. Aurea)

Greek or Latin, meaning either "soft breeze" or "gold." An aura is the perceived field of energy surrounding people and objects in various spiritual beliefs.

Aurelia
(alt. Aurelie)

Latin, meaning gold. The mother of Julius Caesar.

Aurora
(alt. Aurore)

Latin, meaning "dawn." In ancient Roman mythology, Aurora was the goddess of sunrise.

Austine
(alt. Austen, Austin)

Latin, meaning "worthy of respect."

Autumn

Latin, from the name of the harvest season.

Ava
(alt. Avia, Avie)

Latin, meaning "like a bird." Associated with actor Ava Gardner.

Avalon
(alt. Avalyn, Aveline)

Celtic, meaning "island of apples." Avalon is the mythological island in the King Arthur legend.

Axelle
Greek, meaning "father of peace."

Aya
(alt. Ayah)

Hebrew, meaning "bird."

Ayanna
(alt. Ayana)

Yoruba, meaning "beautiful flower."

Ayesha
(alt. Aisha, Aysha)

Persian, meaning "small one."

Azalea
Latin, meaning "dry earth." Also the name of a flowering shrub.

Azalia
Hebrew, meaning "aided by God."

Names of First Ladies

Barbara (Bush)
Edith (Roosevelt)
Elizabeth (Ford)
Grace (Coolidge)
Hillary (Clinton)
Jacqueline (Kennedy)
Martha (Washington)
Mary (Lincoln)
Melania (Trump)
Michelle (Obama)
Nancy (Reagan)

Aziza
Hebrew, meaning "mighty"; Arabic meaning "precious." Female variation of Aziz.

Azure
(alt. Azaria)

French, meaning "sky-blue." Refers to the bright blue color of the sky on a clear day.

B

Girls' names

Babette
(alt. Babe)

French version of Barbara; Greek meaning "foreign." Babette Cole is the author of children's books *Mommy Laid an Egg* and *Princess Smartypants*.

Bailey
(alt. Baeli, Bailee)

English, meaning "law enforcer."

Bambi
(alt. Bambina)

Shortened version of the Italian "bambina," meaning "child." Made famous by the Disney movie *Bambi*.

Barbara
(alt. Barbra; abbrev. Barb, Barbie)

Greek, meaning "foreign." Famous Barbaras include journalist Barbara Walters, and singer and actor Barbra Streisand.

Basma

Arabic, meaning "smile."

Bathsheba

Hebrew, meaning "daughter of the oath." Bathsheba was a key biblical figure, and mother of King Solomon.

Bay
(alt. Bae, Baya)

From the edible plant the bay leaf, or the geographical name for a large inlet of water.

Beata

Latin, meaning "blessed."

Beatrice
(alt. Beatrix, Beatriz, Bee, Bellatrix; abbrev. Bea)

Latin, meaning "bringer of gladness." Beatrice is a character in Dante's *Divine Comedy* and Shakespeare's *Much Ado About Nothing*.

Belinda
(alt. Belen, Belina)

Contraction of Belle and Linda, meaning "beautiful." Well-known Belindas include singer Belinda Carlisle.

Bella
(alt. Béla)

Latin, meaning "beautiful." Bella (Isabella) Swan is the main female character in the "Twilight" series.

Belle
(alt. Bell)

French, meaning "beautiful." Popularized by the Disney princess in *Beauty and the Beast*.

Belva

Latin, meaning "beautiful view." The inspiration for one of the characters in the musical *Chicago* was real-life murderer Belva Gaertner.

Bénédicta
(alt. Benedetta; abbrev. Bennie)

Latin, the feminine of Benedict, meaning "blessed." Associated with Benedicta Henrietta of the Palatinate.

Benita
(alt. Bernita; abbrev. Bennie)

Spanish, meaning "blessed."

Berit
(alt. Beret)

Scandinavian, meaning "splendid" or "gorgeous."

Bernadette
(alt. Bernadine; abbrev. Bernie)

French, meaning "courageous." St. Bernadette was known for her visions of the Virgin Mary.

Bernice
(alt. Berenice, Berniece, Burnice)

Greek, meaning "she who brings victory." The name of Herod's daughter in the Bible.

Bertha
(alt. Berta, Berthe, Bertie)

German, meaning "bright." There are four saints called Bertha, all from the Middle Ages.

Beryl

Greek, meaning "pale, green gemstone." The name of a precious mineral.

Bess
(alt. Bessie)

Shortened form of Elizabeth, meaning "consecrated to God." Queen Elizabeth I's nickname was Good Queen Bess.

Beth

Hebrew, meaning "house." Also shortened form of Elizabeth, meaning "consecrated to God."

Bethany
(alt. Bethan)

Hebrew, referring to a geographical location in the Bible.

Bethel

Hebrew, meaning "house of God." A city in the Bible.

Bettina

(alt. Battina, Betiana, Betina, Bettine; abbrev. Betty, Ina, Tina)

Latin, derived from Benedetta or German derived from Elizabeth. Bettina Bush was the voice for *Rainbow Brite*.

Betty

(alt. Betsy, Bette, Bettie, Bettye)

Originally a shortened version of Elizabeth, meaning "consecrated to God," now often used as a name in its own right. Famous Bettys include cartoon character Betty Boop, actor Betty Grable, and glamor model Bettie Page.

Beulah

Hebrew, meaning "married." The name of the place that exists between Earth and Heaven.

Beverly

(alt. Beverlee, Beverley)

English, meaning "beaver stream." Made famous by Beverly Hills, CA, and actor Beverley Mitchell.

Beyoncé

American English, made popular by the singer.

Bianca

(alt. Blanca)

Italian, meaning "white." Bianca is a character from Shakespeare's *Othello*.

Bijou

French, meaning "precious ring."

Billie

(alt. Bill, Billy, Billye)

Originally used for girls as a shortened version of Wilhelmina, meaning "determined." Now used almost universally as a standalone name, made popular as the stage name chosen by jazz singer Billie Holiday and tennis legend Billie Jean King.

Bina

Hebrew, meaning "knowledge."

Birgit

(alt. Birgitta)

German, meaning "power and strength." Used as a variation of Bridget.

Blaer

Icelandic, meaning "light breeze."

Blair

Scottish Gaelic, meaning "flat, plain area." Well-known Blairs include actor Blair Underwood.

Blake
(alt. Blakely, Blakelyn)

English, meaning either "pale skinned" or "dark." Associated with actor Blake Lively. Can be used for girls or boys.

Blanche
(alt. Blanch)

French, meaning "white or pale." Famous Blanches include the characters of Blanche Devereaux in *The Golden Girls*, and Blanche DuBois in *A Streetcar Named Desire*.

Bliss

English, meaning "intense happiness."

Blithe

English, meaning "joyous."

Blodwen

Welsh, meaning "white flower." The name of a Welsh opera.

Blossom

English, meaning "flowerlike." *Blossom* was a 1990s sitcom.

Blythe
(alt. Bly)

English, meaning "happy and carefree." Blythe Danner starred in sitcom *Will and Grace* and is the mother of actor Gwyneth Paltrow.

Bobbi
(alt. Bobbie, Bobby)

Shortened version of Roberta, meaning "bright fame." Associated with cosmetics brand Bobbi Brown.

Bonita
(alt. Bo)

Spanish, meaning "pretty." "La Isla Bonita" is a song by Madonna.

Bonnie
(alt. Bonny)

Scottish, meaning "fair of face." One half of the outlaw duo Bonnie and Clyde.

Brandy
(alt. Brandee, Brandi, Brandie)

Dutch, meaning "burnt wine." Name of the liquor.

Brea
(alt. Bree, Bria)

Shortened form of Brianna, meaning "strong." Also the name of an ancient Irish god.

Brenda

Old Norse, meaning "sword."

Brianna
(alt. Breana, Breann, Breanna, Breanne, Brenna, Brenyn, Briana, Brianne, Bryanna)

Irish Gaelic, meaning "strong."

Bridget

(alt. Bridgett, Bridgette, Brigette, Brigid, Brigitta, Brigitte)

Irish Gaelic, meaning "strength and power." Famous Bridgets include actors Bridget Fonda and Brigitte Bardot, and the novel and movie *Bridget Jones's Diary*.

Brier

(alt. Briar)

French, meaning "heather." Sleeping Beauty's pseudonym is Briar Rose in the Disney movie.

Brit

(alt. Britt, Britta)

Celtic, meaning "spotted" or "freckled." Name of actor Britt Ekland.

Britannia

Latin, meaning "Britain." Britannia is the female personification of Great Britain.

Brittany

(alt. Britany, Britney, Britni, Brittani, Brittanie, Brittney, Brittni, Brittny)

Latin, meaning "from Britain." Famous Brittanys include the French province, singer Britney Spears, and actor Brittany Murphy.

Bronwen

(alt. Bronwyn)

Welsh, meaning "fair breast." The spelling of Bronwen is more common for baby girls, and Bronwyn for baby boys.

Brooke

(alt. Brook)

English, meaning "small stream." Brooke Shields is an actor and model. Can be used for girls or boys.

Brooklyn

(alt. Brooklynn)

Name of a New York borough. Associated with model Brooklyn Decker.

Brunhilda

(alt. Brunhilde, Brynhildr)

German, meaning "armor-wearing fighting maid." Brynhildr was an important character in Old German mythology.

Bryn

(alt. Brynn)

Welsh, meaning "mount" or "hill."

Bryony

(alt. Briony)

English, from bryonia, the name of a European vine.

Buffy

American English alternative of Elizabeth, meaning "consecrated to God." The protagonist of the sci-fi series *Buffy the Vampire Slayer*.

C

Girls' names

Cadence
(alt. Candenza)
Latin, meaning "with rhythm." Also used beginning with K.

Cai
Vietnamese, meaning "feminine."

Caitlin
(alt. Cadyn, Caitlann, Caitlyn, Caitlyn, Kaitlin)
Greek, meaning "pure." Catelyn Stark is a central character from *Game of Thrones*. Also used beginning with K, as for Kaitlin Doubleday. Caitlyn Jenner is a former Olympian athlete and member of the Jenner/Kardashian clan.

Calandra
Greek, meaning "lark." A small Mediterranean bird.

Calantha
(alt. Calanthe)
Greek, meaning "lovely flower."

Caledonia
Latin, meaning Scotland.

Calla
Greek, meaning "beautiful." Associated with the calla lily.

Callie
(alt. Caleigh, Cali, Calleigh, Cally)
Greek, meaning "beauty." Callie Khouri is a screenwriter.

Calliope
(alt. Kalliope)
Greek, meaning "beautiful voice." From the muse of epic poetry in Greek mythology.

Callista
(alt. Calista, Callisto, Kallista)
Greek, meaning "most beautiful." Best-known as the name of actor Calista Flockhart.

Camas

Native American, from the root and bulb of the same name.

Cambria

Welsh, from the alternate name for Wales.

Camden

(alt. Camdyn)

English, meaning "winding valley." Also a part of London, England.

Cameo

Italian, meaning "skin." Associated with the notion of a cameo role in film or television.

Cameron

(alt. Camryn)

Scottish Gaelic, meaning "bent nose." Used for boys and girls. The best known female Cameron (Diaz) was reported to be the highest-paid female actor over the age of 40.

Camilla

(alt. Camelia, Camellia, Camila, Camille, Camillia)

Latin, meaning "spiritual serving girl." Made famous by model Camilla Alves, and Camilla, Duchess of Cornwall, who is married to Prince Charles.

Candace

(alt. Candice, Candis, Kandace)

Latin, meaning "brilliant white." Famous Candaces include actor Candace Cameron Bure, basketball player Candace Parker, and Candace Bushnell, author of *Sex and the City*.

Candida

Latin, meaning "white."

Candra

Latin, meaning "glowing."

Candy

(alt. Candi, Kandy)

Shortened form of Candace, meaning "brilliant white." Also a name for sweets or confectionery.

Caoimhe

Celtic, meaning "gentleness." Has many different pronounciations, including "Kyva" and "Keeva," depending on where in Ireland you hear it.

Caprice

Italian, meaning "ruled by whim." Made famous by model and actor Caprice.

Cara

Latin, meaning "darling." Cara Delevingne is a model and Cara Black a bestselling mystery novelist.

Carey
(alt. Cari, Carie, Carri, Carrie, Cary)

Welsh, meaning "near the castle."
Famous Careys include actor Carey
Mulligan and singer Mariah Carey.

Carina
(alt. Corina)

Italian, meaning "dearest little one."
Also the name of a star constellation.

Carissa
(alt. Carisa)

Greek, meaning "grace."

Carla
(alt. Charl, Karla)

Feminine of the Old Norse Carl,
meaning "free man." Carla Bruni-
Sarkozy is the singer-songwriter
married to former French president
Nicolas Sarkozy.

Carlin
(alt. Carleen, Carlene)

Gaelic, meaning "little champion."

Carlotta
(alt. Carlota)

Italian, meaning "free man." Carlotta
is a character from *The Phantom of
the Opera*.

Carly
*(alt. Carlee, Carley, Carli, Carlie, Karly,
Karlie)*

Feminine of the German Charles,
meaning "man." Famous Carlys
include singers Carly Simon and Carly
Rae Jepson, and model Karlie Kloss.

Carmel
(alt. Carmela, Carmelita, Carmella)

Hebrew, meaning "garden."
American Carmelita Jeter is an
Olympic medal-winning
100-meter sprinter.

Carmen
(alt. Carma, Carmina)

Latin, meaning "song." The opera
Carmen was composed by Georges
Bizet.

Carol
*(alt. Carole, Carrol, Carroll, Caryl,
Karol)*

Originally the short form of Caroline,
meaning "man." Famous Carols
include actor Carol Burnett.

Caroline
*(alt. Carolann, Carolina, Carolyn,
Carolynn)*

German, meaning "man." A
feminine form of Charles. Caroline
Kennedy is the daughter of John
F. Kennedy.

Carrington

English, meaning "Charles's
town."

Carys
(alt. Cerys)

Welsh, meaning "love."

Casey
(alt. Casy, Casie, Kasey)

Irish Gaelic, meaning "watchful."
Used for girls and boys.

Cassandra

(alt. Casandra, Cassandre, Kassandra; abbrev. Cassie)

Greek, meaning "one who prophesies doom" or "entangler of men." Cassandra was a seer in ancient Greek mythology.

Cassia

(alt. Casia, Casie, Cassie)

Greek, meaning "cinnamon."

Cassidy

Irish, meaning "clever."

Catherine

(alt. Catalina, Catarina, Caterina, Catharine, Cathleen, Cathrine, Cathryn; abbrev. Cate, Cathy, Cathie, Caity, Caty)

Greek, meaning "pure." Famous Catherines include Catherine, Duchess of Cambridge, actor Catherine Zeta Jones, and Russia's Catherine the Great. Cathleen is the Irish variant of Catherine, and Catalina the Spanish version. All variations and abbreviations can also be spelled starting with a K rather than a C.

Cayley

(alt. Cayla, Caylee, Caylen)

Gaelic, meaning "slim" and "fair."

Cecilia

(alt. Cecelia, Cecile, Cecilie, Cecily, Cicely, Cicily)

Latin, meaning "blind one."

Celena

Greek, meaning "goddess of the moon." Also a spelling variation for Selena.

Celeste

(alt. Celestina, Celestine)

Latin, meaning "heavenly." Associated with actor Celeste Holm.

Celine

(alt. Celia, Celina)

French version of Celeste, meaning "heavenly." Associated with singer Celine Dion.

Cerise

French, meaning "cherry." The color cerise is a deep, pink-red shade.

Chanah

(alt. Chana)

Hebrew, meaning "grace." Also a spelling variation for Hannah.

Chance

Middle English, meaning "good fortune."

Chandler

(alt. Chandell)

English, meaning "candle maker." Can be used for girls or, more commonly, boys.

Chandra
(alt. Chanda, Chandry)
Sanskrit, meaning "like the moon." Chandra is a god of the moon in Hinduism.

Chanel
(alt. Chanelle)
French, meaning "pipe." Name of the French fashion house founded by designer Coco Chanel.

Chantal
(alt. Chantel, Chantelle, Chantilly)
French, meaning "stony spot."

Chardonnay
French, from the wine variety of the same name.

Charis
(alt. Charice, Charissa, Charisse)
Greek, meaning "grace." One of the graces in ancient Greek mythology.

Charity
Latin, meaning "brotherly love."

Charlene
(alt. Charleen, Charline)
German, meaning "man." Associated with actor Charlene Tilton.

Charlize
French form of Charlotte, meaning "little and feminine". Made famous by actor Charlize Theron.

Charlotte
(alt. Charnette, Charolette; abbrev. Charlie, Charley, Charly, Lottie)
French, meaning "little and feminine." Famous Charlottes include Princess Charlotte, author Charlotte Bronte, and the novel *Charlotte's Web* by E. B. White. Charlie is also the abbreviation for the boys' name Charles.

Charmaine
Latin, meaning "clan." Derived from Charmain, a favorite servant of Cleopatra.

Chastity
Latin, meaning "purity."

Chava
(alt. Chaya)
Hebrew, meaning "beloved."

Chelsea
(alt. Chelsee, Chelsey, Chelsi, Chelsie)
English, meaning "port or landing place." Famous Chelseas include comedian Chelsea Handler and advocate Chelsea Clinton.

Cher
French, meaning "beloved." Made famous by the singer Cher.

Cherie
(alt. Cheri, Cherise)
French, meaning "dear."

Cherish
(alt. Cherith)

English, meaning "to treasure." The title of a song by Madonna.

Chermona

Hebrew, meaning "sacred mountain."

Cherry
(alt. Cherri)

French, meaning "cherry fruit."

Cheryl
(alt. Cheryle)

English, meaning "little and womanly." Made famous by dancer Cheryl Burke from *Dancing With The Stars*.

Chesney

English, meaning "place to camp." Can be used for girls or, more commonly, boys.

Cheyenne
(alt. Cheyanne)

Native American, from the tribe of the same name in Wyoming.

Chiara
(alt. Ceara, Chiarina, Ciara)

Italian, meaning "light." Associated with the singer Ciara.

China

From the country of the same name.

Chiquita

Spanish, meaning "little one."

Chloe
(alt. Cloe)

Greek, meaning "pale green shoot." Famous Chloes include actors Chloe Grace Moretz and Chloe Sevigny, and author Toni Morrison—whose birth name was Chloe Wofford.

Chloris
(alt. Cloris)

Greek, meaning "pale." Made famous by actor and comedian Cloris Leachman.

Christabel
(alt. Christobel)

Latin and French, meaning "fair Christian." The title of a poem by Samuel Taylor Coleridge.

Christina
(alt. Christine, Christen, Christene, Christian, Christiana, Christiane, Christin, Cristina; abbrev. Chris, Chrissy, Christa, Christie, Christy, Crissy, Cristy)

Greek, meaning "anointed Christian." Famous Christinas include singer Christina Aguilera and actors Christina Ricci and Christine Taylor.

Chuma

Aramaic, meaning "warmth."

Cierra
(alt. Ciera)

Irish, meaning "black."

Cinderella

French, meaning "little ashgirl." Subject of the children's fairy tale.

Cinnamon

Greek, from the exotic spice of the same name.

Citlali

(alt. Citlalli)

Nahuatl, meaning "star." An ancient Aztec name.

Citrine

Latin, from the gemstone of the same name.

Claire

(alt. Clara, Clare, Claira)

Latin, meaning "bright." Associated with actor Claire Danes.

Clarabelle

(alt. Claribel)

Contraction of Clare and Isobel, meaning "bright" and "consecrated to God." Clarabelle is a Disney cow cartoon character.

Clarissa

(alt. Clarice, Clarisse)

Variation of Claire, meaning "bright." The title character from the sitcom Clarissa Explains It All.

Clarity

Latin, meaning "lucid."

Claudia

(alt. Claudetta, Claudette, Claudie, Claudine)

Latin, meaning "lame." The first female president of Haiti was Claudette Werleigh. Claudia Schiffer is a German supermodel.

Clematis

Greek, meaning "vine." A type of flowering plant.

Clementine

(alt. Clemency, Clementina, Clemmie)

Latin, meaning "mild and merciful." Also the small orange fruit.

Cleopatra

Greek, meaning "her father's renown." Famed as an ancient Egyptian queen.

Clio

(alt. Cleo, Cliona)

Greek, from the ancient Greek muse of the same name.

Clodagh

Irish, meaning "river."

Clotilda

(alt. Clothilda, Clothilde, Clotilde)

German, meaning "renowned battle." St. Clotilde was known for her works of charity.

Clover

English, from the flower of the same name.

Coby

Diminutive of Jacob, meaning "supplanter." More commonly used as a boy's name.

Coco

Spanish, an abbreviation of *socorro*, meaning "help." Name of the French fashion designer Coco Chanel.

Cody

English, meaning "pillow."

Colleen
(alt. Coleen)

Irish Gaelic, meaning "girl." Colleen Camp is an actor.

Collette
(alt. Colette)

Greek/French, meaning "people of victory." Sidonie-Gabrielle Colette was the author of *Gigi*.

Constance
(alt. Constanza, Constantina, Konstance; abbrev. Connie)

Latin, meaning "steadfast." Oscar Wilde's wife was Constance Lloyd. Famous Connies include actors Connie Britton and Connie Nielsen, and journalist Connie Chung.

Consuelo
(alt. Consuela)

Spanish, meaning "comfort." Originally from the Virgin Mary, who was Our Lady of Consolation in Spanish.

Cora
(alt. Kora)

Greek, meaning "maiden."

Coral
(alt. Coralie, Coraline, Corelia, Corene)

Latin, from the marine life of the same name.

Corazon

Spanish, meaning "heart" or "darling."

Cordelia
(alt. Cordia, Cordie)

Latin, meaning "heart." Famous fictional Cordelias include characters in Shakespeare's *King Lear* and TV's *Buffy the Vampire Slayer*.

Corey
(alt. Cori, Corrie, Cory)

Irish Gaelic, meaning "the hollow."

Corin
(alt. Corine)

Latin, meaning "spear."

Corinne
(alt. Corinna, Corrine)

French version of Cora, meaning "maiden." Associated with singer Corinne Bailey Rae.

Corliss

English, meaning "cheery."

Cornelia

Latin, meaning "like a horn." The name of several influential ancient Roman women.

Cosette

French, meaning "people of victory." Name of a key character in Victor Hugo's *Les Misérables*.

Cosima
(alt. Cosmina)

Greek, meaning "order." One of the clones in *Orphan Black*.

Courtney
(alt. Cortney)

English, meaning "court-dweller." Famous Courtneys include actor Courtney Cox and singer Courtney Love.

Creola

French, meaning "American-born, English descent." Associated with the Creole language and people.

Crescent

French, meaning "increasing."

Cressida

From the Trojan heroine in Greek mythology of the same name.

Crystal
(alt. Christal, Chrystal, Cristal, Krystal)

Greek, meaning "ice." A kind of manufactured precious stone.

Csilla

Hungarian, meaning "defenses."

Cyd

Shortened form of Sidney, meaning "wide island." Cyd Charisse was a dancer and actor.

Cynara

Greek, meaning "thistly plant."

Cynthia
(abbrev. Cinda, Cindi, Cindy, Cyndi)

Greek, meaning "goddess from the mountain." Famous Cynthias include actor Cynthia Nixon and designer Cynthia Rowley. Famous Cindys include 1980s supermodel Cindy Crawford and singer Cindi Lauper.

Cyra

Persian, meaning "sun." Also a genus of ladybugs.

Cyrilla

Latin, meaning "lordly." Also a type of flowering plant.

D Girls' names

Dacey

Irish Gaelic, meaning "from the south."

Dada

Yoruba, meaning "curly haired." Associated with the art movement Dadaism.

Daenerys

Literary, from the fictional character in *Game of Thrones*.

Dagmar

German, meaning "day's glory." Dagmar was the stage name of Virginia Egnor.

Dagny

Nordic, meaning "new day."

Dahlia

Scandinavian, from the flowering plant of the same name.

Dai

Welsh, meaning "darling." Used for girls or, more commonly, boys.

Daisy

(alt. Daisey, Dasia)

English, meaning "eye of the day." A flowering plant.

Dakota

Native American, meaning "allies." Associated with actor Dakota Fanning, and the states of North and South Dakota.

Dalia

(alt. Daliah, Dalila)

Hebrew, meaning "delicate branch." A Lithuanian goddess.

Dallas

Scottish Gaelic, from the village of the same name. Also the city in Texas.

Damaris

Greek, meaning "calf." A character in the Bible.

Damita

Spanish, meaning "little noblewoman."

Dana

(alt. Dania, Danna, Dayna)

English, meaning "from Denmark"; Persian, meaning "a perfect and valuable pearl."

Danae

Greek, from the mythological heroine of the same name.

Danica

(alt. Danika)

Latin, meaning "from Denmark." Famous Danicas include racing driver Danica Patrick, and actor and author Danica McKellar.

Danielle

(alt. Danelle, Daniela, Daniella, Danila, Danita, Danyell; abbrev. Dani, Danni)

The feminine form of the Hebrew Daniel, meaning "God is my judge." The name of actor Danielle Fischel.

Daphne

(alt. Dafne, Daphna)

Greek, meaning "laurel tree." Daphne was a water nymph in Greek mythology.

Dara

Hebrew/Persian, meaning "wisdom." A character in the Bible.

Darby

(alt. Darbi, Darbie)

Irish, meaning "park with deer."

Darcy

(alt. Darcey, Darci, Darcie)

Irish Gaelic, meaning "dark." Famous Darcys include ballerina Darcey Bussell, and Pride and Prejudice character Mr. Darcy.

Daria

Greek, meaning "rich." Associated with cartoon series Daria.

Darla

English, meaning "darling." Made famous by the child star Darla Hood.

Darlene

(alt. Darleen, Darline)

American English, meaning "darling." Darlene Gillespie is a member of the Mickey Mouse Club.

Daryl

(alt. Darryl)

Old English, and possibly also Old French, meaning "loved." Daryl is usually the female spelling and Darryl the male. Daryl Hannah is an actor.

Davina

Hebrew, meaning "loved one."
Davina Claire is a character in *The Vampire Diaries*.

Dawn
(alt. Dawna)

English, meaning "to become day."

Daya

Hebrew, meaning "bird of prey." A form of teaching in the Sikh religion.

Deanna
(alt. Dayana, Deana, Deanna, Deanne)

English, meaning "girl from the valley." The name of singer and actor Deanna Durbin.

Deborah
(alt. Debbra, Debra, Debrah; abbrev. Debbi, Debbie, Debby, Debi)

Hebrew, meaning "bee." A prophetess in the Bible.

December

Latin, meaning "tenth month."

Dee
(alt. Dea)

Welsh, meaning "swarthy." Also a shortened form of many names beginning with "De-."

Deidre
(alt. Deidra, Deirdre)

Irish, meaning "raging woman."

Deja
(alt. Dejah)

French, meaning "already." The French term for "already seen" is "déjà vu."

Delaney
(alt. Delany)

Irish Gaelic, meaning "offspring of the challenger."

Delia

Greek, meaning "from Delos." Associated with the ancient Greek island of Delos.

Delilah
(alt. Delina)

Hebrew, meaning "seductive." Famous Delilahs include the lover of Samson in the Bible, and the songs "Delilah" by Tom Jones and "Hey There Delilah" by Plain White T's.

Della
(alt. Dell)

Shortened form of Adele, meaning "nobility." Donald Duck's twin sister is called Della Duck.

Delores
(alt. Deloris)

Spanish, meaning "sorrows."

Delphine
(alt. Delpha, Delphia, Delphina, Delphinia)

Greek, meaning "dolphin."

Delta

Greek, meaning "fourth child."
Also the fourth letter of the Greek
alphabet.

Demetria

(alt. Demetrice, Dimitria)
Greek, from the mythological
heroine of the same name.

Demi

French, meaning "half." Name of
the actor Demi Moore.

Dena

(alt. Deena)
English, meaning "from the
valley."

Denise

(alt. Denice, Denisa, Denisse)
French, meaning "to be devoted to
Bacchus." Name of the actor Denise
Richards.

Desdemona

Greek, meaning "wretchedness."
Desdemona is Othello's love interest
in Shakespeare's *Othello*.

Desiree

(alt. Desirae, Des'ree)
French, meaning "much desired."
Associated with singer Des'ree.

Desma

Greek, meaning "blinding oath."

Destiny

*(alt. Destany, Destinee, Destiney,
Destini)*
French, meaning "fate." Associated
with the former girl group Destiny's
Child.

Deva

Hindi, meaning "God-like." Deva
is also a name for several Buddhist,
Hindu, and New Age spiritual entities
or people.

Devin

(alt. Devinne)
Irish Gaelic, meaning "poet." Used
as a girls' or, more commonly, boys'
name.

Devon

English, from the county of the same
name. Also female variant of Devin,
meaning "poet."

Diamond

English, meaning "brilliant." One
of the hardest and most valuable
substances on Earth.

Diana

(alt. Dian, Diane, Dianna, Dianne)
Roman, meaning "divine." Made
famous by Diana, the former Princess
of Wales.

Diandra

Greek, meaning "two males."

Dilys

Welsh, meaning "reliable."

Dimona

Hebrew, meaning "south." A town in the Bible.

Dinah

(alt. Dina)

Hebrew, meaning "justified." A character in the Bible.

Dionne

Greek, from the mythological heroine of the same name. Famous Dionnes include singers Dionne Warwick and Dionne Bromfield, and the infamous Dionne quintuplets.

Divine

Italian, meaning "heavenly." Associated with divinity or Dante's *Divine Comedy*.

Dixie

French, meaning "tenth." Also an old term for the South.

Dodie

Hebrew, meaning "well-loved." Dodie Smith was the author of *101 Dalmations*.

Dolores

(alt. Doloris)

Spanish, meaning "sorrows."

Names for triplets

Abel, Bela, and Elba (anagrams)

Aidan, Diana, and Nadia (anagrams)

Amber, Jade, and Ruby (jewels)

Amy, May, and Mya (anagrams)

April, May, and June (months)

Ava, Eva, and Iva (similar)

Daisy, Lily, and Rose (flowers)

Jay, Raven, and Robin (birds)

Leah, Lianne, and Liam (similar)

Olive, Violet, and Sage (colors)

River, Rain, and Summer (nature)

Dominique

(alt. Domenica, Dominica, Domonique)

Latin, meaning "Lord." The name of a song by Soeur Sourire.

Donata

Latin, meaning "given."

Donna

(alt. Dona, Donnie)

Italian, meaning "lady." Famous Donnas include singer Donna Summer and actor Donna Reed.

Dora

Greek, meaning "gift." The title character in Dora the Explorer.

Doran

Irish Gaelic, meaning "fist" or "stranger."

Dorcas

Greek, meaning "gazelle." Character in the Bible.

Doreen

(alt. Dorene, Dorine)

Irish Gaelic, meaning "brooding"; Greek, meaning "gift."

Doris

(alt. Dorris)

Greek, from the place of the same name. Made famous by singer and actor Doris Day.

Dorothy

(alt. Dorathy, Doretha, Dorotha, Dorothea, Dorthy; abbrev. Dolly, Dottie, Dotty)

Greek, meaning "gift of God." Most commonly associated with Dorothy from The Wizard of Oz.

Dorrit

(alt. Dorit)

Greek, meaning "gift of God." Little Dorrit is a novel by Charles Dickens.

Dory

(alt. Dori)

French, meaning "gilded." Associated with Dory from Finding Nemo and its sequel Finding Dory.

Dove

(alt. Dovie)

English, from the bird of the same name. Used as a symbol of peace.

Dream

English, meaning "rejoice."

Drew

Greek, meaning "masculine." Can be used for girls or boys (as a nickname for Andrew). Made famous by actor Drew Barrymore.

Drusilla

(alt. Drucilla)

Latin, meaning "of the Drusus clan."

Dulcie

(alt. Dulce, Dulcia)

Latin, meaning "sweet."

Dusty

(alt. Dusti)

Old German, meaning "brave warrior." Famous as the name of singer Dusty Springfield.

E Girls' names

Earla
English, meaning "leader."

Eartha
English, meaning "earth." Associated with singer Eartha Kitt.

Easter
Egyptian, from the festival and Pacific island of the same name.

Ebba
English, meaning "fortress of riches." A Top 10 name for girls in Sweden.

Ebony
(alt. Eboni)

Latin, meaning "deep, black wood." Made famous by the song "Ebony and Ivory" by Paul McCartney and Stevie Wonder.

Echo
Greek, meaning "reflected sound." Echo was the name of a nymph in Greek mythology.

Eda
(alt. Edda)

English, meaning "wealthy and happy." An ancient goddess of time and wealth.

Edelmira
Spanish, meaning "admired for nobility."

Eden
(alt. Edie, Eddie)

Hebrew, meaning "pleasure."

Edina
Scottish, meaning "from Edinburgh."

Edith
(alt. Edyth)

English, meaning "prosperity through battle." Edith Wharton was a Pulitzer Prize-winning author.

Edna
Hebrew, meaning "enjoyment."

Edrea

English, meaning "wealthy and powerful." Edrea Vorsal is an opera singer.

Edwina

English, meaning "wealthy friend." Associated with socialite Edwina Mountbatten.

Effie

Greek, meaning "pleasant speech." Effie Trinket is a character in "The Hunger Games" series.

Eglantine

French, from the flowering shrub of the same name.

Eileen
(alt. Eibhlín)

Irish, meaning "shining and brilliant." Associated with the song "Come on Eileen" by Dexys Midnight Runners.

Ekaterina
(alt. Ekaterini)

Slavic, meaning "pure."

Elaine
(alt. Elaina, Elayne)

French, meaning "bright, shining light." Elaine Stritch is an actor and singer.

Elba

Italian, from the island of the same name.

Elberta

English, meaning "high-born."

Eldora

Spanish, meaning "covered with gold."

Eleanor
(alt. Alienor, Aliana, Elana, Elanor, Eleanora, Eleanore, Elena, Eleni, Elenor, Elenora, Elina, Elinor, Elinore; abbrev. Elie, Ellie)

Greek, meaning "light." Queen Eleanor of Aquitane was married to England's Henry II and was one of the most influential, wealthy, and powerful women of the Middle Ages.

Electra
(alt. Elektra)

Greek, meaning "shining." Famous as a character in ancient Greek myth.

Elfrida
(alt. Elfrieda)

English, meaning "elf power." Elfrida Andree is a composer.

Eliane
(alt. Eliana)

Hebrew, meaning "Jehovah is God."

Elissa
(alt. Elise)

French, meaning "pledged to God." The other name of Dido, the ancient Roman Queen of Carthage.

Eliza
(alt. Elisha, Elise)

Hebrew, meaning "pledged to God." Made famous by the character Eliza Doolittle from the play *Pygmalion* and film adaptation *My Fair Lady*.

Elizabeth
(alt. Elisabet, Elisabeth, Elizabella, Elsbeth, Elspet; abbrev. Bess, Bessie, Bet, Beth, Betty, Libby, Liz, Lizzie)

Hebrew, meaning "pledged to God." The name of the current Queen of England, Elizabeth II. The previous Queen Elizabeth I was also known as "Good Queen Bess."

Elke
German, meaning "nobility."

Ella
German, meaning "completely."

Elle
(alt. Ellie)

French, meaning "she." Elle Macpherson was one of the original 1980s supermodels, known as "The Body."

Ellen
(alt. Elin, Eline, Ellyn)

Greek, meaning "shining." Associated with comedian and TV host Ellen DeGeneres.

Ellice
(alt. Elyse)

Greek, meaning "the Lord is God."

Elma
(alt. Elna)

Latin, meaning "soul." Elma Napier is a pioneering Caribbean politician.

Elmira
(alt. Elmyra)

Arabic, meaning "aristocratic lady." Elmyra Duff is a cartoon character.

Elodie
French, meaning "marsh flower."

Eloise
(alt. Elois, Eloisa, Elouise)

French, meaning "renowned in battle."

Elsa
(alt. Else, Elsie)

Hebrew, meaning "pledged to God." Elsa is a character from Disney's *Frozen*.

Elula
Hebrew, meaning "August."

Elva
Irish, meaning "noble."

Elvina
English, meaning "noble friend."

Elvira
(alt. Elvera)

Spanish, from the place of the same name. Associated with the 1980s film *Elvira, Mistress of the Dark*.

Ember
(alt. Embry)

English, meaning "spark."

Emeline
German, meaning "industrious."

Emerald
English, meaning "green gemstone." A precious stone.

Emery
(alt. Emory)

German, meaning "ruler of work." A dark rock used in the manufacture of nail files.

Emilia
Latin, meaning "rival, eager." Associated with *Game of Thrones* actor Emilia Clarke.

Emily
(alt. Emelie, Emilee, Emilie, Emlyn)

Latin, meaning "rival, eager." Famous Emilys include actor Emily Blunt and author Emily Dickinson.

Emma
(alt. Emme, Emmi, Emmie, Emmy)

German, meaning "embraces everything." Made famous by Jane Austen's novel *Emma*.

Emmanuelle
Hebrew, meaning "God is among us."

Emmeline
(alt. Emmelina; abbrev. Emi, Emme, Emmie, Emmy)

German, meaning "embraces everything." Emmeline Pankhurst was a British activist and suffragette, named by *Time* magazine as "One of the 100 Most Important People of the Twentieth Century."

Ena
Shortened form of Georgina, meaning "farmer."

Enid
(alt. Eneida)

Welsh, meaning "life spirit." Enid Blyton was an English children's novelist.

Enola
Native American, meaning "solitary." Associated with the song "Enola Gay."

Ensley
English, meaning "one's own meadow."

Enya
Irish Gaelic, meaning "fire." Irish singer Enya's birth name was Eithne.

Erica
(alt. Ericka, Erika)

Scandinavian, meaning "ruler forever." Erica Durance is an actor.

Erin
(alt. Eryn)

Irish Gaelic, meaning "from the isle to the west." An old name for Ireland. Erin Brockovich is a legal clerk and activist, portrayed by Julia Roberts in the film of the same name.

Eris

Greek, from the mythological heroine of the same name. Eris is responsible for chaos, strife, and discord.

Erlinda

Hebrew, meaning "spirited."

Erma

German, meaning "universal."

Ermine

French, meaning "weasel." The fur of a stoat or weasel is known as ermine.

Erna

English, meaning "sincere." A character in Norse mythology.

Ernestine
(alt. Ernestina)

English, meaning "sincere." Ernestine Gilbreth Carey is the author of *Cheaper By the Dozen*.

Esme

French, meaning "esteemed." Esme Cullen is a character in *Twilight*.

Esmeralda

Spanish, meaning "emerald." Esmeralda is a lead character in *The Hunchback of Notre Dame*.

Esperanza

Spanish, meaning "hope."

Estelle
(alt. Estela, Estell, Estella)

French, meaning "star." Associated with R&B singer Estelle.

Esther
(alt. Esta, Ester, Etha, Ethna, Ethne)

Persian, meaning "star." A character in the biblical Book of Esther.

Eternity

Latin, meaning "forever."

Ethel
(alt. Ethyl)

English, meaning "noble." Ethel Merman was an actor and singer, best known for rousing musical theater.

Etta
(alt. Etter, Ettie)

Shortened form of Henrietta, meaning "ruler of the house." Famous Ettas include singer Etta James (real name Janesetta), and DC Comic character Etta Candy.

Eudora

Greek, meaning "generous gift." Eudora is a character in Disney's *Princess and the Frog*.

Eugenia
(alt. Eugenie)

Greek, meaning "well born." Princess Eugenie is a granddaughter of Queen Elizabeth II.

Eulalia
(alt. Eula, Eulah, Eulalie)

Greek, meaning "sweetspeaking." Associated with St. Eulalia.

Eunice
(alt. Unice)

Greek, meaning "victorious." Eunice Kennedy Shriver was John F. Kennedy's sister and the founder of the Special Olympics.

Euphemia

Greek, meaning " favorable speech."

Eva

Hebrew, meaning "life." Eva Peron was the real-life inspiration for the musical *Evita*.

Evadne

Greek, meaning "pleasing one."

Evangeline
(alt. Evangelina)

Greek, meaning "good news." The very first musical comedy was called *Evangeline*, in 1874.

Evanthe

Greek, meaning "good flower."

Eve
(alt. Evie)

Hebrew, meaning "life." The Bible story names Eve as the first woman to walk on the Earth.

Evelina
(alt. Evelia)

German, meaning "hazelnut." The title of a novel by 18th-century author Fanny Burney.

Evelyn
(alt. Evalyn, Evelin, Eveline, Evelyne)

German, meaning "hazelnut." Famous Evelyns include singer Evelyn "Champagne" King, deaf virtuoso percussionist Evelyn Glennie and novelist Evelyn Waugh (who was in fact a man).

Everly
(alt. Everleigh, Everley)

English, meaning "grazing meadow."

Evette

French, meaning "yew wood."

Evonne
(alt. Evon)

French, meaning "yew wood." Made famous by Australian tennis pro Evonne Goolagong.

Girls' names

Fabia

(alt. *Fabiana, Fabienne, Fabiola, Fabriana*)

Latin, meaning "from the Fabian clan."

Fabrizia

Italian, meaning "works with hands."

Faith

English, meaning "loyalty." Famous Faiths include singers Faith Hill and Faith Evans.

Faiza

Arabic, meaning "victorious."

Fallon

Irish Gaelic, meaning "descended from a ruler."

Fanny

(alt. *Fannie*)

Latin, meaning "from France." The heroine of Jane Austen's *Mansfield Park* is Fanny Price.

Farica

German, meaning "peaceful ruler."

Farrah

English, meaning "lovely and pleasant." Associated with actor Farrah Fawcett and reality TV star Farrah Abraham.

Fatima

Arabic, meaning "baby's nurse."

Faustine

Latin, meaning "fortunate."

Fawn

(alt. *Fawne*)

French, meaning "young deer." Also the light brown color.

Fay

(alt. *Fae, Faye*)

French, meaning "fairy." Famous Fays include author Fay Weldon and original *King Kong* actor Fay Wray.

Felicia

(alt. Felecia, Felice, Felicita, Felisha)

Latin, meaning "lucky and happy." Famous Felicias include actors Felicia Day and Felicia Farr, and *American Idol*'s Felicia Barton.

Felicity

Latin, meaning "fortunate."

Fenella

Irish Gaelic, meaning "white shoulder." Made famous by actor Fenella Fielding.

Fenia

Scandinavian, from the mythological giantess of the same name.

Fern

(alt. Fearn, Fearne, Ferne, Ferrin)

English, from the plant of the same name.

Fernanda

German, meaning "peace and courage."

Ffion

(alt. Fion)

Irish Gaelic, meaning "fair and pale" or "foxglove." Very popular name for baby girls in Wales.

Fia

Italian, meaning "flame." Also a nickname for Fiona.

Fifi

Hebrew, meaning "Jehovah increases."

Filomena

Greek, meaning "loved one."

Finlay

(alt. Finley)

Irish Gaelic, meaning "fair-headed courageous one." Used for girls or, more commonly, boys.

Finola

(alt. Fionnula)

Irish Gaelic, meaning "fair shoulder." Associated with actor Finola Hughes.

Fiona

(alt. Fiora)

Irish Gaelic and Scottish, meaning "fair and pale." Princess Fiona is a character in *Shrek*.

Flanna

(alt. Flannery)

Irish Gaelic, meaning "russet hair" or "red hair."

Flavia

Latin, meaning "yellow hair."

Fleur

(alt. Flor)

French, meaning "flower." Fleur Delacour is a character in the *Harry Potter* series.

Flora

Latin, meaning "flower." A fairy godmother in Disney's *Sleeping Beauty* (she was the red one).

Florence

(alt. Florencia, Florene, Florine; abbrev. Flo, Florrie, Flossie, Floy)

Latin, meaning "in bloom." Associated with the Italian city of the same name.

Florida

Latin, meaning "flowery." Also the southern state.

Frances

(alt. Francine, Francis; abbrev. Fanny, Fran, Frankie, Frannie, Franny)

Latin, meaning "from France." Famous Franceses include actor Frances McDormand and playwright Frances Hodgson Burnett.

Francesca

(alt. Franchesca, Francisca)

Latin, meaning "from France." Francesca Simon is a children's author.

Freda

(alt. Freida, Frida, Frieda)

German, meaning "peaceful." Associated with artist Frida Kahlo.

Frederica

German, meaning "peaceful ruler." Popular name for modern European princesses.

Fuchsia

German, from the flower of the same name.

Girls' names

Gabrielle
(alt. Gabriel, Gabriela, Gabriella; abbrev. Gabbi, Gabby)
Hebrew, meaning "heroine of God."
A character in *Xena: Warrior Princess.*

Gaia
(alt. Gaea)
Greek, meaning "the earth." Gaia was the ancient Greek Mother Goddess.

Gail
(alt. Gale, Gayla, Gayle)
Hebrew, meaning "my father rejoices." Gail O'Grady is an actor and producer.

Gal
Hebrew, meaning "wave." Made famous by *Wonder Woman* actor Gal Gadot.

Gala
French, meaning "festive merrymaking."

Galiena
German, meaning "high one."

Galina
Russian, meaning "shining brightly."

Garnet
(alt. Garnett)
English, meaning "red gemstone." Can be used as a twin name alongside Ruby.

Gay
(alt. Gaye)
French, meaning "glad and lighthearted."

Gaynor
Welsh, meaning "white and smooth." Associated with singer Gloria Gaynor.

Gemini

Greek, meaning "twin." The third astrological sign in the Zodiac.

Gemma
(alt. Jemma)

Italian, meaning "precious stone." Well-known Gemmas include actor Gemma Arterton.

Gene

Greek, meaning "well born." Usually a boys' name, as with actor and dancer Gene Kelly, but can be used for girls.

Genesis

Greek, meaning "beginning." Associated with the first book of the Old Testament, and the band Genesis.

Geneva
(alt. Genevra)

French, meaning "juniper tree." A city in Switzerland.

Genevieve
(alt. Genie)

German, meaning "white wave." St. Genevieve is said to have saved Paris.

Georgia
(alt. Georgie)

Greek, meaning "farmer." Also the southern US state and a European country.

Georgina
(alt. Georgene, Georgette, Georgiana, Georgianna, Georgine, Giorgina; abbrev. Giget, Gigi)

Greek, meaning "farmer." Georgina Chapman is an actor and fashion designer. Gigi is the title of the novel and musical.

Geraldine
(abbrev. Geri)

German, meaning "spear ruler." Geraldine Chaplin is an actor and Geri Halliwell is "Ginger Spice" of the Spice Girls.

Gerda

Nordic, meaning "shelter." A character from Hans Christian Andersen's Snow Queen.

Germaine

French, meaning "from Germany." Germaine Greer is an author and activist.

Gertrude
(alt. Gertie)

German, meaning "strength of a spear." Made famous by author Gertrude Stein.

Gia
(alt. Ghia)

Italian, meaning "God is gracious."

Gianina
(alt. Giana)

Hebrew, meaning "God's graciousness."

Gilda

English, meaning "gilded." A character from Verdi's opera *Rigoletto*.

Gilia

Hebrew, meaning "joy of the Lord." Also a genus of flowering plants.

Gillian

Latin, meaning "youthful." Famous Gillians include actor Gillian Anderson and author Gillian Cross.

Ginger

Latin, from the root of the same name.

Giovanna

Italian, meaning "God is gracious."

Giselle
(alt. Gisela, Gisele, Giselle, Gisselle)

German, meaning "pledge." Famous Giselles include the romantic ballet, and supermodel Gisele Bündchen.

Gita
(alt. Geeta)

Sanskrit, meaning "song." The Bhagavad Gita is an important part of Hindu scripture, and is often simply known as the Gita.

Giulia
(alt. Giuliana)

Italian, meaning "youthful." Associated with TV host Giuliana Rancic.

Gladys
(alt. Gladyce)

Welsh, meaning "lame." Gladys Knight is a singer.

Glenda

Welsh, meaning "fair and good."

Glenna
(alt. Glennie)

Irish Gaelic, meaning "glen."

Gloria
(alt. Glory)

Latin, meaning "glory." Famous Glorias include singers Gloria Estefan and Gloria Gaynor.

Glynda
(alt. Glinda)

Welsh, meaning "fair." Name of the good witch in *The Wizard of Oz*.

Glynis

Welsh, meaning "small glen." Glynis Nunn is a heptathlon athlete.

Golda
(alt. Goldia, Goldie)

English, meaning "gold." Golda Meir is the former Israeli Prime Minister.

Grace
(alt. Graça, Gracie, Gracin, Grayce)

Latin, meaning "grace." The actor Grace Kelly became Princess Grace of Monaco.

Grainne
(alt. Grania)

Irish Gaelic, meaning "love." Also an ancient goddess of corn.

Gratia
(alt. Grasia)

Latin, meaning "blessing." Gratia was the ancient Greek goddess of charm, beauty, and fertility.

Greer
(alt. Grier)

Latin, meaning "alert and watchful."

Gregoria

Latin, meaning "alert."

Greta
(alt. Gretel)

Greek, meaning "pearl." One of the characters in the fairy tale *Hansel and Gretel*.

Gretchen

German, meaning "pearl." Gretchen Mol is an actor.

Griselda
(alt. Griselle)

German, meaning "gray fighting maid."

Gudrun

Scandinavian, meaning "battle."

Guinevere

Welsh, meaning "white and smooth." The legendary Queen consort of King Arthur.

Gwenda

Welsh, meaning "fair and good."

Gwendolyn
(alt. Gwen, Gwendolen, Gwenel)

Welsh, meaning "fair bow." Gwendolyn Brooks is a poet.

Gwyneth
(alt. Gwynneth, Gwynyth)

Welsh, meaning "happiness." Made famous by actor Gwyneth Paltrow.

Gwynn
(alt. Gwyn)

Welsh, meaning "fair blessed."

Gypsy

English, meaning "of the Roman tribe." Associated with the movie *Gypsy*.

H Girls' names

Hadassah

Hebrew, meaning "myrtle tree." The Hebrew name for Esther in the Bible.

Hadley

English, meaning "heather meadow." Hadley Richardson was the wife of Ernest Hemingway.

Hadria

Latin, meaning "from Hadria." The name of two ancient cities in Italy.

Hala

Arabic, meaning "halo." A female weather demon in Serbian mythology.

Haley

(alt. Hailee, Hailey, Hailie, Haleigh, Hali, Halie, Haylee, Hayleigh, Hayley, Haylie)

English, meaning "hay meadow." Famous Haleys include singer Haley Reinhart and singer Hayley Mills.

Halima

(alt. Halimah, Halina)

Arabic, meaning "gentle." The prophet Mohammad's foster mother was called Halimah.

Hallie

(alt. Halle, Halley)

German, meaning "ruler of the home or estate." Associated with actor Halle Berry.

Hannah

(alt. Haana, Hana, Hanna)

Hebrew, meaning "grace." Famous Hannahs include actor Hannah Gordon and musical comedy Hannah Montana.

Harley

(alt. Harlene)

English, meaning "the long field." Used for girls and boys. Made famous by the Harley-Davidson motorbike company.

Harlow

English, meaning "army hill."

Harmony

Latin, meaning "harmony."

Harper

English, meaning "minstrel." Has risen in popularity after its use by Victoria and David Beckham for their daughter Harper Seven.

Harriet

(alt. Harriett, Harriette, Hattie)

German, meaning "ruler of the home or estate." Famous Harriets include activist Harriet Tubman and author Harriet Beecher Stowe.

Haven

English, meaning "a place of sanctuary."

Hayden

Old English, meaning "hedged valley."

Hazel

(alt. Hazle)

English, from the tree of the same name. Also an eye color.

Heather

English, from the flower of the same name. Famous Heathers include actors Heather Graham and Heather Locklear, and model Heather Mills.

Heaven

English, meaning "everlasting bliss."

Hedda

German, meaning "warfare." *Hedda Gabler* is a play by Henrik Ibsen.

Hedwig

German, meaning "warfare and strife." Also Harry Potter's constant owl companion.

Heidi

(alt. Heidy)

German, meaning "nobility." The title of a children's book *Heidi* by Johanna Spyri.

Helen

(alt. Halen, Helena, Helene, Hellen)

Greek, meaning "light." In Greek mythology Helen of Troy was considered to be the most beautiful woman in the world.

Helga

German, meaning "holy and sacred."

Heloise

French, meaning "renowned in war." Heloise d'Argenteuil was a nun and writer.

Henrietta

(alt. Henriette)

German, meaning "ruler of the house." Henrietta Maria of France was queen consort to England's King Charles I.

Long names

Alexandria
Bernadette
Christabelle
Constantina
Evangeline
Gabrielle
Henrietta
Jacqueline
Marguerite
Wilhelmina

Hephzibah

Hebrew, meaning "my delight is in her." A character in the Bible.

Hera

Greek, meaning "queen." Hera is the ancient Greek Queen of the Gods and the goddess of marriage, women, and births.

Hermia
(alt. Hermina, Hermine, Herminia)

Greek, meaning "messenger." A character from Shakespeare's play *A Midsummer Night's Dream.*

Hermione

Greek, meaning "earthly." Harry Potter's closest (and smartest) female friend.

Hero

Greek, meaning "brave one of the people."

Hertha

English, meaning "earth." Another name for Nerthus, the goddess of fertility in ancient German mythology.

Hesper
(alt. Hesperia)

Greek, meaning "evening star." The first evening star in ancient Greece.

Hester
(alt. Hestia)

Greek, meaning "star." Hester Prynne is a character from *The Scarlet Letter.*

Hilary
(alt. Hillary)

Greek, meaning "cheerful and happy." Famous Hilarys include actor Hilary Swank and politician Hillary Rodham Clinton.

Hilda
(alt. Hildur)

German, meaning "battle woman." The first female pilot to own a license was Hilda Hewlett.

Hildegarde
(alt. Hildegard)

German, meaning "battle stronghold."

Hildred

German, meaning "battle counselor."

Hilma

German, meaning "helmet."

Hollis

English, meaning "near the holly bushes."

Holly
(alt. Holli, Hollie)

English, from the tree of the same name. Famous Hollys include writer Holly Black and actor Holly Hunter.

Honey

English, meaning "sweet nectar."

Honor
(alt. Honora, Honoria, Honour)

Latin, meaning "woman of worth and respect." Actor Honor Blackman played Bond girl Pussy Galore in *Goldfinger*.

Hope

English, meaning "desire and expectation." One of the three virtues: faith, hope, and charity.

Hortense
(alt. Hortencia, Hortensia)

Latin, meaning "of the garden." The name of Napoleon Bonaparte's mother.

Hulda

German, meaning "loved one." A prophetess in the Bible.

Hyacinth

Greek, from the flower of the same name. A hero in ancient Greek mythology.

I Girls' names

Ianthe
(alt. Iantha)
Greek, meaning "purple flower."

Ida
(alt. Idell, Idella)
English, meaning "prosperous." Ida B. Wells was a prominent African-American civil rights activist and journalist.

Idona
Nordic, meaning "renewal."

Ignacia
Latin, meaning "ardent."

Ila
French, meaning "island." In Hindu mythology, Ila is a character able to change sexes at will.

Ilana
Hebrew, meaning "tree." Famous Ilanas include pianist Ilana Vered and a character in TV series *Lost*.

Ilaria
Italian, meaning "cheerful."

Ilene
American English, meaning "light." Ilene Woods was the voice of Disney's *Cinderella*.

Iliana
(alt. Ileana)
Greek, meaning "Trojan."

Ilona
Hungarian, meaning "light." The name of the Queen of the Fairies in Magyar mythology.

Ilsa
German, meaning "pledged to God." The character played by Ingrid Bergman in *Casablanca*.

Ima

German, meaning "embraces everything."

Iman

Arabic, meaning "faith." Associated with the model, actor and entrepreneur known simply as Iman.

Imelda

German, meaning "all-consuming fight." Imelda Staunton is an Oscar nominated British actor.

Imogen
(alt. Imogene)

Latin, meaning "last-born."

Ina

Latin, meaning "to make feminine." Famous Inas include author and presenter Ina Garten, childbirth pioneer Ina May Gaskin, and the Ina language of Brazil.

Inaya

Arabic, meaning "taking care."

India
(alt. Indie)

Hindi, from the country of the same name. India Arie is a singer.

Indiana

Latin, meaning "from India." Also the Midwestern state.

Indigo

Greek, meaning "deep blue dye." One of the seven colors of the rainbow.

Indira
(alt. Inira)

Sanskrit, meaning "beauty." Indira Gandhi was the first and only female prime minister of India.

Inez
(alt. Ines)

Spanish, meaning "pure."

Inga
(alt. Inge, Ingeborg, Inger)

Scandinavian, meaning "guarded by Ing."

Ingrid

Scandinavian, meaning "beautiful." Made famous by actor Ingrid Bergman.

Io
(alt. Eye)

Greek, from the mythological priestess and heroine of the same name.

Ioanna

Greek, meaning "grace."

Iola
(alt. Iole)

Greek, meaning "cloud of dawn." Iola Leory by Frances Harper is one of the first published novels by a black female author.

Iolanthe

Greek, meaning "violet flower." The title of a comic opera by Gilbert and Sullivan.

Iona

Greek, from the island of the same name.

Ione

Greek, meaning "violet." Also a genus of orchid.

Iphigenia

Greek, meaning "sacrifice." The ancient Greek victim of slaughter, who became known as the mother of all strong children.

Ira

(alt. Iva)

Hebrew, meaning "watchful."

Irene

(alt. Irelyn, Irena, Irina, Irini)

Greek, meaning "peace." Singer Irene Cara won an Academy Award for Best Original Song.

Iris

Greek, meaning "rainbow." Also a flower and the Greek goddess who travels with the speed of wind from one end of the rainbow to the other, and from sea to sky, and connects the gods with humanity.

Irma

German, meaning "universal."

Isabel

(alt. Isabela, Isabell, Isabella, Isabelle, Isobel, Izabella, Izabelle; abbrev. Izzie, Izzy)

Spanish, meaning "pledged to God." The name of various historical members of European royal families, including Queen Isabella I of Spain. Isabella Swan is the lead character in the "Twilight" series.

Isadora

Latin, meaning "gift of Isis."

Ishana

Hindi, meaning "desire." One of the names for Shiva in the Hindu faith.

Isis

Egyptian, from the goddess of the same name. She was worshipped as the ideal mother and wife, and the goddess of nature and magic.

Isla

(alt. Isa, Isela, Isley)

Scottish Gaelic, meaning "river." Isla Fischer is an actor.

Isolde

Welsh, meaning "fair lady." A character in Richard Wagner's opera *Tristan und Isolde*.

Istas

Native American, meaning "snow."

Ivana

(alt. Iva, Ivanka)

Slavic, meaning "Jehovah is gracious." Associated with model Ivana Trump.

Ivory

Latin, meaning "white as elephant tusks."

Ivy

English, from the plant of the same name. Beyoncé and Jay-Z's daughter is Blue Ivy.

Ixia

South African, from the flower of the same name.

J

Girls' names

Jacinda
(alt. Jacinta)

Spanish, meaning "hyacinth." Jacinda Barrett is an actor.

Jacqueline
(alt. Jacalyn, Jacklyn, Jaclyn, Jacquelin, Jacquelyn, Jacquline, Jaquelin, Jaqueline; abbrev. Jackie, Jacky, Jacqui)

French, meaning "he who supplants." Famous Jacquelines include actor Jacqueline Bisset, cellist Jacqueline du Pré, First Lady Jacqueline (Jackie) Kennedy Onassis, and singer Jackie Evancho.

Jade
(alt. Jada, Jaida, Jayda, Jayde)

Spanish, meaning "green stone." Associated with TV host Jade McCarthy.

Jaden
(alt. Jadyn, Jaiden, Jayden)

Contraction of Jade and Hayden, meaning "green hedged valley." Used for girls as well as for boys.

Jael

Hebrew, meaning "mountain goat." A character in the Bible.

Jaime
(alt. Jaima, Jaimie, Jami, Jamie)

Spanish, meaning "he who supplants." J'aime is also French for "I love."

Jamila

Arabic, meaning "lovely." Jamila Gavin is a children's author.

Jan
(alt. Jana, Janae, Janay, Jann, Janna, Joana)

Hebrew, meaning "the Lord is gracious"; Arabic, meaning "dear"; and Persian, meaning "life."

Jane
(alt. Jayne)

Feminine form of John, meaning "the Lord is gracious." Famous Janes include actors Jane Lynch, Jane Seymour, and Jayne Mansfield.

Janelle
(alt. Janael, Janel, Janell, Jenelle)

American English, derived from Jane, meaning "the Lord is gracious." Janelle Monae is a singer and Janell Burse is a professional basketball player.

Janet
(alt. Janette)

Scottish, meaning "the Lord is gracious." Famous Janets include singer Janet Jackson and Olympic champion swimmer Janet Evans.

Janice
(alt. Janis)

American, meaning "the Lord is gracious." Janice Dickinson is a former supermodel.

Janie
(alt. Janey, Janney, Jannie)

Derived from Jane or short form of Janet, meaning "the Lord is gracious." Famous Janies include Motown songwriter Janie Bradford, country singer Janie Frickie and Janie Hendrix, the sister of musician Jimi.

Janine
(alt. Janeen)

English, meaning "the Lord is gracious." Associated with actor Janine Turner.

Janoah
(alt. Janiya, Janiyah)

Hebrew, meaning "quiet and calm."

January

Latin, meaning "the first month." January Jones is an actor.

Jasmine
(alt. Jasmin, Jazim, Jazmine)

Persian, meaning "jasmine flower." Also the princess in Disney's Aladdin.

Jay

Latin, meaning "jaybird."

Jayna

Sanskrit, meaning "bringer of victory."

Jean

(alt. Jeane, Jeanie, Jeanne, Jeannie)

Scottish, meaning "the Lord is gracious." Jean Harlow was a glamorous acting star of the 1930s. Also associated with the sitcom *I Dream of Jeannie*.

Jeana

(alt. Jeanna)

Latin, meaning "queen."

Jeanette

(alt. Jeannette, Janette)

French, meaning "the Lord is gracious." Jeanette MacDonald is an actor.

Jeanine

(alt. Jeannine)

Latin, meaning "the Lord is gracious."

Jemima

Hebrew, meaning "dove." Famous Jemimas include writer Jemima Khan, actor Jemima Kirke, and the children's character Jemima Puddle-Duck.

Jena

Arabic, meaning "little bird."

Jennifer

(alt. Jenifer; abbrev. Jenna, Jennie, Jenny)

Cornish alternative to Guinevere, meaning "white and smooth." Famous Jennifers include actors

Jennifer Lawrence, Jennifer Aniston, Jenna Elfman, Jenna Dewan, and singer Jennifer Hudson.

Jerrie

(alt. Jeri, Jerri, Jerrie, Jerry)

German, meaning "spear ruler." Jerry Hall is a model and actor, known also for her marriage to Mick Jagger.

Jerusha

Hebrew, meaning "married." Jerusha Hess is a film maker.

Jeryl

English, meaning "spear ruler." Associated with actor Jeryl Prescott.

Jessamy

(alt. Jessame, Jessamine, Jessamyn)

Persian, meaning "jasmine flower." Also a children's book by Barbara Sleigh.

Jessica

(alt. Jesica, Jessika; abbrev. Jess, Jessa, Jessie)

Hebrew, meaning "He sees." Famous Jessicas include actors Jessica Alba and Jessica Lange, singer Jessie J and the character Jess from *Girls*.

Jesusa

Spanish, meaning "mother of the Lord."

Jette
(alt. Jetta, Jettie)
Danish, meaning "black as coal."

Jewel
(alt. Jewell)
French, meaning "delight." Associated with singer songwriter Jewel.

Jezebel
(alt. Jezabel, Jezabelle)
Hebrew, meaning "pure and virginal." The misbehaving wife of King Ahab in the Bible.

Jill
Latin, meaning "youthful."

Jillian
Latin, meaning "youthful." Jillian Michaels is a personal trainer and TV personality.

Jimena
Spanish, meaning "heard."

Joan
Hebrew, meaning "the Lord is gracious." Famous Joans include St. Joan of Arc, actor Joan Collins, and comedian Joan Rivers.

Short names
Bea
Bo
Fay
Jan
Jo
Kay
Kim
May
Mia
Val

Joanna
(alt. Joana, Joanie, Joann, Joanne, Johanna, Joni; abbrev. Jo)
Hebrew, meaning "the Lord is gracious." Famous Joannas include author J. K. Rowling (real name Joanne), and actors Joanna Lumley and Joanna Page.

Jocasta
Italian, meaning "lighthearted." A character in ancient Greek mythology.

Jocelyn
(alt. Jauslyn, Jocelyne, Joscelin, Joslyn; abbrev. Joss)
German, meaning "cheerful." Famous Jocelyns include renowned American socialite Jocelyn Wildenstein, singer Jocelyn Brown, and English soul singer songwriter Joss Stone.

Jody
(alt. Jodee, Jodi, Jodie)

Shortened form of Judith, meaning "Jewish." Made famous by actor Jodie Foster.

Joelle
(alt. Joela)

Hebrew, meaning "Jehovah is the Lord."

Joie

French, meaning "joy."

Jolene

Contraction of Joanna and Darlene, meaning "gracious darling." The title of a song by Dolly Parton.

Jolie
(alt. Joely)

French, meaning "pretty." Made famous by actor and director Angelina Jolie.

Jonisa
(alt. Jonisha)

Hebrew and French, meaning "God is gracious."

Jordan
(alt. Jordana, Jordin, Jordyn)

Hebrew, meaning "descend." Made famous by singer Jordan Sparks.

Jorgina

Dutch, meaning "farmer."

Josephine
(alt. Josefina, Josephina; abbrev. Jo, Josie, Joss)

Hebrew, meaning "Jehovah increases." Famous Josephines include actor Josephine Baker, author Josephine Bell, and comedian Josie Lawrence.

Jovita
(alt. Jovie)

Latin, meaning "made glad." Associated with St. Jovita.

Joy

Latin, meaning "joy." Joy Behar is a comedian.

Joyce

Latin, meaning "joyous." Famous Joyces include author Joyce Carol Oates and actors Joyce Blair and Joyce DeWitt.

Juanita
(alt. Juana)

Spanish, meaning "the Lord is gracious." Associated with the ice maiden Mummy Juanita.

Jubilee

Hebrew, meaning "ram's horn" or "special anniversary." The celebration of an anniversary.

Judith

(alt. Judit; abbrev. Jude, Judi, Judy)

Hebrew, meaning "Jewish." Famous Judiths include the character in the Bible and actors Judy Garland and Judi Dench.

Jules

French, meaning "Jove's child." Also an abbreviation of Julian used for boys.

Julia

(alt. Juli, Julie)

Latin, meaning "youthful." Famous Julias include actor Julia Roberts, TV chef Julia Childs, and actor and singer Julie Andrews.

Julianne

(alt. Juliana, Juliann, Julianna)

Latin, meaning "youthful." Julianne Moore and Julianna Margulies are both actors.

Juliet

(alt. Joliet, Juliette)

Latin, meaning "youthful." A character in Shakespeare's play *Romeo and Juliet*.

June

(alt. Juna)

Latin, after the month of the same name. The name of several American actors famous in the period 1930–60, and country singer June Carter Cash.

Juniper

Dutch, from the shrub of the same name used in the production of gin.

Juno

(alt. Juneau)

Latin, meaning "queen of heaven." Juno was an ancient Roman goddess of marriage and Rome.

Justice

English, meaning "to deliver what is just." The female spirit of Justice is depicted with balance scales, a blindfold, and a sword.

Justine

(alt. Justina)

Latin, meaning "fair and righteous." Famous Justines include the Christian saint, and actor Justine Bateman.

K Girls' names

Kady
(alt. Kadi, Kadie)
Irish Gaelic, meaning "a rhythmic flow of sounds."

Kailani
(alt. Kehlani)
Hawaiian, meaning "sea and sky."

Kala
(alt. Kaela, Kaiala, Kaila)
Sanskrit, meaning "black one." The great ape that saved Tarzan as a baby.

Kali
(alt. Kailey, Kaleigh, Kaley, Kalie, Kalli, Kally, Kaylee, Kayleigh)
Sanskrit, meaning "black one." Also the Hindu goddess of time and change.

Kalila
Arabic, meaning "beloved."

Kalina
Slavic, meaning "flower."

Kama
Sanskrit, meaning "love." Associated with the Hindu goal of intellectual fulfillment.

Kami
Japanese, meaning "lord."

Kamilla
(alt. Kamilah)
Slavic, meaning "serving girl."

Kana
Hawaiian, from the demi-god of the same name who could take the form of a rope that could stretch from Molokai to Hawaii.

Kara
Latin, meaning "dear one." The bracelet worn by Sikhs.

Karen
(alt. Caren, Carin, Caron, Caryn, Karan, Karin, Karina, Karon, Karren; abbrev. Kari)

Greek, meaning "pure." Famous Karens include singer Karen Carpenter, actor Karen Gillan, and TV host and scientist Kari Byron.

Karimah

Arabic, meaning "giving."

Karishma
(alt. Karisma)

Sanskrit, meaning "miracle." Karisma Kapoor is an actor.

Karissa
(alt. Carissa, Korissa)

Greek, meaning "very dear."

Karma

Hindi, meaning "destiny." Karma is the principle of good and bad deeds being returned to you.

Kate
(alt. Kat, Katie, Kathi, Kathie, Kathy, Kati, Katy)

Derived from or used as a shortened form of Catherine or Katherine, meaning "pure." Actors Kate Winslet and Kate Hudson were given the name Kate. The Duchess of Cambridge, formerly Kate Middleton, was given the name Catherine.

Katherine
(alt. Katharine, Kathrine, Kathryn, Katrina, Katya, Katyea; abbrev. Kate, Kathy, Katie, Katy, Kay, Kitty)

Greek, meaning "pure." Also spelled with a C rather than a K, both forms

are frequently used. Katya is the Russian form of Katherine.

Kathleen
(alt. Kathlyn)

Greek, meaning "pure." Kathleen Robertson is an actor.

Katniss

From one of the common names of the aquatic plant genus Sagittaria. Made famous by the character Katniss Everdeen from "The Hunger Games" trilogy.

Kaya

Sanskrit, meaning "nature," or Turkish, meaning "rock." Also a sweet coconut jam.

Kayla
(alt. Kaylah)

Greek, meaning "pure." Also Gaelic, meaning "slim" and "fair."

Kaylee
(alt. Kayley, Kayleigh, Kayli, Kaylin)

Derived from Kayla, meaning "pure." Kayley is a character from The Magic Sword: Quest for Camelot.

Keeley
(alt. Keely)

Irish, meaning "battle maid." Keeley Hawes is an actor.

Keila

Hebrew, meaning "citadel."

Keira

Irish Gaelic, meaning "dark." Name of actor Keira Knightley.

Keisha
(alt. Keesha)

Arabic, meaning "woman." Name of actor Keisha Pulliam.

Kelila

Hebrew, meaning "crown of laurel."

Kelis

American English, meaning "beautiful." Kelis is an R&B singer.

Kelly
(alt. Keli, Kelley, Kelli, Kellie)

Irish Gaelic, meaning "battle maid." Famous Kellys include singer Kelly Clarkson and TV personality Kelly Osbourne.

Kelsey
(alt. Kelcie, Kelsea, Kelsi, Kelsie)

English, meaning "island."

Kendall
(alt. Kendal)

English, meaning "the valley of the Kent."

Kendra

English, meaning "knowing." Kendra Wilkinson is a reality TV star.

Kenna

Irish Gaelic, meaning "handsome."

Kennedy
(alt. Kenadee, Kennedi)

Irish Gaelic, meaning "helmet head." Made famous by the Kennedy family.

Kenya

African, from the eponymous country.

Kenzie

Shortened form of Mackenzie, meaning "son of the wise ruler."

Kerensa

Cornish, meaning "love." Also used as a spelling variation of Karen.

Kerrigan

Irish, meaning "black haired."

Kerry
(alt. Keri, Kerri, Kerrie)

Irish, from the eponymous county.

Khadijah
(alt. Khadejah)

Arabic, meaning "premature baby." Khadija bint Khuwaylid was the first wife of Muhammad and known as the "Mother of Islam."

Kiana
(alt. Kia, Kianna)

American English, meaning "fibre." Associated with TV personality Kiana.

Kiara

Italian, meaning "light." St. Kiara saved an Irish town from a fire through prayer.

Kiki

Spanish, meaning "home ruler." "Let's Have a Kiki" is a song by the Scissor Sisters. Kiki Dee was the stage name of a pop singer from the 1970s.

Kimberly

(alt. Kimberleigh, Kimberley; abbrev. Kim, Kimmy)

Old English, meaning "royal forest." Also a town in South Africa. Famous Kimberlys include reality star Kim Kardashian and singer Lil' Kim.

Kingsley

(alt. Kinsley)

English, meaning "king's meadow." Used for boys as well as girls.

Kinsey

English, meaning "king's victory."

Kira

Greek, meaning "lady." The antagonist in the popular Japanese anime Death Note.

Kiri

Maori, meaning "tree bark." Dame Kiri Te Kanawa is an opera singer.

Kirsten

(alt. Kirstin; abbrev. Kirstie, Kirsty)

Scandinavian, meaning "Christian." Kirsten Dunst and Kirstie Alley are actors and Kirsten Gillibrand a politician.

Kizzy

Hebrew, meaning the plant cassia.

Klara

Hungarian, meaning "bright."

Komal

Hindi, meaning "soft and tender."

Kristen

(alt. Kristan, Kristin, Kristine; abbrev. Kri, Krista, Kristi, Kristie, Kristy)

Greek, meaning "Christian." Famous Kristens include actor Kristen Stewart and reality TV star Kris Jenner.

Kwanza

(alt. Kwanzaa)

African, meaning "beginning." Also the name of the African-American festival in December and January.

Kyla

(alt. Kya, Kylah, Kyle)

Scottish, meaning "narrow spit of land." The name of actor Kyla Pratt.

Kylie

(alt. Kiley, Kylee)

Irish Gaelic, meaning "graceful." The name of singer Kylie Minogue.

Kyra

Greek, meaning "lady."

Kyrie

Greek, meaning "the Lord." Also a prayer sung at the beginning of Christian masses.

L Girls' names

Lacey
(alt. Laci, Lacie, Lacy)

French, from the town of the same name. Famous Laceys include actor Lacey Turner and dancer Lacey Schwimmer.

Ladonna
Italian, meaning "lady." A spelling alternative to Madonna.

Lady
English, meaning "bread kneader." A character from Disney's Lady and the Tramp.

Laila
(alt. Layla, Leila, Lejla, Lela, Lelah, Lelia)

Arabic, meaning "night." Famous Lailas include boxer Laila Ali, and the song "Layla" by Eric Clapton.

Lainey
(alt. Laine, Laney)

French, meaning "bright light."

Lakeisha
(alt. Lakeshia)

American English, meaning "woman." A contraction of La and Keisha.

Lakshmi
(alt. Laxmi)

Sanskrit, meaning "good omen." The Hindu goddess of wealth.

Lana
Greek, meaning "light." Famous Lanas include singer Lana Del Rey, and actor Lana Turner.

Lani
(alt. Lanie)

Hawaiian, meaning "heaven and sky."

Lara
Latin, meaning "famous." Famous Laras include actor Lara Flynn Boyle, Tomb Raider star Lara Croft, and an ancient Roman nymph.

Laraine

French, meaning "from Lorraine."

Larissa

(alt. Larisa)

Greek, meaning "light-hearted." Larissa was a nymph in ancient Greek mythology.

Lark

(alt. Larkin)

English, meaning "playful songbird."

Larsen

(alt. Larsan)

Scandinavian, meaning "son of Lars."

Latifa

Arabic, meaning "gentle and pleasant."

Latika

(alt. Lotika)

Hindi, meaning "a plant." Also a character in Slumdog Millionaire.

Latisha

Latin, meaning "happiness."

Latona

(alt. Latonia)

Latin, from the mythological ancient Roman heroine of the same name who had twin boys with Zeus.

Latoya

Spanish, meaning "victorious one." Name of singer LaToya Jackson.

Latrice

(alt. Latricia)

Latin, meaning "noble."

Laura

(alt. Lora)

Latin, meaning "laurel." Famous Lauras include actor Laura Dern, author Laura Ingalls Wilder, and designer Laura Ashley.

Laurel

Latin, meaning "laurel tree." Also a term used for young women in the Mormon Church.

Lauren

(alt. Lauran, Loren)

Latin, meaning "laurel." Famous Laurens include actors Lauren Bacall and Lauran Grace.

Laveda

(alt. Lavada)

Latin, meaning "cleansed."

Lavender

Latin, from the plant of the same name. A character from the Harry Potter series.

Laverne

(alt. Lavern, Laverna)

Latin, from the goddess of the same name. Famous Lavernes include Laverne Andrews, of the Andrews Sisters, and sitcom Laverne & Shirley.

Lavinia
(alt. Lavina)

Latin, meaning "woman of Rome." In Roman mythology Lavinia is a heroine whose hair caught fire, creating a prophecy.

Lavonne
(alt. Lavon)

French, meaning "yew wood."

Leah
(alt. Lea, Leia)

Hebrew, meaning "weary." Name of musical actor Lea Michele.

Leandra

Greek, meaning "lion man." A character in *Don Quixote*.

Leanne
(alt. Leann, Leanna, Leeann)

Contraction of Lee and Ann, meaning "meadow grace." Famous Leannes include singers LeAnn Rimes and Lee Ann Womack.

Leda

Greek, meaning "gladness." The ancient Greek heroine Leda was seduced by Zeus in the form of a swan.

Lee
(alt. Leigh)

English, meaning "pasture or meadow."

Leilani

Hawaiian, meaning "flower from heaven." Name of actor Leilani Jones.

Leith

Scottish Gaelic, meaning "broad river."

Lena
(alt. Leena, Lina)

Latin, meaning "light." Famous Lenas include actor and filmmaker Lena Dunham and actor Lena Headey.

Lenna
(alt. Lennie)

German, meaning "lion's strength." The Lenna photograph is a standard test image used in image processing.

Léonie
(alt. Leona, Leone)

Latin, meaning "lioness." Leonie Adams is a poet.

Leonora
(alt. Lenora, Lenore, Leonor, Leonore, Leora)

Greek, meaning "light." Leonora Braham is an opera singer.

Leslie
(alt. Leslee, Lesley)

Scottish Gaelic, meaning "the gray castle." Famous Leslies include actor and dancer Leslie Caron, and singer Leslie Feist. Lesley is more commonly the female spelling and Leslie the male.

Leta

Latin, meaning "glad and joyful."
Leta Hollingworth is a child
psychologist.

Letha

Greek, meaning "forgetfulness." Also
a type of butterfly.

Letitia
(alt. Leticia, Lettice, Lettie)

Latin, meaning "joy and gladness."
St. Leticia was a Spanish virgin
martyr.

Lexia
(alt. Lexi, Lexie)

Greek, meaning "defender of
mankind." Also a genus of butterfly.

Lia

Italian, meaning "bringer of the
gospel." Lia Williams is an actor.

Liana

French, meaning "to twine around."

Libby
(alt. Libbie)

Originally a shortened form of
Elizabeth, meaning "pledged to
God." Name of singer Libby Holman.

Liberty

English, meaning "freedom." Made
famous by the Statue of Liberty in
New York, NY.

Lida

Slavic, meaning "loved by the
people."

Liese
(alt. Liesel, Liesl)

German, meaning "pledged to God."
Liesl is a character in *The Sound of
Music*.

Lila
(alt. Lilah)

Arabic, meaning "night." In the
Hindu faith, Lila refers to playtime or
pastimes.

Lilac

Latin, from the flower of the
same name. Also the pale purple
color.

Lilia
(alt. Lilias)

Scottish, meaning "lily."

Lilith

Arabic, meaning "ghost." In Jewish
mythology Lilith was thought to be a
female demon.

Lillian
(alt. Lilian, Liliana, Lilla, Lillianna)

Latin, meaning "lily." Famous Lillians
include actor Lillian Gish, playwright
Lillian Hellman, and nursing pioneer
Lillian Wald.

Lily
(alt. Lili, Lillie, Lilly)

Latin, from the flower of the same name. Famous Lilys include singer Lily Allen, actor Lily Collins, and model Lily Cole.

Linda
(alt. Lynda)

Spanish, meaning "pretty." Famous Lindas include actor Linda Blair and singer Linda Ronstadt.

Linden
(alt. Lindie, Lindy)

European, from the tree of the same name.

Lindsay
(alt. Lindsey, Linsey, Lynsey)

English, meaning "island of linden trees." Famous Lindsays include actor Lindsay Lohan and skier Lindsay Vonn. Can be used for both girls and boys.

Linette
(alt. Lynette)

Welsh, meaning "idol."

Linnea
(alt. Linnae, Linny)

Scandinavian, meaning "lime or linden tree." An extremely popular name for baby girls in Sweden.

Liora
(alt. Lior)

Hebrew, meaning "I have a light." Also a spelling alternative to Leora.

Lisa
(alt. Leesa, Lise, Liza)

Hebrew, meaning "pledged to God." Famous Lisas include singer Lisa Bonet, actor Lisa Kudrow, and The Simpsons character Lisa Simpson.

Lish

Shortened form of Elisha, meaning "my God is salvation."

Lissa

Greek, meaning "bee." Also a shortened form of Melissa.

Lissandra
(alt. Lisandra)

Greek, meaning "man's defender."

Liv

Nordic, meaning "defense." Also a short form of Olivia. Actor Liv Tyler is an original Liv, although she did change her surname!

Livia

Latin, meaning "olive." Livia Drusilla was the wife of Roman Emperor Augustus.

Logan

Irish Gaelic, meaning "small hollow." Used more commonly for boys.

Lois

German, meaning "renowned in battle." Made famous by *Superman* heroine Lois Lane.

Lolita

(alt. Lola; abbrev. Lollie)

Spanish, meaning "sorrows." The title of a novel by Vladimir Nabokov.

Lona

Latin, meaning "lion." Lona is a moon deity in Hawaiian mythology.

Lorelei

(alt. Loralai, Loralie)

German, meaning "dangerous rock." Associated with the Lorelei myth in Germany.

Lorenza

Latin, meaning "from Laurentium."

Loretta

(alt. Loreto)

Latin, meaning "laurel." Loretta Devine is an actor.

Lori

(alt. Laurie, Lorie, Lorri)

Latin, meaning "laurel." Name of actor Lori Petty.

Lorna

Scottish, from the place of the same name. The title character in R. D. Blackmore's novel *Lorna Doone*.

Lorraine

(alt. Loraine)

French, meaning "from Lorraine." Famous Lorraines include actor Lorraine Bracco, paranormal investigator Lorraine Warren, and playwright Lorraine Hansberry.

Lottie

(alt. Lotta, Lotte)

French, meaning "little and womanly." Also a shortened form of Charlotte.

Lotus

Greek, meaning "lotus flower."

Louise

(alt. Lou, Louie, Louisa, Luisa)

German, meaning "renowned in battle." Famous Louises include actors Louise Fletcher and Louise Lasser.

Lourdes

French, from the town of the same name. Chosen by Madonna for her daughter.

Love

English, meaning "deep affection and attraction."

Lowri

Welsh, meaning "crowned with laurels."

Luanne
(alt. Luann, Luanna)

German, meaning "renowned in battle"; Hawaiian, meaning "enjoyment." Famous Luannes include author Luanne Rice and *Real Housewife* LuAnn de Lesseps.

Lucia
(alt. Luciana)

Italian, meaning "light."

Lucille
(alt. Lucile, Lucilla)

French, meaning "light." Name of actor Lucille Ball.

Lucinda

English, meaning "light." Famous Lucindas include actor Lucinda Jenney and singer Lucinda Williams.

Lucretia
(alt. Lucrece)

Spanish, meaning "light." Important figure in ancient Roman history.

Lucy
(alt. Lucie)

Latin, meaning "light." Associated with the sitcom *I Love Lucy*.

Ludmilla

Slavic, meaning "beloved of the people."

Luella
(alt. Lue)

English, meaning "renowned in battle." Luella Bartley is a designer.

Lulu
(alt. Lula)

German, meaning "renowned in battle." Name of the singer.

Luna

Latin, meaning "moon." Luna was the personification of the moon in ancient Roman mythology.

Lupita

Spanish, from the town of the same name. Lupita Nyong'o is an actor.

Luz

Spanish, meaning "light."

Lydia
(alt. Lidia)

Greek, meaning "from Lydia." Lydia Bennet is one of the five sisters in Jane Austen's *Pride and Prejudice*.

Lynn
(alt. Lyn, Lynna, Lynne)

Spanish, meaning "pretty"; English, meaning "waterfall." Name of the actor Lynn Redgrave.

Lyra

Latin, meaning "lyre." The main female character in Philip Pullman's trilogy *His Dark Materials*.

M Girls' names

Mab
(alt. Mabe)

Irish Gaelic, meaning "joy."
Queen Mab is a character from
Shakespeare's *Romeo and Juliet*.

Mabel
(alt. Mabelle, Mable)

Latin, meaning "loveable." Dates
from the fifth century.

Macaria

Spanish, meaning "blessed."

Mackenzie
(alt. Mackenzy, McKenzie)

Irish Gaelic, meaning "son of the
wise ruler." Used for girls and boys.

Macy
(alt. Macey, Maci, Macie)

French, meaning "Matthew's estate."
Famous Macys include department
store Macy's and reality TV star Maci
Bookout.

Mada

English, meaning "from Magdala."
In Hindu mythology, Mada is an
enormous monster who is able to
swallow the universe.

Madden
(alt. Maddyn)

Irish, meaning "little dog." Associated
with the video game series.

Madeline
(alt. Madaline, Madalyn, Madeleine,
Madelyn, Madilyn; abbrev. Maddi,
Maddie, Madie)

Greek, meaning "from Magdala."
Associated with Ludwig Bemelmans's
"Madeline" novels.

Madge

Greek, meaning "pearl." Also
the short form of Marjorie
and the nickname of singer
Madonna.

Madhuri

Hindi, meaning "sweet girl."

Madison

(alt. Maddison, Madisen, Madisyn)

English, meaning "son of the mighty warrior." Made famous by *Splash* character Madison, and President James Madison.

Madonna

Latin, meaning "my lady." Made famous by pop legend Madonna and the Virgin Madonna.

Maeve

Irish Gaelic, meaning "intoxicating." Queen Maeve appears in Irish mythology and Maeve Binchy was an Irish author.

Mafalda

Spanish, meaning "battlemighty." Mafalda Hopkirk is a character in the *Harry Potter* series.

Magali

Greek, meaning "pearl."

Magdalene

(alt. Magdalen, Magdalena)

Greek, meaning "from Magdala." Associated with Mary Magdalene from the Bible.

Maggie

Shortened form of Margaret, meaning "pearl." Famous Maggies include actors Maggie Gyllenhaal and Maggie Grace, and *The Simpsons* character Maggie Simpson.

Magnolia

Latin, from the flowering plant of the same name. Also the name of a movie.

Mahala

(alt. Mahalia)

Hebrew, meaning "tender affection."

Maia

(alt. Maja)

Greek, meaning "mother." An important character in ancient Greek mythology.

Maida

English, meaning "maiden."

Maisie

(alt. Maisey, Maisy, Maizie, Masie, Mazie)

Greek, meaning "pearl." Name of actor Maisie Williams.

Malin

(alt. Maline)

Hebrew, meaning "of Magda." Famous Malins include actor Malin Akerman, singer Malin Berggren, and infamous alleged Swedish witch Malin Matsdotter.

Maliyah
(alt. Malia)

Hawaiian, meaning "beloved." Also the name of one of former President Barack Obama's daughters.

Malka

Hebrew, meaning "queen."

Mallory
(alt. Malorie)

French, meaning "unhappy." The name of children's author Malorie Blackman.

Malvina

Gaelic, meaning "smooth brow."

Mamie
(alt. Mammie)

Shortened form of Margaret, meaning "pearl." Famous Mamies include former First Lady Mamie Eisenhower, actor Mamie Gummer, and infamous midwife Mamie Cadden.

Mandy
(alt. Mandie)

Shortened form of Amanda, meaning "much loved." Famous Mandys include actor Mandy Moore, performer Mandy Miller, and the song "Mandy" by Barry Manilow.

Manisha

Sanskrit, meaning "desire." Manisha is the goddess of wisdom in the Hindu faith.

Mansi

Hopi, meaning "plucked flower."

Manuela

Spanish, meaning "the Lord is among us."

Mara

Hebrew, meaning "bitter." Famous Maras include actors Mara Wilson and Rooney Mara, and author Mara Bergman.

Marcy
(alt. Marci, Marcie, Marcia, Marcela, Marceline, Marcella, Marcelle)

Latin, meaning "war-like." Famous Marcias include actor Marcia Cross and voice actor Marcia Wallace.

Margaret
(alt. Margarete, Margaretta, Margarette, Margret, Margarita, Margeurite; abbrev. Maggie, Margot, Meg)

Greek, meaning "pearl." Famous Margarets include author Margaret Atwood, actor Margaret Rutherford, and former Prime Minister of Great Britain Margaret Thatcher. Margot is the abbreviation of the French form, Marguerite, used by dancer Margot Fonteyn.

Maria
(alt. Mariah)

Latin, meaning "bitter." Famous Marias include tennis pro Maria Sharapova, performer Maria Von Trapp, and singer Mariah Carey.

Marian
(alt. Marianne, Mariam, Mariana, Marion)

French, meaning "bitter grace." Maid Marian is a character from the Robin Hood legend.

Maribel
Hebrew, meaning "beautiful."

Marie
French, meaning "bitter." Famous Maries include French Queen consort Marie Antoinette, physicist Marie Curie, and singer Marie Osmond.

Mariel
(alt. Mariela, Mariella, Marika)

Dutch, meaning "bitter."

Marietta
(alt. Marieta)

French, meaning "bitter." Marietta Stow was a suffragist.

Marigold
English, from the flowering plant of the same name. Associated with the movie *The Best Exotic Marigold Hotel*.

Marilyn
(alt. Marilee, Marilene, Marilynn)

English, meaning "bitter." Made famous by actor and singer Marilyn Monroe.

Marin
American English, from the county of the same name.

Marina
(alt. Marine)

Latin, meaning "from the sea."

Mariposa
Spanish, meaning "butterfly."

Marisa
(alt. Maris, Marissa)

Latin, meaning "of the sea." Famous Marisas include actors Marisa Tomei, Marissa Ribisi, and Marissa Jaret Winokur.

Marisol
Spanish, meaning "bitter sun." Associated with Maria de la Soledad, which is a Spanish title for the Virgin Mary.

Marjolaine
French, meaning "marjoram."

Marjorie
(alt. Margery, Marjory; abbrev. Madge, Marge, Margie, Margit, Margy)

French, meaning "pearl." Famous Marjories include actors Marjorie Reynolds and Marjorie Main, socialite Marjorie Bridges, and autobiographer Margery Kempe.

Marlene
(alt. Marla, Marlen, Marlena)

Hebrew, meaning "bitter." Name of the actor Marlene Dietrich.

Marley
(alt. Marlee)

American English, meaning "bitter." Made famous by singer Bob Marley.

Marlo
(alt. Marlowe)

American English, meaning "bitter."

Marnie
(alt. Marney)

Scottish, meaning "from the sea." Famous Marnies include the character of Marnie from *Girls*, the movie *Marnie* by Alfred Hitchcock, and the birth name of ballerina Darcey Bussell.

Marseille

French, from the city of the same name.

Marsha

English, meaning "war-like." Famous Marshas include singer Marsha Hunt, playwright Marsha Norman, and *Brady Bunch* character Marsha.

Martha
(alt. Marta)

Aramaic, meaning "lady." A character in the Bible.

Martina
(alt. Martine)

Latin, meaning "war-like." Famous Martinas include singer Martina McBride, and tennis pros Martina Hingis and Martina Navratilova.

Marvel

French, meaning "something to wonder at." Also a comic book brand.

Mary

Hebrew, meaning "bitter." Famous Marys include the Virgin Mary and Mary Magdalene from the Bible, and author Mary Shelley.

Masada

Hebrew, meaning "foundation."

Matilda
(alt. Mathilda, Mathilde; abbrev. Tilly)

German, meaning "battlemighty." *Matilda* is a novel by Roald Dahl, and a movie from the book.

Mattea

Hebrew, meaning "gift of God."

Maude
(alt. Maud)

German, meaning "battlemighty." Maude Flanders is a character from *The Simpsons*.

Maura

Irish, meaning "bitter."

Maureen
(alt. Maurine)

Irish, meaning "bitter."

Mavis

French, meaning "thrush." Mavis is a character in *Hotel Transylvania*.

Maxine
(abbrev. Maxie)

Latin, meaning "greatest." Maxine Andrews was one of the singing group the Andrews Sisters.

May
(alt. Mae, Maya, Maye, Mayra)

Hebrew, meaning "gift of God." Also the fifth month.

Mckenna
(alt. Mackenna)

Irish Gaelic, meaning "son of the handsome one." Used more commonly for boys.

Medea
(alt. Madea, Meda)

Greek, meaning "ruling." Associated with the Tyler Perry character Madea.

Meg

Shortened form of Margaret, meaning "pearl." Famous Megs include actor Meg Ryan, and the characters of Meg from Disney's *Hercules* and Meg Griffin from *Family Guy*.

Megan
(alt. Meagan, Meghan)

Welsh, meaning "pearl." Famous Megans include actor Megan Fox and the Duchess of Sussex, Meghan Markle.

Mehitabel

Hebrew, meaning "benefited by God."

Mehri

Persian, meaning "kind."

Melanie
(alt. Melania, Melany, Melonie; abbrev. Mel)

Greek, meaning "dark-skinned." Famous Melanies include actor Melanie Griffith and singers Melanie Brown and Melanie Chisholm of the Spice Girls.

Melba

Australian, meaning "from Melbourne." Made famous by Melba toast and the dessert Peach Melba.

Melia
(alt. Meliah)

German, meaning "industrious."

Melina

Greek, meaning "honey." Name of actor Melina Kanakaredes.

Melinda

Latin, meaning "honey."
Philanthropist Melinda Gates is the wife of Microsoft founder Bill Gates.

Melisande
(alt. Melisende)

French, meaning "bee." Melisandre is a character from *Game of Thrones*.

Melissa
(alt. Melisa, Mellissa)

Greek, meaning "bee." Famous Melissas include singer Melissa Etheridge and actor Melissa Joan Hart.

Melody
(alt. Melodie)

Greek, meaning "song."

Melvina

Celtic, meaning "chieftain."

Menora
(alt. Menorah)

Hebrew, meaning "candlestick." A Menorah is a candalabrum with seven branches, used in Jewish worship; a symbol of Judaism.

Mercedes

Spanish, meaning "mercies." Made famous by the car company Mercedes-Benz.

Mercy

English, meaning "mercy."

Meredith
(alt. Meridith)

Welsh, meaning "great ruler." Meredith Brooks is a singer. Also the name of the title character Meredith Grey in *Grey's Anatomy*.

Merle

French, meaning "blackbird." Also the term for the patterning on the coat of a dog.

Merry

English, meaning "lighthearted."

Meryl
(alt. Merrill)

Irish Gaelic, meaning "seabright." The name of actor Meryl Streep and ice dancer Meryl Davis.

Meta

German, meaning "pearl."

Mia

Italian, meaning "mine." Famous Mias include actors Mia Farrow and Mia Wasikowskaa, and singer M.I.A.

Michaela
(alt. Makaela, Makaila, Makayla, McKayla, Micaela, Mikaela, Mikaila, Mikala, Mikayla)

Hebrew, meaning "who is like the Lord." The name of gymnast McKayla Maroney.

Michelle

(alt. Machelle, Mechelle, Michaele, Michal, Michele; abbrev. Micki, Mickie, Micky)

French, meaning "who is like the Lord." Famous Michelles include former First Lady Michelle Obama, and actor Michelle Rodriguez.

Migdalia

Greek, meaning "from Magdala."

Mignon

French, meaning "cute." Also a cut of steak.

Mika

(alt. Micah)

Hebrew, meaning "who resembles God." Associated with singer Mika.

Milada

Czech, meaning "my love."

Milagros

Spanish, meaning "miracles." Also a type of Mexican folk charm.

Milan

Italian, from the city of the same name.

Mildred

English, meaning "gentle strength." The title character from the movie and TV series Mildred Pierce.

Milena

Czech, meaning "love and warmth."

Miley

American English, meaning "smiley." Name of singer and actor Miley Cyrus.

Millicent

(alt. Milicent; abbrev. Millie, Milly)

German, meaning "high-born power." Famous Millicents include suffragist Millicent Fawcett, British spy Milicent Bagot, and the musical Thoroughly Modern Millie.

Mimi

Italian, meaning "bitter." Mimi is a character from Giacome Puccini's opera La boheme.

Mina

(alt. Mena)

German, meaning "love"; Persian, meaning "colored glass."

Mindy

(alt. Mindi)

Latin, meaning "honey." Famous Mindys include comedian Mindy Kaling, singer Mindy McCready, and actor Mindy Sterling.

Minerva

Roman, from the goddess of the same name. Minerva was the goddess of wisdom, arts, and defense.

Ming

Chinese, meaning "bright." Associated with the Ming Dynasty in China.

Minnie
(alt. Minna)

German, meaning "helmet." Made famous by Disney's Minnie Mouse.

Mira
(alt. Meera)

Latin, meaning "admirable."

Mirabel
(alt. Mirabella, Mirabelle)

Latin, meaning "wonderful." Also a type of plum.

Miranda
(alt. Meranda)

Latin, meaning "admirable." Famous Mirandas include actors Miranda Richardson and Miranda Hart, and model Miranda Kerr.

Mirella
(alt. Mireille, Mirela)

Latin, meaning "admirable." Mirella Freni is an opera singer.

Miriam

Hebrew, meaning "bitter." A prophetess in the Bible.

Mirta

Spanish, meaning "crown of thorns."

Missy
(alt. Missie)

Shortened form of Melissa, meaning "bee." The name of singer and producer Missy Elliot.

Misty
(alt. Misti)

English, meaning "mist." Associated with Misty from Pokémon.

Mitzi

German, meaning "bitter." Name of actor Mitzi Gaynor.

Miu

Japanese, meaning "beautiful feather."

Moira
(alt. Maira)

Irish, meaning "bitter." Associated with actor Moira Kelly.

Molly
(alt. Mollie)

American English, meaning "bitter." Famous Mollys include actors Molly Ringwald and Molly Sims.

Mona

Irish Gaelic, meaning "aristocratic." The vampire from Mona the Vampire.

Monica
(alt. Monika, Monique)

Latin, meaning "advisor." Famous Monicas include intern Monica Lewinsky, tennis pro Monica Seles, and Friends character Monica Geller.

Monroe

Gaelic, meaning "mouth of the river Rotha." Made famous by singer and actor Marilyn Monroe.

Montserrat

(alt. Monserrate)

Spanish, from the town of the same name. Montserrat Caballe is an opera singer.

Morag

Scottish, meaning "star of the sea." Also the name of the Loch Moror monster in Scotland.

Morgan

(alt. Morgann)

Welsh, meaning "great and bright." Used for girls and boys.

Moriah

Hebrew, meaning "the Lord is my teacher."

Morwenna

Welsh, meaning "maiden." St. Morwenna is the patron saint of Cornwall, England.

Moselle

(alt. Mozell, Mozella, Mozelle)

Hebrew, meaning "savior."

Mulan

Chinese, meaning "wood orchid." The name of the Disney movie *Mulan*.

Muriel

Irish Gaelic, meaning "seabright." Name of the novelist Muriel Spark.

Mya

(alt. Maya, Myah)

Greek, meaning "mother." Famous Myas include author Maya Angelou, comedian Maya Rudolph, and the Mayan people of Central America.

Myfanwy

Welsh, meaning "my little lovely one."

Myla

English, meaning "merciful."

Myra

Latin, meaning "scented oil." Name of the pioneering lawyer Myra Bradwell.

Myrna

(alt. Mirna)

Irish Gaelic, meaning "tender and beloved." Associated with actor Myrna Fahey.

Myrtle

Irish, from the shrub of the same name. Myrtle Wilson is a character from *The Great Gatsby*.

N Girls' names

Nadia
(alt. Nadya)

Russian, meaning "hope."
Nadia Comaneci was the first
gymnast to be awarded a perfect
score of ten in an Olympic
event.

Nadine

French, meaning "hope."
Name of the socialite Nadine
Caridi.

Nahara

Aramaic, meaning "light."

Naima

Arabic, meaning "water nymph."

Nalani

Hawaiian, meaning "serenity of
the skies."

Nancy
*(alt. Nanci, Nancie; abbrev. Nan,
Nanna, Nannie)*

Hebrew, meaning "grace." Famous
Nancys include former First Lady
Nancy Reagan and figure skater
Nancy Kerrigan.

Nanette
(alt. Nannette)

French, meaning "grace." Associated
with musical *No, No, Nanette*.

Naomi
(alt. Naoma, Noemi)

Hebrew, meaning "pleasant."
Famous Naomis include actor Naomi
Watts, author Naomi Wolf, and an
important character in the Bible.

Narcissa

Greek, meaning "daffodil." Narcissa
Malfoy is a character in the *Harry
Potter* series.

Nastasia

Greek, meaning "resurrection." Can also refer to a baby born on Christmas Day.

Natalie

(alt. Natalia, Natalya, Nathalie)

Latin, meaning "birth day." Natalie Wood was an actor.

Natasha

(alt. Natasa; abbrev. Nat, Tasha)

Russian, meaning "birth day." A character from Leo Tolstoy's War and Peace.

Neda

English, meaning "wealthy." An ancient Greek nymph.

Nedra

English, meaning "underground."

Neema

Swahili, meaning "born of prosperity."

Neka

Native American, meaning "goose."

Nell

(alt. Nelda, Nella, Nellie, Nelly)

Originally a shortened form of Eleanor, meaning "light." The title of a movie. Singer Nelly Furtado was given the name at birth, but Nell Gwynn, mistress of King Charles II, was an Eleanor.

Nemi

Italian, from the lake of the same name.

Neoma

Greek, meaning "new moon."

Nereida

Spanish, meaning "sea nymph."

Nerissa

Greek, meaning "sea nymph." A character in Shakespeare's The Merchant of Venice.

Nettie

(alt. Neta)

Shortened form of Henrietta, meaning "ruler of the house."

Neva

Spanish, meaning "snowy."

Nevaeh

American English, meaning "heaven" (and spelled that way backwards).

Niamh

(alt. Neve)

Irish, meaning "brightness." An Irish goddess.

Nicola

(abbrev. Nicki, Nicky, Nikki)

Greek, meaning "victory of the people." Famous Nicolas include actor Nicola Peltz and singer Nicola Roberts.

Nicole

(alt. Nichol, Nichole, Nicolette, Nicolle, Nikole)

Greek, meaning "victory of the people." Famous Nicoles include actor Nicole Kidman, socialite Nicole Richie, and singer Nicole Scherzinger.

Nidia

Spanish, meaning "graceful."

Nigella

Irish Gaelic, meaning "champion." Name of chef Nigella Lawson.

Nikita

Greek, meaning "unconquered." Also a song by Elton John.

Nila

Egyptian, meaning "Nile." Associated with Nila wafers.

Nilda

German, meaning "battle woman."

Nina

Spanish, meaning "girl." Nina Simone is a singer.

Nissa

Hebrew, meaning "sign."

Nita

Spanish, meaning "gracious."

Old name, new fashion

Bella	Hazel
Carolyn	Matilda
Clara	Nora
Dorothy	Penelope
Emmeline	Rosalie

Nixie

German, meaning "water sprite."

Noelle

(alt. Noel)

French, meaning "Christmas." Noelle is usually the female form and Noel the male form.

Nola

(alt. Nuala)

Irish Gaelic, meaning "white shoulder." Often refers to someone with white or very blonde hair.

Nona

Latin, meaning "ninth."

Nora

(alt. Norah)

Shortened form of Eleanor, meaning "light." The name of screenwriter Nora Ephron, singer Norah Jones, and author Nora Roberts.

Noreen
(alt. Norine)

Irish, meaning "light." Noreen Murray was a scientist who helped develop the vaccine against hepatitis B.

Norma

Latin, meaning "pattern." Marilyn Monroe's birth name was Norma Jean Mortenson.

Normandie
(alt. Normandy)

French, from the province of the same name.

Novia
(alt. Nova)

Latin, meaning "new."

Nydia

Latin, meaning "nest."

Nysa
(alt. Nyssa)

Greek, meaning "ambition." A district in ancient Greek mythology.

O

Girls' names

Oaklyn
(alt. Oaklynn)

English, meaning "from the oak meadow."

Oceana
(alt. Ocean, Océane, Ocie)

Greek, meaning "ocean."

Octavia

Latin, meaning "eighth." Famous Octavias include actor Octavia Spencer, and Octavia in Shakespeare's *Antony and Cleopatra*.

Oda
(alt. Odie)

Shortened form of Odessa, meaning "long voyage"; German, meaning "wealth" or "inheritance."

Odele
(alt. Odell)

English, meaning "woad hill." Woad is a dye for the color indigo.

Odelia

Hebrew, meaning "I will praise the Lord." Associated with St. Odelia.

Odessa

Greek, meaning "long voyage."

Odette
(alt. Odetta)

French, meaning "wealthy." Name of the "good" swan in *Swan Lake*.

Odile
(alt. Odilia)

French, meaning "prospers in battle." Name of the "bad" swan in *Swan Lake*.

Odina

Feminine form of Odin, meaning "creative inspiration," from the Nordic god of the same name.

Odyssey

Greek, meaning "long journey."
Title of the epic poem by Homer.

Oksana

Russian, meaning "praise to God."

Ola
(alt. Olie)

Greek, meaning "man's defender."

Olena
(alt. Olene)

Russian, meaning "light."

Olga

Russian, meaning "holy." Name of the model and actor Olga Kurylenko, and gymnast Olga Korbut.

Olivia
(alt. Olivev, Oliviana, Olivié, Ollie; abbrev. Liv, Livia)

Latin, meaning "olive." Famous Olivias include actors Olivia Munn and Olivia Wilde, and Scandal character Olivia Pope.

Olwen

Welsh, meaning "white footprint."

Olympia
(alt. Olimpia)

Greek, meaning "from Mount Olympus." Name of actor Olympia Dukakis.

Oma
(alt. Omie)

Arabic, meaning "leader." In some communities, Oma refers to a grandmother.

Omyra

Latin, meaning "scented oil."

Oneida
(abbrev. Ona, Onnie)

Native American, meaning "long awaited." The name of a tribe.

Onyx

Latin, meaning "veined gem." Also a semiprecious stone.

Oona
(alt. Oonagh)

Irish, meaning "unity."

Opal

Sanskrit, meaning "gem." Also a precious stone.

Ophelia
(alt. Ophélie)

Greek, meaning "help." A character in Shakespeare's Hamlet.

Oprah

Hebrew, meaning "young deer." Name of the legendary TV host Oprah Winfrey.

Ora

Latin, meaning "prayer." Also a platinum metal.

Orabela

Latin, meaning "prayer."

Oralie
(alt. Oralia)

French, meaning "golden."

Orane

French, meaning "rising."

Orchid

Greek, from the flower of the same name.

Oriana
(alt. Oriane)

Latin, meaning "dawning." One of the many nicknames of Queen Elizabeth I.

Orla
(alt. Orlaith, Orly)

Irish Gaelic, meaning "golden lady."

Orlean

French, meaning "plum." The city of New Orleans in Louisiana.

Orsa
(alt. Osia, Ossie)

Latin, meaning "bear."

Otthid

Greek, meaning "prospers in battle."

Ottilie
(alt. Ottie)

French, meaning "prospers in battle." Name of the opera singer Ottilie Metzger.

Ouida

French, meaning "renowned in battle."

Ozette

Native American, from the village of the same name.

P

Girls' names

Padma

Sanskrit, meaning "lotus." Padma Lakshmi is an Indian born American cookery book writer, actor, and TV host.

Paige
(alt. Page)

French, meaning "serving boy." Paige Turco is an actor.

Paisley

Scottish, from the town of the same name. The name of a fabric pattern.

Palma
(alt. Palmira)

Latin, meaning "palm tree."

Paloma

Spanish, meaning "dove." Famous Palomas include singer Paloma Faith and designer Paloma Picasso.

Pamela
(alt. Pamala, Pamella; abbrev. Pam, Pammie)

Greek, meaning "all honey." Famous Pamelas include actors Pamela Anderson and Pamela Adlon, and author Pamela (P. L.) Travers.

Pandora

Greek, meaning "all gifted." Associated with the myth of Pandora's box in ancient Greek mythology.

Pangiota

Greek, meaning "all is holy."

Pansy

French, from the flower of the same name.

Paradisa
(alt. Paradis)

Greek, meaning "garden orchard."

Paris
(alt. Parisa)

Greek, from the mythological hero of the same name. Famous Parises include the city in France and socialite Paris Hilton.

Parker

English, meaning "park keeper." Parker Posey is an actor.

Parthenia

Greek, meaning "virginal."

Parthenope

Greek, from the mythological Siren of the same name. Parthenope Nightingale was sister of nurse Florence Nightingale.

Parvati

Sanskrit, meaning "daughter of the mountain." The Hindu goddess of love and devotion. Also a character in the *Harry Potter* series.

Pascale

Latin, meaning "Easterchild." Also a boys' name, usually spelt Pascal.

Patience

French, meaning "the state of being patient."

Patricia
(abbrev. Pat, Patsy, Patti, Pattie, Patty, Trisha)

Latin, meaning "noble." Famous Patricias include actors Patricia Arquette and Patricia O'Neal.

Paula

Latin, meaning "small." Famous Paulas include singer Paula Abdul, actor Paula Patton, and chef Paula Deen.

Pauline
(alt. Paulette, Paulina)

Latin, meaning "small." Associated with actor Pauline Collins.

Paxton

Latin, meaning "peaceful town."

Paz

Spanish, meaning "peace."

Pazia

Hebrew, meaning "golden."

Peace

English, meaning "peace."

Pearl
(alt. Pearle, Pearlie, Perla)

Latin, meaning "pale gemstone."

Peggy
(alt. Peggie)

Greek, meaning "pearl." The name of actor Peggy Lipton and figure skater Peggy Fleming; also the movie *Peggy Sue Got Married*.

Pelia

Hebrew, meaning "marvel of God."

Penelope

(abbrev. Penni, Pennie, Penny)

Greek, meaning "bobbin worker." Penelope was also the loyal wife of Odysseus in Greek mythology.

Peony

Greek, from the flower of the same name.

Perdita

Latin, meaning "lost." A character in William Shakespeare's play The Winter's Tale.

Peri

(alt. Perri)

Hebrew, meaning "outcome." Associated with Peri spirits in Persian mythology.

Perry

French, meaning "pear tree."

Persephone

Greek, meaning "bringer of destruction." The Queen of the Underworld in ancient Greek mythology.

Petra

(alt. Petrina)

Greek, meaning "rock."

Petula

Latin, meaning "to seek." Name of the singer Petula Clark.

Petunia

Greek, from the flower of the same name.

Peyton

(alt. Payton)

Old English, meaning "fighting man's estate." Associated with TV series Peyton Place.

Phaedra

Greek, meaning "bright."

Philippa

(abbrev. Pippa)

Greek, meaning "horse lover." Philippa Gregory is an author.

Philomena

(alt. Philoma)

Greek, meaning "loved one." Title of the book and movie Philomena.

Phoebe

Greek, meaning "shining and brilliant." Name of actor Phoebe Cates, and Friends character Phoebe Buffay.

Phoenix

Greek, meaning "red as blood." The city in Arizona and the mythical bird.

Phyllis
(alt. Phillia, Phyllida, Phylis)
Greek, meaning "leafy bough."
Name of comedian Phyllis Diller.

Pia
Latin, meaning "pious."

Pilar
Spanish, meaning "pillar."

Piper
English, meaning "pipe player." Piper
Laurie is an actor.

Plum
Latin, from the fruit of the same
name.

Polly
Hebrew, meaning "bitter." Associated
with the classic Polly Pocket toy.

Pomona
Latin, meaning "apple." Name of
the goddess of fruitful abundance in
ancient Roman mythology.

Poppy
Latin, from the flower of the
same name. Name of model
Poppy Delevingne, sister of Cara
Delevingne.

Portia
(alt. Porsha)
Latin, meaning "from the Portia
clan." Portia de Rossi is an actor.

Posy
(alt. Posie)
English, meaning "small flower."

Precious
Latin, meaning "of great worth." Title
of the movie *Precious*.

Priela
Hebrew, meaning "fruit of God."

Primrose
English, meaning "first rose."

Princess
English, meaning "daughter of the
monarch."

Priscilla
(alt. Priscila)
Latin, meaning "ancient." Name of
the actor Priscilla Presley.

Priya
Hindi, meaning "loved one."

Prudence
(abbrev. Pru, Prudie)
Latin, meaning "caution." Prudence
is the mother of all virtues.

Prunella
Latin, meaning "small plum." Name
of the actor Prunella Scales.

Psyche
Greek, meaning "breath." The name
of TV show *Psyche*.

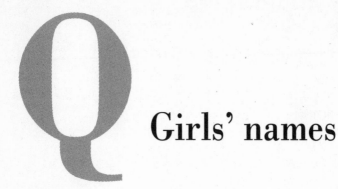

Girls' names

Qiturah

Arabic, meaning "incense."

Queen
(alt. Queenie)

English, meaning "queen." The name of rapper and actor Queen Latifah.

Quiana

American English, meaning "silky." Name of the model Quiana Grant.

Quincy
(alt. Quincey)

French, meaning "estate of the fifth son."

Quinn
(alt. Quinnie)

Irish Gaelic, meaning "counsel." Quinn is a character from *Glee*.

R Girls' names

Rachel
(alt. *Rachael, Rachelle, Raquel;* abbrev. *Rach*)

Hebrew, meaning "ewe." Famous Rachels include the character in the Bible, actors Rachel Weisz and Rachel Bilson, and the *Glee* character Rachel Berry.

Radhika
Sanskrit, meaning "prosperous."

Rae
(alt. *Ray*)

Feminine form of Ray, meaning "ray," or shortened form of Rachel, meaning "ewe." Rae Armantrout is a poet.

Rahima
Arabic, meaning "compassionate." Name of smallpox survivor Rahima Banu.

Raina
(alt. *Rain, Raine, Rainey, Rayne*)

Latin, meaning "queen."

Raissa
(alt. *Raisa*)

Yiddish, meaning "rose." Name of former Russian First Lady Raisa Gorbacheva.

Raleigh
(alt. *Rayleigh*)

English, meaning "meadow of roe deer."

Rama
(alt. *Ramey, Ramya*)

Hebrew, meaning "exalted." Associated with the Vishnu's avatars in the Hindu faith.

Ramona
(alt. *Romona*)

Spanish, meaning "wise guardian." Associated with the "Ramona" books, and the movie *Ramona and Beezus*.

Ramsey
(alt. Ramsay)

English, meaning "raven island."

Rana
(alt. Rania, Rayna)

Arabic, meaning "beautiful thing."

Randy
(alt. Randi)

Shortened form of Miranda, meaning "admirable." More commonly used for boys, as a short form of Randall.

Rani

Sanskrit, meaning "queen."

Raphaela
(alt. Rafaela, Raffaella)

Spanish, meaning "healing God."

Rashida

Turkish, meaning "righteous." Name of actor Rashida Jones.

Raven
(alt. Ravyn)

English, from the bird of the same name. Raven-Symoné is an actor.

Razia

Arabic, meaning "contented."

Reagan
(alt. Reagen, Regan)

Irish Gaelic, meaning "descendant of Riagán." Associated with former President and First Lady Ronald and Nancy Reagan.

Reba

Shortened form of Rebecca, meaning "joined." Name of singer and actor Reba McEntire.

Rebecca
(alt. Rebekah; abbrev. Reb, Reba, Becca, Bex)

Hebrew, meaning "joined." Famous Rebeccas include the character from the Bible, designer Rebecca Minkoff, and one-hit-wonder Rebecca Black.

Reese
(alt. Reece)

Welsh, meaning "fiery and zealous." Name of actor Reese Witherspoon.

Regina
(abbrev. Geena, Gena, Gina)

Latin, meaning "queen." Famous Reginas include actors Regina Hall and Regina King, and singer Regina Spektor. Geena Davis is an actor.

Reina
(alt. Reyna, Rheyna)

Spanish, meaning "queen."

Rena
(alt. Reena, Rina)

Hebrew, meaning "serene."

Renata

Latin, meaning "reborn." Renata Tebaldi is an opera singer.

Rene

Greek, meaning "peace." Rene Russo is an actor.

Renée
(alt. Renae)

French, meaning "reborn." Name of actor Renée Zellweger.

Renita
(alt. Renira)

Latin, meaning "resistant."

Reshma
(alt. Resha)

Sanskrit, meaning "silk."

Reta
(alt. Retha, Retta)

Portuguese, meaning "straight." Also a shortened form of Margaret.

Rhea

Greek, meaning "earth." Also a type of ostrich-like bird. Name of actor Rhea Perlman.

Rheta

Greek, meaning "eloquent speaker." Flora Rheta Schreiber is an author.

Rhiannon
(alt. Rhian)

Welsh, meaning "witch." A prominent figure in Welsh mythology.

Rhoda

Greek, meaning "rose." Title of the sitcom *Rhoda*.

Rhona

Nordic, meaning "rough island." Rhona Mitra is a model and actor.

Rhonda
(alt. Ronda)

Welsh, meaning "noisy." "Help Me Rhonda" is a song by the Beach Boys.

Ria
(alt. Rie, Riya)

Shortened form of Victoria, meaning "victor."

Ricki
(alt. Rieko, Rika, Rikki)

Shortened form of Frederica, meaning "peaceful ruler." Name of the TV host Ricki Lake.

Rihanna
(alt. Reanna, Rhianna)

Welsh, meaning "witch." Name of singer Rihanna.

Riley

Irish Gaelic, meaning "courageous."

Rilla

German, meaning "small brook."

Rima

Arabic, meaning "antelope." Name of the comic book character *Rima the Jungle Girl*.

Riona

Irish Gaelic, meaning "like a queen."

Ripley

English, meaning "shouting man's meadow."

Risa

Latin, meaning "laughter."

Rita

Shortened form of Margaret, meaning "pearl." Famous Ritas include actors Rita Hayworth and Rita Moreno, and singer Rita Coolidge.

River

(alt. Riviera)

English, from the body of water of the same name. Famous Rivers include actor River Phoenix, singer Rivers Cuoma, and comedian Joan Rivers.

Roberta

(abbrev. Bobbi, Bobby, Robbie, Robi, Roby)

English, meaning "bright fame." Name of singer Roberta Flack.

Robin

(alt. Robbin, Robyn)

English, meaning "bright fame." Famous Robins include actor Robin Wright Penn, and singers Robyn and Robin Thicke. Used for both girls and boys.

Rochelle

(alt. Richelle, Rochel)

French, meaning "little rock." Name of actor Rochelle Aytes.

Rogue

French, meaning "beggar." Also an "X-Men" character.

Rohina

(alt. Rohini)

Sanskrit, meaning "sandalwood."

Roisin

Irish Gaelic, meaning "little rose."

Rolanda

German, meaning "famous land." Rolanda Watts is a voice actor.

Roma

Italian, meaning "Rome." Also the name of an ancient Roman deity, and a group of nomadic people.

Romaine

(alt. Romina)

French, meaning "from Rome."

Romola

(alt. Romilda, Romily)

Latin, meaning "Roman woman." Name of the actor Romola Garai.

Romy

Shortened form of Rosemary, meaning "dew of the sea." Famous Romys include actor Romy Rosemont and the movie *Romy and Michele's High School Reunion*.

Rona
(alt. Ronia, Ronja, Ronna)

Nordic, meaning "rough island."

Ronnie
(alt. Roni, Ronnie)

English, meaning "strong counsel."

Rosa

Italian, meaning "rose." Made famous by Civil Rights activist Rosa Parks.

Rosabel
(alt. Rosabella)

Contraction of Rose and Belle, meaning "beautiful rose."

Rosalie
(alt. Rosale, Rosalia, Rosalina)

French, meaning "rose garden." Actor Andie MacDowell's birth name is actually Rosalie.

Rosalind
(alt. Rosalinda)

Spanish, meaning "pretty rose." A character in Shakespeare's play *As You Like It*.

Rosalyn
(alt. Rosaleen, Rosaline, Roselyn)

Contraction of Rose and Lynn, meaning "pretty rose."

Rosamund
(alt. Rosamond)

German, meaning "renowned protector." Famous Rosamunds include actor Rosamund Pike and author Rosamunde Pilcher.

Rose
(alt. Rosie, Rosia)

Latin, from the flower of the same name. Famous Roses include actors Rose Byrne and Rose McGowan, and the character of Rose DeWitt Bukater from *Titanic*.

Roseanne
(alt. Rosana, Rosanna, Rosanne, Roseann, Roseanna)

Contraction of Rose and Anne, meaning "graceful rose." Name of comedian and actor Roseanne Barr.

Rosemary
(alt. Rosemarie; abbrev. Rosie, Rosy)

Latin, meaning "dew of the sea." Famous Rosemarys include actor Rosemary Clooney and the film *Rosemary's Baby*.

Rosita

Spanish, meaning "rose." Also a character on *Sesame Street*.

Rowena
(alt. Rowan)

Welsh, meaning "slender and fair." Rowena was a powerful and beautiful seductress in ancient Welsh mythology.

Roxanne
(alt. Roxana, Roxane, Roxanna; abbrev. Roxie)

Persian, meaning "dawn." Also a song by The Police. Famous Roxies include the character of Roxie Hart from the musical *Chicago*, inventor Roxey Ann Caplin, and the band Roxy Music.

Rubina
(alt. Rubena)

Hebrew, meaning "behold, a son."

Ruby
(alt. Rubi, Rubie)

English, meaning "red gemstone." Made famous by the song "Ruby Tuesday" by the Rolling Stones.

"Bad girl" names

Delilah	Roxy
Desdemona	Salome
Jezebel	Scarlett
Lilith	Tallulah
Pandora	Trixie

Ruth
(alt. Ruthe, Ruthie)

Hebrew, meaning "friend and companion." Famous Ruths include the character from the Bible and Supreme Court Justice Ruth Bader Ginsburg.

Ryan
(alt. Riaan)

Gaelic, meaning "little king." Used for girls or, more commonly, boys.

Girls' names

Saba
(alt. Sabah)

Greek, meaning "from Sheba."

Sabina
(alt. Sabine)

Latin, meaning "from the Sabine tribe." The title given to political women in ancient Rome.

Sabrina

Latin, meaning "the River Severn." Famous Sabrinas include the movie *Sabrina*, the sitcom *Sabrina, the Teenage Witch*, and the character from *Charlie's Angels*.

Sadie
(alt. Sade, Sadye)

Hebrew, meaning "princess." Name of designer Sadie Frost.

Saffron

English, from the reddish-yellow spice of the same name.

Safiyya
(alt. Safiya)

Arabic, meaning "sincere friend." One of Muhammad's wives in the Qur'an.

Sage
(alt. Saga, Saige)

Latin, meaning "wise and healthy." Also an aromatic herb.

Sahara

Arabic, meaning "desert."

Sakura

Japanese, meaning "cherry blossom."

Sally
(alt. Sallie)

Hebrew, meaning "princess." Name of the actor Sally Field.

Salome
(alt. Salma)

Hebrew, meaning "peace." The name of a seductress in the Bible.

Samantha
(abbrev. Sam, Sammie, Sammy)

Hebrew, meaning "told by God." Famous Samanthas include TV host Samantha Brown and actors Samantha Lewes and Samantha Morton.

Samara
(alt. Samaria, Samira)

Hebrew, meaning "under God's rule."

Sanaa

Arabic, meaning "brilliance." Also the capital of Yemen.

Sandra
(alt. Saundra; abbrev. Sandy)

Shortened form of Alexandra, meaning "defender of mankind." Famous Sandras include actor Sandra Bullock and the character Sandy from Grease.

Sangeetha
(alt. Sangeeta)

Hindi, meaning "musical."

Sanna
(alt. Saniya, Sanne, Sanni)

Hebrew, meaning "lily."

Santana
(alt. Santina)

Spanish, meaning "holy."

Saoirse

Irish Gaelic, meaning "freedom."

Sapphire
(alt. Saphira)

Hebrew, meaning "blue gemstone." Associated with Push (or Precious) author Sapphire.

Sarah
(alt. Sara, Sarai, Sariah)

Hebrew, meaning "princess." Famous Sarahs include actors Sarah Michelle Gellar and Sarah Hyland, and reality TV star Sarah Palin.

Sasha
(alt. Sacha, Sascha)

Russian, meaning "man's defender." Name of former President Barack Obama's daughter.

Saskia
(alt. Saskie)

Dutch, meaning "the Saxon people"; Danish, meaning "valley of light."

Savannah
(alt. Savanah, Savanna, Savina)

Spanish, meaning "treeless."

Scarlett
(alt. Scarlet)

English, meaning "scarlet." Scarlett O'Hara is the protagonist of Margaret Mitchell's novel *Gone With The Wind*.

Scout

French, meaning "to listen." Also the lead character in Harper Lee's novel *To Kill a Mockingbird*.

Sedona
(alt. Sedonia, Sedna)

Spanish, from the city of the same name.

Selah
(alt. Sela)

Hebrew, meaning "cliff"; Hebrew, meaning "stop and listen."

Selby

English, meaning "manor village."

Selena
(alt. Salena, Salima, Salina, Selene, Selina)

Greek, meaning "moon goddess." Famous Selenas include singers Selena Gomez and Selena Quintanilla-Perez (known simply as Selena), and actor Selena Royle.

Selma

German, meaning "Godly helmet." Name of actor Selma Blair.

Seneca

Native American, meaning "from the Seneca tribe."

Sephora

Hebrew, meaning "bird"; Greek, meaning "beauty."

September

Latin, meaning "seventh month." The ninth month.

Seraphina
(alt. Serafina, Seraphia, Seraphine)

Hebrew, meaning "ardent." St. Serafina was known for her strong faith despite illness and suffering.

Serena
(alt. Sarina, Sereana)

Latin, meaning "tranquil." Name of tennis pro Serena Williams.

Serenity

Latin, meaning "serene." Also a sci-fi movie.

Shakira

Arabic, meaning "thankful." Name of the singer Shakira.

Shania
(alt. Shaina, Shana, Shaniya)

Hebrew, meaning "beautiful." Name of the singer Shania Twain.

Shanice

American English, meaning "from Africa." Name of the singer Shanice.

Shaniqua

(alt. Shanika)

African, meaning "warrior princess."

Shanna

English, meaning "old."

Shannon

(alt. Shannan, Shanon)

Irish Gaelic, meaning "old and ancient." Shannon Elizabeth is an actor.

Shantal

(alt. Shantel, Shantell)

French, from the place of the same name.

Shanti

(alt. Shantih)

Hindi, meaning "peaceful."

Sharlene

German, meaning "man."

Sharon

(alt. Sharen, Sharona, Sharron)

Hebrew, meaning "a plain." Famous Sharons include reality TV star Sharon Osbourne and actors Sharon Stone and Sharon Tate.

Shasta

American English, from the mountain and Native American tribe of the same name.

Shauna

(alt. Sharna, Shawna)

Irish, meaning "the Lord is gracious." Sharna Burgess is a dancer.

Shayla

(alt. Shaylie, Shayna, Sheyla)

Irish, meaning "blind."

Shea

Irish Gaelic, meaning "from the fairy fort." The tree and nut of the same name.

Sheena

Irish, meaning "the Lord is gracious." Name of the singer Sheena Easton.

Sheila

(alt. Shelia, Shila)

Irish, meaning "blind." Name of singer Sheila E.

Shelby

(alt. Shelba, Shelbie)

English, meaning "estate on the ledge."

Shelley
(alt. Shellie, Shelly)

English, meaning "meadow on the ledge." Famous Shelleys include actor Shelley Fabares and Shelley Duvall, and author Mary Shelley.

Shenandoah

Native American, meaning "after an Oneida chief." Also the name of a national park.

Sheridan

Irish Gaelic, meaning "wild man."

Sheryl
(alt. Sherryl; abbrev. Sheri, Sherie, Sherri, Sherrie)

German, meaning "man." Famous Sheryls include singer Sheryl Crow, businesswoman Sheryl Sandberg, and host Sheryl Underwood. Also comedian and host Sherri Shepherd.

Shiloh

Hebrew, meaning "his gift." Name of Angelina Jolie and Brad Pitt's daughter.

Shirley
(alt. Shirlee)

English, meaning "bright meadow." Famous Shirleys include singer Dame Shirley Bassey, actor Shirley MacLaine, and child star Shirley Temple.

Shivani

Sanskrit, meaning "wife of Shiva."

Shona

Irish Gaelic, meaning "God is gracious."

Shoshana
(alt. Shoshanna)

Hebrew, meaning "lily." Shoshanna Shapiro is a character from *Girls*.

Shura

Russian, meaning "man's defender"; Arabic, meaning "consultation."

Sian
(alt. Sianna)

Welsh, meaning "the Lord is gracious."

Sibyl
(alt. Sybil)

Greek, meaning "seer and oracle." Sibyl was a prophetess in ancient Greek mythology.

Sidney
(alt. Sydney)

English, meaning "from St. Denis." Name of the city in Australia.

Sidonie
(alt. Sidonia, Sidony)

Latin, meaning "from Sidonia."

Great female singers

Adele (Adkins)

Aretha (Franklin)

Billie (Holiday)

Dionne (Warwick)

Dolly (Parton)

Ella (Fitzgerald)

Gladys (Knight)

Jennifer (Hudson)

Judy (Garland)

Nina (Simone)

Siena
(alt. Sienna)

Latin, from the town of the same name.

Sierra

Spanish, meaning "saw."

Signa
(alt. Signe)

Scandinavian, meaning "victory."

Sigrid

Nordic, meaning "fair victory." Sigrid the Haughty was an important figure in ancient Norse mythology.

Silja

Scandinavian, meaning "blind."

Simcha

Hebrew, meaning "joy."

Simone
(alt. Simona)

Hebrew, meaning "listening intently." Famous Simones include singer Nina Simone, and philosopher Simone de Beauvoir.

Sinead

Irish, meaning "the Lord is gracious." Name of singer Sinead O'Connor.

Siobhan

Irish, meaning "the Lord is gracious." Siobhan Fallon Hogan is an actor.

Siren
(alt. Sirena)

Greek, meaning "entangler." In ancient Greek mythology, sirens were beautiful and dangerous creatures who lured sailors to their deaths.

Siria

Spanish, meaning "glowing."

Skye
(alt. Sky)

Scottish, from the island of the same name in Scotland.

Skylar
(alt. Skyla, Skyler)

Dutch, meaning "giving shelter." Skylar White is a character from *Breaking Bad*.

Sloane
(alt. Sloan)

Irish Gaelic, meaning "man of arms." Famous Sloanes include Sloane Stephens, the infamous Sloane Rangers, and the character of Sloane Sabbith on *Newsroom*.

Socorro

Spanish, meaning "to aid."

Sojourner

English, meaning "temporary stay." Name of the women's rights and civil rights activist Sojourner Truth.

Solana

Spanish, meaning "sunlight."

Solange

French, meaning "with dignity." Solange Knowles is a singer.

Soledad

Spanish, meaning "solitude."

Soleil

French, meaning "sun." Cirque du Soleil is a performance group.

Solveig

Scandinavian, meaning "woman of the house."

Sonia
(alt. Sonja, Sonya)

Greek, meaning "wisdom." Sonia Kasuk is a designer.

Sophia
(alt. Sofia, Sofie, Sophie)

Greek, meaning "wisdom." Famous Sophias include director Sofia Coppola and actors Sofia Vergara and Sophia Loren.

Sophronia

Greek, meaning "sensible."

Soraya

Persian, meaning "princess."

Sorcha

Irish Gaelic, meaning "bright and shining."

Sorrel

English, from the herb of the same name.

Spirit

Latin, meaning "breath."

Stacey
(alt. Stacie, Stacy)

Greek, meaning "resurrection." Famous Staceys include actors Stacey Keibler and Stacey Dash, and presenter Stacey Dales.

Star
(alt. Starla, Starr)

English, meaning "star." The name of reality TV star Star Jones.

Stella

Latin, meaning "star." Stella McCartney is a designer.

Stephanie
(alt. Stefanie, Stephani, Stephany, Stephenie; abbrev. Steph)

Greek, meaning "crowned." Famous Stephanies include actor Stephanie Beacham, tennis pro Stefanie Graf, and author Stephenie Meyer.

Storm
(alt. Stormi, Stormy)

English, from the weather feature. Ktlie Jenner's daughter is Stormi.

Sukey
(alt. Sukey, Sukie)

Derived from Susan, meaning "lily."

Sula

American English, meaning "peace" or "little she-bear." Also the novel *Sula* by Toni Morrison.

Summer

English, from the season of the same name. Summer Glau is an actor.

Sunday

English, meaning "the first day." Nicole Kidman and Keith Urban's daughter is Sunday Rose.

Sunny
(alt. Sun)

English, meaning "of a pleasant temperament."

Suri

Persian, meaning "red rose." Tom Cruise and Katie Holmes's daughter is Suri.

Surya

Hindi, from the sun god of the same name.

Susan
(alt. Susann, Suzan; abbrev. Sue, Susie, Suzy)

Hebrew, meaning "lily." Famous Susans include actor Susan Sarandon, singer Susan Boyle, and suffragist Susan B. Anthony.

Susannah
(alt. Susana, Susanna, Susanne, Suzanna, Suzanne)

Hebrew, meaning "lily."

Svetlana

Russian, meaning "star."

Swanhild

Saxon, meaning "battle swan."

Sylvia
(alt. Silvia, Sylvie)

Latin, meaning "from the forest." Famous Sylvias include authors Sylvia Plath and Sylvia Day, and singer Sylvia Robinson.

Girls' names

Tabitha
(alt. *Tabatha, Tabetha*)

Aramaic, meaning "gazelle." A character in the Bible who was raised from the dead.

Tahira

Arabic, meaning "virginal."

Tai

Chinese, meaning "big."

Taima
(alt. *Taina, Tayna*)

Native American, meaning "peal of thunder."

Talia
(alt. *Tali*)

Hebrew, meaning "heaven's dew." Talia Shire is an actor.

Taliesin

Welsh, meaning "shining brow." The name of a Welsh poet Taliesin.

Talise
(alt. *Talisa, Talyse*)

Native American, meaning "lovely water." Talisa Stark is a character from *Game of Thrones*.

Talitha

Aramaic, meaning "young girl."

Tallulah
(alt. *Taliyah*)

Native American, meaning "leaping water." Famous Tallulahs include actors Tallulah Bankhead and Tallulah Riley, and *Bugsy Malone* character Tallulah.

Tamara
(alt. *Tamera*)

Hebrew, meaning "palm tree." Famous Tamaras include actors Tamara Taylor and Tamera Mowry.

Tamatha
(alt. Tametha)

American English, meaning "dear Tammy."

Tamika
(alt. Tameka)

American English, meaning "people."

Tamsin
(abbrev. Tami, Tammie, Tammy)

Hebrew, meaning "twin." Tammy Wynette is the name used by the legendary country singer—her real first name was Virginia.

Tanis

Spanish, meaning "to make famous."

Tanya
(alt. Tania, Tanya, Tonya)

Shortened form of Tatiana, meaning "from the Tatius clan." The name of actor Tanya Roberts and figure skater Tonya Harding.

Tara
(alt. Tahra, Tarah, Tera)

Irish Gaelic, meaning "rocky hill." Famous Taras include actors Tara Reid and Tara Fitzgerald.

Tatiana
(alt. Tatyana)

Russian, meaning "from the Tatius clan." Famous Tatianas include actors Tatyana Ali and Tatiana Maslany, and author Tatiana de Rosnay.

Tatum

English, meaning "lighthearted." Famous Tatums include actors Tatum O'Neal and Channing Tatum.

Tawny
(alt. Tawanaa, Tawnee, Tawnya)

English, meaning "golden brown."

Taya

Greek, meaning "poor one." In several languages the name also means "princess" or "goddess."

Taylor
(alt. Tayler)

English, meaning "tailor." Famous Taylors include singer Taylor Swift and actors Taylor Lautner and Taylor Schilling.

Tea

Greek, meaning "goddess." Tea Leoni is an actor.

Teagan
(alt. Teague, Tegan)

Irish Gaelic, meaning "poet."

Teal

English, from the bird of the same name. Also the blue-green color.

Tecla

Greek, meaning "fame of God."

Temperance

English, meaning "virtue."
Temperance Brennan is a character
from *Bones*.

Tempest

French, meaning "storm." The
Shakespeare play of the same name.

Teresa

(*alt. Terese, Tereza, Theresa, Therese*)
Greek, meaning "harvest." Famous
Teresas include nun Mother Teresa,
and actor Teresa Graves.

Terri

(*alt. Teri, Terrie, Terry*)
Derived from the short form of
Teresa, meaning "harvest." Teri
Hatcher is an actor, given this short
name at birth.

Tessa

(*alt. Tess, Tessie*)
Derived from the short form of
Teresa, meaning "harvest." Famous
Tessas include ice dancer Tessa
Virtue and literary heroine *Tess of the
D'Urbervilles* by Thomas Hardy.

Thais

Greek, from the mythological
heroine of the same name.

Thalia

Greek, meaning "blooming." The
name of numerous ancient Greek
muses, nymphs, and graces.

Thandie

(*alt. Thana, Thandi*)
Arabic, meaning "thanksgiving."
Thandie Newton is an actor.

Thea

Greek, meaning "goddess." Can be
a shortened form of Theodora or
Dorothea.

Theda

German, meaning "people." Name
of the silent movie actor Theda
Bara.

Thelma

Greek, meaning "will." Famous
Thelmas include singer Thelma
Houston, and the movie *Thelma &
Louise*.

Theodora

Greek, meaning "gift of God." The
name of numerous ancient Roman
figures.

Theodosia

Greek, meaning "gift of God."

Thisbe

Greek, from the mythological
heroine of the same name.

Thomasina

(*alt. Thomasin, Thomasine, Thomasyn*)
Greek, meaning "twin." The birth
name of singer Tammi Terrell was
Thomasina Montgomery.

Thora

Scandinavian, meaning "Thor's struggle." Name of the actor Thora Birch.

Tia
(alt. Tiana)

Spanish, meaning "aunt." Tia Mowry is an actor.

Tiara

Latin, meaning "jeweled headband."

Tierney

Irish Gaelic, meaning "Lord."

Tierra
(alt. Tiera)

Spanish, meaning "land."

Tiffany
(alt. Tiffani, Tiffanie)

Greek, meaning "God's appearance." Name of the one-hit-wonder singer Tiffany.

Tigris
(alt. Tiggy)

Irish Gaelic, meaning "tiger."

Tilly
(alt. Tilda, Tillie)

Shortened form of Matilda, meaning "battle-mighty."

Timothea

Greek, meaning "honoring God."

Tina
(alt. Teena, Tena)

Shortened form of Christina, meaning "anointed Christian." Famous Tinas include comedian Tina Fey and singer Tina Turner.

Tirion

Welsh, meaning "kind and gentle."

Tirzah

Hebrew, meaning "pleasantness." A character in the Bible.

Titania

Greek, meaning "giant." The Queen of the Fairies from Shakespeare's *A Midsummer Night's Dream*.

Toby
(alt. Tobi)

Hebrew, meaning "God is good." Usually a boy's name but can be used for girls.

Toni
(alt. Tony)

Latin, meaning "invaluable." Female version of Tony, or short form of Antoinette. Famous Tonis include singer Toni Braxton, author Toni Morrison, and choreographer Toni Basil.

Tonia
(alt. Tonja, Tonya)

Russian, meaning "praiseworthy."

Topaz

Latin, meaning "golden gemstone."

Tori
(alt. Tora)

Shortened form of Victoria, meaning "victory." Famous Toris include actor Tori Spelling and singer Tori Amos.

Tova
(alt. Tovah, Tove)

Hebrew, meaning "good."

Tracy
(alt. Tracey, Tracie)

Greek, meaning "harvest." Famous Tracys include singer Tracy Chapman, actor Tracey Ullman, and artist Tracey Emin.

Treva

Welsh, meaning "homestead."

Trilby

English, meaning "vocal trills." Also the name of a style of men's hat.

Trina
(alt. Trena)

Greek, meaning "pure."

Trinity

Latin, meaning "triad." Associated with the Christian Holy Trinity. The lead female character from the film series *The Matrix*.

Trisha
(alt. Tricia)

Shortened form of Patricia, meaning "noble." Name of singer Trisha Yearwood.

Trista

Latin, meaning "sad."

Trixie

Shortened form of Beatrix, meaning "bringer of gladness."

Trudie
(alt. Tru, Trudy)

Shortened form of Gertrude, meaning "strength of a spear."

True

English, meaning "loyal."

Tullia

Roman, meaning "bound for glory."

Twyla
(alt. Twila)

American English, meaning "star." Name of the choreographer Twyla Tharp.

Tyler

English, meaning "tiler." Used for girls and also for boys.

Tyra

Scandinavian, meaning "Thor's struggle." Tyra Banks is a model.

Tzipporah

Hebrew, meaning "bird."

U

Girls' names

Ula
(alt. Ulla)
Celtic, meaning "gem of the sea."

Ulrika
(alt. Urica)
German, meaning "power of the wolf."

Uma
Sanskrit, meaning "flax." Uma Thurman is an actor.

Una
Latin, meaning "one."

Undine
Latin, meaning "little wave."

Unique
Latin, meaning "only one."

Unity
English, meaning "oneness."

Uriela
(alt. Uriella)
Hebrew, meaning "God's light."

Ursula
Latin, meaning "little female bear." The villain from Disney's *The Little Mermaid*.

Uta
German, meaning "prospers in battle."

Girls' names

Vada

German, meaning "famous ruler."

Valdis

(alt. Valdiss, Valdys, Valdyss)

Norse, meaning "goddess of the dead," from the mythological goddess of the same name.

Valencia

(alt. Valancy, Valarece)

Latin, meaning "strong and healthy." A city in Spain.

Valentina

Latin, meaning "strong and healthy."

Valentine

Latin, from the saint of the same name.

Valerie

(alt. Valarie, Valeria, Valery, Valorie; abbrev. Val, Vale, Valia, Vallie)

Latin, meaning "to be healthy and strong." Famous Valeries include actors Valerie Bertinelli and Valerie Harper, and the song "Valerie" by Mark Ronson and Amy Winehouse.

Vandana

Sanskrit, meaning "worship."

Vanessa

(alt. Vanesa)

Greek, meaning "butterfly." Famous Vanessas include actor Vanessa Hudgens and singer Vanessa Williams.

Vanity

Latin, meaning "self-obsessed."

Vashti

Persian, meaning "beauty." A Persian queen in the Bible.

Veda

Sanskrit, meaning "knowledge and wisdom."

Vega

Arabic, meaning "falling vulture."

Velda

German, meaning "ruler."

Vella

American English, meaning "beautiful."

Velma

English, meaning "determined protector." A character from *Scooby Doo*.

Venice
(alt. Venetia, Venita)

Latin, meaning "city of canals." An Italian city.

Venus

Latin, from the Roman goddess of the same name. Venus was the goddess of love, beauty, sex, and fertility.

Vera
(alt. Verla, Verlie)

Slavic, meaning "faith." Famous Veras include designer Vera Wang, actor Vera Farmiga, and singer Vera Lynn.

Verda
(alt. Verdie)

Latin, meaning "spring-like."

Verena

Latin, meaning "true." Associated with St. Verena.

Verity

Latin, meaning "truth."

Verna
(alt. Vernie)

Latin, meaning "spring green."

Verona

Latin, from the Italian city of the same name.

Veronica
(alt. Verica, Veronique)

Latin, meaning "true image." Famous Veronicas include actors Veronica Lake and Veronica Carlson, and the "Veronica Mars" series and movie.

Veruca

Latin, meaning "wart." Veruca Salt is a character from *Charlie and the Chocolate Factory*.

Vesta

Latin, from the Roman goddess of the same name.

Vicenta

Latin, meaning "prevailing."

Victoria

(abbrev. Tori, Vicki, Vicky, Vikki, Vix)

Latin, meaning "victory." Famous Victorias include designer Victoria Beckham, England's Queen Victoria, and chain store Victoria's Secret.

Vida

Spanish, meaning "life."

Vidya

Sanskrit, meaning "knowledge." Refers to learning and knowledge in the Hindu faith.

Vienna

Latin, from the city of the same name in Austria.

Vigdis

Scandinavian, meaning "war goddess."

Vina

(alt. Vena)

Spanish, meaning "vineyard."

Viola

Latin, meaning "violet." Name of the actor Viola Davis.

Violet

(alt. Violetta)

Latin, meaning "purple." The famed nurse and survivor Violet Jessop.

Virginia

(alt. Virgie, Virginie; abbrev. Ginnie, Ginny)

Latin, meaning "maiden." Famous Virginias include author Virginia Woolf, *Raising Hope* character Virginia Chance, and the eastern states of Virginia and West Virginia.

Vita

Latin, meaning "life."

Vittoria

Variation of Victoria, meaning "victory."

Viva

Latin, meaning "alive." Name of the actor Viva.

Vivian

(alt. Vivien, Vivienne, Vyvian)

Latin, meaning "lively." Famous Vivians include actor Vivian Leigh, designer Vivienne Westwood, and photographer Vivian Maier.

Vivica

(alt. Viveca)

Scandinavian, meaning "war fortress." Name of the actor Vivica A. Fox.

Vonda

Czech, meaning "from the tribe of Vandals." Vonda Shepard is a singer.

Girls' names

Waleska
Polish, meaning "beautiful."

Wallis
English, meaning "from Wales."
Name of socialite Wallis Simpson,
the woman responsible for the
abdication of Great Britain's King
Edward VIII.

Wanda
(alt. Waneta, Wanita)
Slavic, meaning "tribe of
the vandals." Name of
comedian and actor Wanda
Sykes.

Wava
English, meaning "way."

Waverly
(alt. Waverley)
Old English, meaning "meadow of
aspens."

Wendy
English, meaning "friend." Famous
Wendys include host Wendy
Williams, the character of Wendy
Darling in *Peter Pan*, and the
hamburger chain Wendy's.

Whisper
English, meaning "whisper."

Whitley
Old English, meaning "white
meadow."

Whitney
(alt. Witney)
Old English, meaning "white
island." Famous Whitneys include
singer Whitney Houston, comedian
Whitney Cummings, and dancer
Witney Carson.

Wilda
German, meaning "willow tree."

Wilhelmina

(abbrev. Mina, Mine, Minna, Willa, Willy, Wilma)

German, meaning "determined to protect." A popular name with the German royal family.

Willa

(alt. Willene, Willia)

German, meaning "helmet." Willa Cather is an author.

Willow

English, from the tree of the same name. Famous celebrity children called Willow include Willow Smith (Will and Jada Pinkett Smith's daughter) and Willow Hart (Pink and Carey Hart's daughter).

Winifred

(alt. Winnie)

Old English, meaning "holy and blessed." South African activist Winifred "Winnie" Madikizela-Mandela was once married to Nelson Mandela.

Winona

(alt. Wynonna)

Indian, meaning "first-born daughter." Famous Winonas include actor Winona Ryder and singer Wynonna Judd.

Winslow

English, meaning "friend's hill."

Winter

English, meaning "winter."

Wisteria

English, meaning "flower."

Wren

English, meaning "wren."

Wynne

(alt. Wynn)

Welsh, meaning "white."

X Girls' names

Xanthe

Greek, meaning "blonde." The name of several ancient Greek mythological characters.

Xanthippe

Greek, meaning "nagging."

Xaverie

Greek, meaning "bright."

Xaviera

Arabic, meaning "bright."

Xena
(alt. Xenia)

Greek, meaning "foreigner." The title character from the TV sci-fi series Xena: Warrior Princess.

Ximena

Greek, meaning "listening."

Xiomara

Spanish, meaning "battleready."

Xochitl

Spanish, meaning "flower." Queen Xochitl was a legendary Toltec ruler.

Xoey

Variation of Zoe, meaning "life." Spelling alternative for Zoey or Joey.

Xristina

Variation of Christina, meaning "follower of Christ." Singer Christina Aguilera often spells her name Xristina.

Xylia
(alt. Xylina, Xyloma)

Greek, meaning "from the woods."

Y

Girls' names

Yadira
Arabic, meaning "worthy."

Yael
Hebrew, meaning "mountain goat."
A figure in the Bible.

Yaffa
(alt. Yahaira, Yajaira)
Hebrew, meaning "lovely."

Yamilet
Arabic, meaning "beautiful."

Yana
Hebrew, meaning "the Lord is gracious." Yana Rudkovskaya is the wife of figure skater Evgeni Plushenko.

Yanira
Hawaiian, meaning "pretty."
A character in ancient Greek mythology.

Yara
Arabic and Persian, meaning "small butterfly."

Yareli
Latin, meaning "golden."

Yaretzi
(alt. Yaritza)
Aztec, meaning "forever beloved."

Yasmin
(alt. Yasmeen, Yasmina, Yasmine)
Persian, meaning "jasmine flower."
Yasmine Bleeth is an actor.

Yelena
Greek, meaning "bright and chosen."

Yesenia
Arabic, meaning "flower."

Yetta
English, from Henrietta, meaning "ruler of the house."

Yeva

Hebrew variant of Eve, meaning "life."

Ylva

Old Norse, meaning "she wolf."

Yoki
(alt. Yoko)

Native American, meaning "rain." Yoko Ono is an artist and peace activist.

Yolanda
(alt. Yolonda)

Spanish, meaning "violet flower." Name of reality TV star Yolanda Foster.

Yoselin

English, meaning "lovely."

Yoshiko

Japanese, meaning "good child." Princess Yoshiko was an important Empress of Japan.

Ysabel

English, meaning "God's promise." Spelling alternative to Isabel.

Ysanne

Contraction of Isabel and Anne, meaning "pledged to God" and "grace."

Yuki

Japanese, meaning "lucky."

Yuliana

Latin, meaning "youthful."

Yuridia

Russian, meaning "farmer."

Yvette
(alt. Ivette, Ivonne, Yvonne)

French, meaning "yew." Yvette Nicole Brown is an actor.

Z Girls' names

Zafira

Arabic, meaning "successful."

Zahara

(alt. Zahava, Zahra)

Arabic, meaning "flowering and shining." Name of Angelina Jolie and Brad Pitt's daughter.

Zaida

(alt. Zaide)

Arabic, meaning "prosperous"; Hebrew, meaning "loved grandfather."

Zalika

Swahili, meaning "well born."

Zaltana

Arabic, meaning "high mountain."

Zamia

Greek, meaning "pine cone."

Zaneta

(alt. Zanceta, Zanetah, Zanett, Zanetta)

Hebrew, meaning "a gracious present from God."

Zaniyah

Arabic, meaning "lily."

Zara

(alt. Zaria, Zariah, Zora)

Arabic, meaning "radiance." A fashion brand.

Zaya

(alt. Zayah)

Tibetan, meaning "victorious woman."

Zelda

German, meaning "dark battle." Associated with the hugely successful video game series *Legend of Zelda*.

Zelia
(alt. Zella)
Scandinavian, meaning "sunshine."

Zelma
German, meaning "helmet."

Zemira
(alt. Zemirah)
Hebrew, meaning "joyous melody." Title of the opera *Zemira* by Francesco Bianchi.

Zena
(alt. Zenia, Zina)
Greek, meaning "hospitable."

Zenaida
Greek, meaning "the life of Zeus." Associated with physician St. Zenaida.

Zenobia
Latin, meaning "the life of Zeus." Zenobia was a queen of ancient Roman Syria.

Zephyr
Greek, meaning "the west wind."

Zetta
Latin, meaning "seven."

Zia
Arabic, meaning "light and splendor."

Zinaida
Greek, meaning "belonging to Zeus."

Zinnia
Latin, meaning "flower."

Zipporah
Hebrew, meaning "bird." Zipporah was one of Moses' wives in the Bible.

Zita
(alt. Ziva)
Spanish, meaning "little girl." St. Zita is the patron saint of maids and domestic servants.

Zizi
(alt. Zizzy)
Hungarian/Hebrew, meaning "God is my oath."

Zoe
(alt. Zoi, Zoie, Zoey, Zoeya, Zooey)
Greek, meaning "life." Famous Zoes include actors Zoe Saldana and Zooey Deschanel.

Zoila
Greek, meaning "life."

Zoraida
Spanish, meaning "captivating woman."

Zosia
(alt. Zosima)
Greek, meaning "wisdom." Zosia Mamet is an actor.

Zoya

Greek, meaning "life." Zoya Kosmodemyanskaya was a Soviet Union heroine.

Zula

African, meaning "brilliant."

Zuleika

Arabic, meaning "fair and intelligent." Zuleika was the name of Potiphar's wife in the Bible.

Zulma

Arabic, meaning "peace."

Zuzana

Hebrew, meaning "lily."

Zuzu

Czech, meaning "flower." Susan (Zuzu) is a character in the movie *It's A Wonderful Life*.

A name for all seasons

Spring	Summer	Fall	Winter
April	August	Autumn	January
Cerelia	June	Demetria	Neva
Kelda	Natsumi	September	Neve
May	Persephone	Theresa	Perdita
Primavera	Soleil	Tracey	Rainer
Verda	Summer		Tahoma
Verna	Suvi		